— Rusty's —
Thanks for having our
send off from Cocoa Beach
"Whatever happens, happens!"

Bob B

Wounded Hero Voyage I
Smallest Powerboat Crossing the Atlantic
(Florida to Greenland)

This book is the black and white picture version.

By Robert Brown

DO MORE than say thanks to our HEROES, which include not only military personnel, but also policemen, firemen, and anyone else who risks their life to save and protect others.

"Failure is not an option!"

bobbrown1408@aol.com Copyright © 2011 by Bob Brown
ISBN: 978-1463725273

Published in the United States of America
Publish Date: April 04, 2012
Advisory Editors who helped with different sections:
Tamara McHatton, Cindie Robinson,
Dean Schaaf, Liz Carroll, and Donna Chesher, and Shannon McGregor
Cover Artist: Bob Brown
Photography Credit: Bob and Ralph Brown, Hahns Kindt, Stevie Hicks, Jim Decker
Maps Credit: NASA (reconstructed by Bob Brown)
Cover Art Copyright by Bob Brown

All rights reserved. Except for brief excerpts for review purposes, no portion of this book may be reproduced or transmitted in any form or by any electronic or mechanical means, including photocopying, recording or by any information retrieval and storage system without permission of the Robert Brown.

Pirating of books is illegal. Criminal Copyright Infringement, *including* infringement without monetary gain, may be investigated by the Federal Bureau of Investigation and is punishable by up to five-years in federal prison and a fine of up to $250,000.

Author contact: Robert Brown can be contacted at bobbrown1408@aol.com or through www.RobertBrownBooks.com

Wounded Hero Voyage I

Dedication

This book is dedicated to the three Marines who died in Operation Eagle Claw April 24th, 1980 trying to rescue the 52 American Hostages in Iran. Ralph, my brother (a Marine), was on the roster to possibly go with them (explained in the book).

The three Marines died instantly in the fiery crash in the RH-53 helicopter:

Marine Sgt. John D. Harvey (21 years old) was an avionics technician with leadership qualities, an intense drive toward excellence, and many high achievements that went with his great sense of humor.

Marine Cpl. George N. Holmes (22 years old) had a goal to become a helicopter crew chief and was chosen for that role in his special elite team of rescue soldiers.

Marine Staff Sgt. Dewey L. Johnson (31 years old) was a devoted family man, considered the best Air Group's RH-53 mechanic, and an instructor. He was a father figure to many of the younger mechanics.

I want to recognize the other Heroes who also died that day in Operation Eagle Claw: April 24th, 1980

The Air Force guys died staying too long rescuing others

Air Force Capt. Harold L. Lewis Jr. (35 years old)
Air Force Capt. Lyn D. McIntosh (33 years old)
Air Force Capt. Richard L. Bakke (33 years old)
Air Force Capt. Charles McMillian (28 years old)
Air Force Sgt. Joel C. Mayo (34 years old)

Special mention of Casey, our golden retriever, who died in our house fire, Nov 15, 2009.

Wounded Hero Foundations promoted during our voyage:

Wounded Warrior Project: (The Wounded Warrior Project (WWP) works to raise awareness and enlist the public's aid for the needs of severely injured service men and women, to help severely injured service members aid and assist each other, and to provide unique, direct programs and services to meet their needs)

Special Operations Warrior Foundation: (The Special Operations Warrior Foundation provides full scholarship grants and educational and family counseling to the surviving children of special operations personnel who die in operational or training missions and immediate financial assistance to severely wounded special operations personnel and their families.)

Help for Heroes (United Kingdom): (Help for Heroes raises money to support members of the Armed Forces who have been wounded in the service of their country. We ask our supporters to "do their bit" to show these extraordinary young men and women that they are cared for by us.)

Military Ministries: (share the Gospel of Jesus Christ with military men and women, veterans and military families. Our ministries, resources, and partnerships are all based on the belief that faith makes a difference in the lives of those in harm's way)

Wounded Warriors in Action: (The WWIA aids in healing the hearts and minds of our Nation's combat wounded heroes (Purple Heart recipients) by providing world-class outdoor sporting activities, chiefly consisting of hunting and fishing opportunities across America.)

Wounded Warrior Regiment (USMC): (is a regiment of the United States Marine Corps formed to allow for recuperation for wounded, ill, and injured Marines and attached Sailors and their family members. It provides facilities and access to medical care to assist them as they return to duty or transition to civilian life.)

Guardian Angels Canada): (is a volunteer organization of non-profit international unarmed citizen crime patrollers.)

USO: (Thousands of USO volunteers do everything possible to provide a home away from home for our troops and to keep them connected to the families they left behind.)

It is my hope this book inspires readers to support at least one of the above foundations. (Google them to learn how)

Team Effort

We especially want to thank God who watched over us and answered our prayers allowing us to remain on the positive side of that fine line on many occasions.

This voyage could have never been possible without "I Am Second," which means **God is First**! The I Am Second Company was our major sponsor.

All the volunteer people behind the scenes that made sure we were as prepared as possible.

All our sponsors and the many people we met along the way that helped us out.

Our families for giving us the time away even when it appeared there was no end in site. And I am including the 2,000 hours of work on the two books associated with the voyage.

Thank you!

Table of Contents

Lucky the First Time..1
Tampa, Florida, Recovered Photographer 33
To Fort Myers, Going back in Time 41
Islamorada, Florida Keys, the Lube Job 49
In Route to South Carolina, Duck 73
Charleston, South Carolina, for Old Glory 79
New York, We Need That 95
Leaving New York, with Unsecured Possessions 117
Boston, Massachusetts, Counter Clockwise 127
Leaving Boston, Wiped Clean 145
Halifax, Nova Scotia, Canada, Playing Hide and Seek 159
To St. Pierre Miquelon, France, *Flummp!* 167
St. John's, Newfoundland, Canada, Secret Benefactors 191
St. Anthony, Newfoundland, Best Deal Ever 211
Cartwright, Labrador, Canada, Travelers' Haven 229
Heading for Greenland, Calling for a Fuel Drop 237
Our Toll Crossing the Atlantic Ocean 267
Boat Stops and the Big Mileages 267
Thank you! 269
About the Author; Robert Brown 272

Wounded Hero Voyage I

Map Pages

Whole North Atlantic viii
Florida to North Carolina 42
North Carolina to Boston, Mass 91
Boston, Mass to Labrador, Canada 148
Labrador to Greenland 240

These are the Wounded Heroes from the Dedication Page

John Harvey   George Holmes   Dewey Johnson

The Wounded Heroes that Died during Operation Eagle Claw April 24, 1980

Harold Lewis   **Richard Bakke**

Joel Mayo   Lyn McIntosh   Charles McMillian

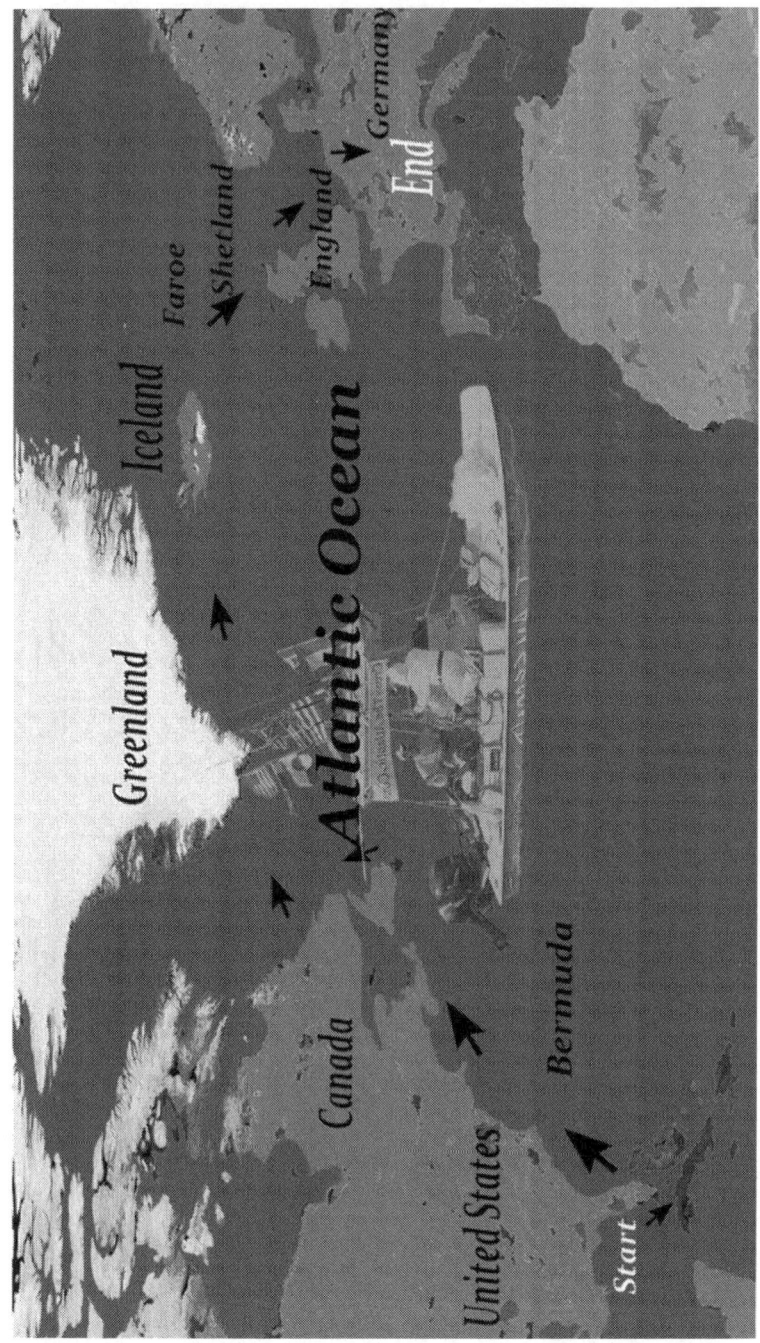

Lucky the First Time

I was driving the boat when out of nowhere our front light exposed the underside of a white crested breaking wave. The wave was pitched over the T-top of the boat. The raging North Atlantic came over and through our boat before we had time to duck. Ralph and I were plastered against the backrest of the captain's seat as the boat was instantly jolted backwards leaving us in waist-deep turbulent foamy water. It happened so fast everything went to slow motion. Whatever wasn't tied down was gone. We were lucky we were both in the cockpit area. Just as soon as the boat started making headway again, another wave crested over us. This one spun us sideways and the boat tilted before it punched through the foam and crashed back down. I instantly thought the storm, we'd been outrunning, had caught us. Without hesitation, I turned the boat seaward directly into the waves, not wanting to get caught sideways. Ralph, the captain, asked if he could drive. He didn't have to ask twice, I moved over.

A smaller wave hit us again. I yelled for Ralph to turn quickly and head for shore. He throttled up and made a quick blind U-turn. The next wave came over the back and a wall of four-foot foam heading into the cockpit area pancaked us against the dash. Ralph yelled that we had to go back out to sea and I was yelling for him to head in and get behind the huge silhouette peaked island. He

Lucky the First Time

argued we had a better chance facing the storm away from land. He waited for the next wave to hit us before spinning the boat around out to sea again. He started praying out loud and I yelled for him not to panic as wave after wave beat us from every direction.

Ralph shouted, "It won't sink! It won't sink! It won't sink! Don't panic, don't panic! Help me Lord, help us Lord, please! Trust your equipment, trust your equipment!"

Ralph pulled the microphone out of the overhead glove box and attempted to contact the fishing trawlers we saw earlier. When he couldn't get a response, I checked our antenna on top of the T-top and it was down. In the dark of night, in between the fifteen-foot crashing waves breaking over us with the boat filled to the rim, I jumped up on one of the fifty-gallon tanks, reached over to the rooftop antenna, and shoved it back up. Ralph thrust me our large crescent wrench for me to whack the locking handle down hard.

Ralph got someone on the radio emergency channel but we could hardly hear a thing. Ralph was trying to drive, so he handed me the microphone. The glove box kept popping open and it was all we could do to keep everything, including the non-bolted-in radio, from flying out. Harbour radio asked if we were alright and if we needed to be rescued. I yelled over the roar of the storm that we did not need to be rescued, but were asking for the directions to the nearest harbour, because I did not want to go back out to sea. As the powerful waves slung us around in the gale force winds, harbour radio wanted to know our location. Our GPS coordinates were on a different navigational page on the Garmin. Ralph didn't want to change pages, since all we had to navigate with was the image of us as a quarter-inch boat on the tiny Garmin Plotter screen. We didn't want to be hit broadside by the next set of incoming waves which would most likely flip us. The sky was cloaked in a blanket of clouds, hiding the stars. We were bashed by wave after wave standing in knee deep water as the radio transmission went in and out a couple of times; and then the signal was lost....

Okay, now let's go back and start at the beginning of the story.

"The Trip is on!" is what Ralph said over a phone call to Bob. In 2007, two-years ago, brothers Bob and Ralph Brown took a flats boat (open fishing boat designed to operate in less than a foot of water) from North Carolina to Bermuda and then back to New York. It was a trip of 1,574-ocean miles. They received two world records for their feat. However, Ralph wasn't satisfied with just doing that, so a year later and after we'd both spent hundreds of hours sending out mailings, emails and phone calls trying to get sponsorship for a bigger and grander adventure... to cross the Atlantic in the exact same 21-foot 1-inch flats boat in the summer of 2008. It would be the smallest powerboat to ever cross the Atlantic Ocean (the current world record is a 21-foot 4-inch boat with a cabin and a keel designed for the ocean). But, early September in 2008, Ralph had to cancel our attempt... not enough funding.

During the next year, both Bob and Ralph continued their efforts contacting many companies trying to get sponsorship. Ralph had several close calls, but with the bad economy, nothing was panning out. That was until Ralph finagled a couple of car rides with Norm Miller during the Tampa Bay Prayer Conference. Norm Miller was the Chairman for Interstate Battery, America's number one automobile battery company and the founder of I Am Second... and to cut to the chase, the trip was funded. The amount was way

Lucky the First Time

below the minimum Ralph estimated it would cost. It was one of those take-it-or-leave-it options; we had to leave by June 27th according to the contract offer or not accept the money. Ralph had a volunteer support team in place, including Larry Garrison who is considered one of the most experienced and best story brokers in the United States. But, out of gratitude to Norm Miller for joining the team, Ralph went with Interstate's PR team instead so they could be in charge. Believing additional funding would be generated once we were underway... the trip was on.

Ralph was originally hoping to start the voyage with $145,000. The money was to be spent on gas, food, some advertising, cold weather gear, helicopter footage, video and camera equipment, and safety equipment required by the Coast Guard. We also needed some high quality radio and navigational equipment, a land promotional support team's fuel and their lodging along the United States, expenses for pulling the boat out of the water to change the oil and other maintenance needs, a team of people calling the media at all our destinations weeks ahead and then making follow up calls days before. We would need a waterproof laptop with editing equipment for sending back footage, a website and a webmaster for updates, air fair for our families to meet with us several times along our journey, including transportation for the boat and us back from Europe, press releases, a few dinners out with an occasional hotel room, rental cars to get around during some of our visits in other countries. We would need money for expenses to bring attention to our voyage and to promote the countries that we visit, so they would in turn promote us so we could promote the Wounded Hero Foundations. We needed to design and print quality "Do More" T-shirts, a team to promote the sale of the "Do More" shirts including packaging and mailing them, business cards and brochures, satellite phones, EPIRB, additional cell phone use, etc.

 Nine days before our departure we received our largest donation. It was the donation from I Am Second presented by Interstate Battery. We had previously received a couple of thousand from some local sponsors. Ralph immediately spent a few thousand on advertising, having a graphic-boat wrap put on, and removing and installing a higher stronger floor in the Intruder 21 boat made by Dreamboats. He also spent a few more thousand on designing and printing T-shirts. I spent about three thousand in supplies I wanted to take and Ralph paid some outstanding bills related to his two years of work trying to put this voyage together.

 Other donations given ***before*** our departure: **Mustang Survivor** gave us two black and bright yellow moderately cold survivor jackets and pants, which I thought was really neat as my boys went to Merritt Island High School; their colors are black and gold (yellow) and their mascot is a Mustang. **Boat US** gave us a towing agreement, a little capital and the EPIRB. **Ideal Image** removed the hair off my back. **Cape Surf** gave us a surfboard bag, two rash guards, and a handful of their T-shirts to give to the Wounded Heroes who might get to ride on some coastal legs with us. **GoPro** gave us two small underwater sport cameras. **NGR Manager** gave us a solar panel for emergency recharging the batteries if we became stranded out at sea. **Interstate Battery** gave us three batteries, hats, shirts, windbreakers, and fleece windbreakers. **Spot** gave us a Spot (position locator). **Suzuki** lent us our big motor and a trolling motor and gave us our banner blanket. **Xterra** gave us two ultra thin triathlon wetsuits. **Georgianna Methodist Church**, our church, gave us a little

Lucky the First Time

capital. **Benco Insurance Planners** gave us some capital. Everything added together was about a third of Ralph's projected cost of the trip.

Here are the World Records from our Bermuda trip in 2007 (our first trip):

<u>Guinness World Records</u>: "Longest Non-stop Ocean Voyage in a Flats boat," is: The longest non-stop ocean voyage in a flats boat was 1245.63 Km (774-miles) was set by Ralph and Robert Brown (USA) who traveled from St. Georges, Bermuda to New York harbor, USA, from 9-11 May, 2007.

<u>The World Record Academy</u>: Ralph Brown of Spring Hill, Fla., and Bob Brown of Merritt Island, Fla., were recognized by the World Record Academy as being the holders of a new record: the longest unescorted oceanic crossing of a flats boat.

A flats boat by definition is a single engine (trolling motors don't count), low-profile, open fishing boat, which can operate in less than 1 foot of water. This particular flats boat, the Intruder 21, made by the brothers' company, Dreamboats, can operate in less than 6 inches of water.

Many smaller boats have made a longer trip, but they have either a keel, considerably more freeboard, a cabin, sail, or escort.

The two world records and Bob's *Bermuda Suicide Challenge* book

Wounded Hero Voyage I

US Congress Honors Cross the Atlantic

Cristin Datch, Congressional assistant to Congressman Gus Bilirakis contacted Ralph from his office to say, "You were honored in the Congressional Record." Ralph had no idea Bruce Schulman had made the recommendation.

Speech by Honorable Gus M. Bilirakis, in the Florida House of Representatives, Tuesday, June 2, 2009.

"Madam Speaker, I rise today to honor two of my constituents, brothers Ralph and Robert Brown. Ralph and Robert will be attempting a 2nd Guinness World Record this summer by sailing non-stop across the Atlantic Ocean from Tampa, Florida to Hamburg, Germany to raise funds for Wounded Warrior Foundations.

In 2007, Ralph and Robert set their first Guinness World Record for the "Longest nonstop ocean voyage in a flats boat" traveling from North Carolina to Bermuda and back to New York in a 21-foot open fishing boat of their own design. This voyage garnered a great deal of publicity and convinced the brothers to use this notoriety to raise money for Wounded Warriors Organizations in the future.

Ralph and Robert will be using the publicity from their second voyage to raise money for six Wounded Warrior and Disabled Veterans Organizations, having set a goal of $3 million.

In 1980, former Marine Ralph Brown was placed on the roster to liberate the American Embassy in Iran during the hostage takeover. However, Ralph's group was replaced by another group of soldiers, out of which three US Marines were killed. Mr. Brown and his brother have since dedicated their lives to honoring the lives of these three Marines and their many other brave countrymen.

Madam Speaker, Ralph and Robert Brown truly are doing more than just saying "thanks," by raising money and awareness for our nation's wounded warriors. And they are doing so in one of the most original manners possible."

Lucky the First Time

I am Bob Brown and this is my account of our voyage starting a few days before our departure on June 27th, 2009.

Wounded Hero Voyage I

After finishing up my two weeks of paint jobs in about a week, I still had a lot of personal things to tie up. Since my auto-driver's license would expire during our trip, I renewed it and looked around for a surf kite. I wanted a kite for emergency. In case we broke down out at sea, at least we would be able to sail, but they were all too expensive. I'd look some more later. I stopped by the Merritt Island Mall to see about getting a new handycam (smaller than a video camcorder). My old one had been acting up and I didn't want to take something untrustworthy for an adventure of this magnitude. I didn't know much about cameras, so I stopped at a shop that specifically catered to cameras and video equipment. Even though I had video taped almost everything imaginable throughout my life, they educated me in the difference between a normal HD, below 480 dots per inch (dpi) while a real HD video camera would have lines between 780 dpi and 1010 dpi. I needed a good video camera because I was planning on finding a producer to make a documentary film of the voyage after it was completed.

I spent the next couple of hours looking at the different cameras. Kevin, the store manager, was good at explaining the differences and did not pressure me like a used car salesman. I went home to think about it and thought I could probably get a better deal if I bought a camera over the Internet. However, I didn't have much time and Kevin was there to explain things to me. He told me when I was finished with the trip; he would help teach me how to edit the video.

When I went back the next day to make the purchase, I elected to buy a wide angle lens since most of the filming would be close up. I wouldn't have the ability to video very often from off the boat. The wide angle lens would make the video much more valuable if someone was going to make a documentary of the trip. I toyed with the idea of using a wireless microphone, but decided against it because of the price. It was over $200 and I had already way overshot my budget for the video camera. I initially thought I could get a good camera in the $300 to $500 range and now I was already drifting over the $1,400 mark.

When I got home, I decided I was going to try to build a Plexiglas case for the camera so it would be usable in all conditions. The camera had a flip-out LCD screen. When you opened it to view the LCD screen, it turned the camera on. The more I thought about it, making a case which would work was more than I had time to fool around with and besides, it would probably leak anyway. It would be worth the investment to purchase the waterproof case designed for the camera. Since the case would make the camera good underwater down to ten meters (about thirty foot), I could take some underwater videos of the boat. If I ordered the case over the Internet through Sony, I would save fifty dollars on the $300 purchase.

I decided to save the money and go with the two-day express mail and have the camera case shipped over to Ralph in Hudson. This would give me a couple of extra days in the event something went wrong with the shipping. After ordering it, I realized the shipping date was the 25th of June even though I was ordering it on the morning of June 23rd. I wasn't sure if the company considered Saturday a business day or not, so the possibility of leaving without a camera case was highly possible and not something I wanted to happen. During our last trip, Ralph brought a new video camera for the second leg of the trip from Bermuda to New York. His camera developed problems; the wide angle and telephoto functions stopped working before we even made it to New York (about 800 miles done in 53 hours). This trip, across the whole Atlantic Ocean, was supposed to be over 6,200 miles and take about 48 days. I did not want to expose the brand new video camera to the corrosive salt air of the Atlantic and have the same thing happen again.

I also decided it would be a good idea to purchase a ten-hour battery. The standard two-hour battery which came with the camera would have me changing it out for charging too often. We were bringing a small twelve-volt inverter for charging, but once out at sea, I didn't want to open the waterproof camera case any more than I had to. Moisture was everywhere and could get in and cause the lens to fog on the inside.

Ralph had been designing the T-shirt picture for the trip over the last couple of weeks. We'd both been talking about it over the phone. It looked as if his shirts might not be ready for the send-off on June 27th. I had also been fooling around with a shirt design as well as business cards for the trip. We were having a problem deciding what type of nautical item to use as a frame for the shirt picture. My first thought was rope, and then I went to chain, before finally deciding to go with the piece of driftwood I found along the Banana River near a Merritt Island bridge. I only had the one piece of wood, but I wanted the frame to have four pieces, all similar but a little different. I used Power Point and Paint on the computer, and was able to stretch the piece and flip it around, essentially making one piece look like four.

The first picture I used inside the driftwood frame was a shot of the boat from our first trip; two years ago going to Bermuda. Over the last six months, I'd been looking everywhere for a good

Lucky the First Time

picture of a wave. I wanted a wave which resembled the waves during our Bermuda trip out at sea. The wave needed to be taller than the boat and still look realistic. I shot close-up pictures at the beach and along the shoreline of both the Banana and Indian Rivers during all types of conditions. I was surprised at how difficult it was to get a good picture. I even had some computer people try to find one on the Internet, but with no luck. Donna Lange, from our Bermuda trip, sent me a picture she had taken on her solo sail around the world. It was pretty close. There was size and texture, but the sun glow on the wave made the photo useless.

One day my son Bryan wanted to go to a local Chinese restaurant and while waiting for our takeout, I noticed a picture of a lighthouse on the wall. There were sections of the surf which looked very promising. I had my camera in the car so I took several close-up shots of some of the individual waves among the twenty or so waves in the picture. I went home and was able to Photoshop the background out of my boat picture, then take that and paste it on top of the best wave picture. I was pretty happy with how it turned out. I wanted a wave in the nine-foot range, something we've been in during our crossing from North Carolina to Bermuda. I liked my final results and locally ordered five hundred business cards to hand out for our *CrossTheAtlantic.com* website.

I wanted to use that same picture in my T-shirt design. Lamar, the owner of Funwear T-Shirts, said the picture would be too dark and not look very good on the shirts. So I went one more time to the beach with my camera. I took about twenty different pictures of some two-foot waves as I stood in the waist-deep water of the Atlantic Ocean. I checked out the photos, but none of them looked good enough, plus the waves were too smooth. All of a sudden the wind picked up and the top of some of the waves started to crest and the wave faces developed ripples. I got excited and took another twenty shots. One of the last pictures I took looked good. Normally the water around Cocoa Beach looks cloudy grayish in color, but on this day, it was a pretty green, almost perfectly clear. This was the picture I selected to use on my group of T-shirts. When I showed Lamar this picture, he agreed it would work much better.

    I wanted the shirts to be a bright gray-blue-green color, but found out that particular color was hard to find. To me that blend of colors looked nautical and fresh, almost unique. Lamar showed me every color sample they had and none were what I wanted. I even cut a color sample out of an old New England lobster tourist T-shirt I had, and they still couldn't find it. The color wasn't available in Florida. My next choice was a teal green, but I was afraid it might look too girlish for the big tough males not wanting to show their feminine side. I decided to order one-hundred white shirts and twenty of the teal color. I also mixed in a few sample colors to see how they would have looked in case we need to order more. I ordered four bright yellow shirts, two beige shirts, and a handful of red. Lamar said they would take about a week. He was going to tweak the design a little and then squeeze the order in when he had a chance.

Lucky the First Time

Bob's Wounded Hero "Do More" T-shirt design

I got a call the morning of Wednesday, June 24th. The shirts were going to be finished midday, so I rushed over to Funwear T-shirts to see if I could get some video of the shirts being printed. I was fascinated with the mass production process and took a few minutes of footage. The shirts were attached to a large rotating machine with a separate stage for each color used. A different silk screen was set up for each color. The paint was thick, almost like the consistency of pancake batter. As the shirts rotated to each different stage, they were mechanically stopped. A screen was lowered in the exact spot needed and the color was mechanically spread through the screen onto the shirt by the use of a large squeegee. After the last color, they were manually removed and laid onto a conveyor belt that went into a drying machine. When they came out, they were folded and put into cardboard boxes. The colored shirts looked good. Now I wished I hadn't printed so many of the white. I like white, but being the slob that I am, I have a bad habit of trashing a white shirt; often the first time wearing it.

The first shirt sold was a bright yellow to Shannon McGregor, a paint customer of mine. Her friend bought a teal one. Yellow was also my favorite color so I kept two out of the mix of shirts for sale. I wanted one to wear on the boat and I thought Ralph might want a yellow one too. I also kept the beige ones for us. Over the next day, I sold mainly the teal and almost everyone wanted the coveted yellow ones. Many of the guys wanted the beige, but I didn't have any to sell. At least I know if I reorder, to make a bunch of yellow, beige and teal shirts. Most girls wear smalls and several asked about tank tops, which was something to think about.

During the last boat trip I spent a lot of time wishing I'd had an audio recorder with me. Trying to remember all the things that happened or remembering what went through my mind while we traveled was forgotten by the time I arrived at our next port where I could write them down. For any lengthy descriptions, the boat was too bumpy and wet for paper. So I'd purchased a digital voice recorder, but I had a trouble keeping the files in order and even more difficulty not accidentally erasing things. To cap that off, what if the recorder broke? How would I recover the files? The digital would make a good backup, but for the actual voyage, I wanted a mini-cassette. This way, at worst, if I lost the recorder or it got wet, I'd only lose one tape not my entire diary. I would keep the rest of the tapes in a secure dry place on the boat.

The last few days I'd started coughing and I was getting a little worried that I might be coming down with a cold. The last thing I wanted to do was to start the trip being sick. Part of it might have been because I was so excited about the trip that I was having trouble sleeping. Many nights I'd gotten up, restless, on edge, and used that time to read some boating books. You can never be too prepared.

I still had a lot of unfinished things to do around the house before I could take off for what Ralph expected to be around two months. I couldn't leave it all for my wife to deal with especially since I would be gone through much of the Florida hurricane season. I just finished putting a new roof on my house and still had the leaking, crumbly stucco around the fireplace to deal with. The fireplace would leak a little due to water peculating through the stucco. I worked on it several times, buttering elastomeric patching compound over the whole thing and embedding it in fiberglass screen to keep it from cracking. I needed only a couple more coats to finish.

I ordered two banners from Lickity Split Signs for advertising our operation when we were in port. These two foot by six-foot signs had the picture from the shirts in the middle with a blank area on each side for writing in any sponsors we picked up along the way. We wanted to promote the website: CrossTheAtlantic.com and our sponsors. Lickity Split made some of our smaller sponsors' decals, for example the one for Georgianna

Wounded Hero Voyage I

Methodist Church. One of the two decals for the church would go on a gas tank and the other would go on my surfboard, mounted on top of the T-top. I thought an ad from our church would be apropos because the name of our boat was *I am Second* which meant *"God is First"*. Also, I wanted to put a decal on the surfboard since their youth program is named *The Wave*. They made a donation for the purchase of a life raft or to go in the general fund for gas and miscellaneous purchases.

Thursday, June 25th

Two days from departure, I went driving around looking for more sponsors now that I knew we were going for sure. I thought it would be a good idea to have a surf-kite on the boat. In the event our engines died, most likely from capsizing or waves crashing over them, I thought it would be good not to be completely helpless. A surf-kite would enable us to move at least slowly downwind to head in the direction of dry land or shipping lanes. I went to several places within fifty miles to look for an inexpensive kite. No luck, they were all over a thousand dollars... too expensive, but I did stop at a surf shop. Cape Surf in Cape Canaveral was a store I had never been in before. I do most of my surfing going south of the 520 Causeway and hardly ever go north to Cape Canaveral. Anyway, I stopped in and talked with the guy behind the counter. He told me to call back and talk to Kevin, one of the owner partners. He thought Kevin would love to be involved with our project. I had already approached other surf shops in Cocoa Beach, but they showed absolutely no interest in our venture. In all fairness, they are probably bombarded by a lot of organizations requesting sponsorships, monies, and free merchandise.

Lunch was at Sonny's Bar-B-Q with a good friend of mine,

Lucky the First Time

Mr. Wonderful, as I was told to call him 25-years ago when I was first introduced to him during a paint job I was doing. He and some of the waitresses were previously involved in helping me make some decisions on the T-shirt designs. Since I'd just gotten the shirts the day before, I showed them the finished product. They liked them and said good luck with that oh-so-familiar side glance, meaning they didn't think we had a chance.

The 500-business boat cards I ordered earlier for the trip, advertised my Bermuda book on the back, so I could promote my book during the voyage. Ralph wanted some with different text on the front and also wanted the back to be blank, for writing notes or phone numbers. He wanted me to order 1,000, and with my 500, we'd start the trip with 1,500-boat cards. I went to Digit Tech, about seven-miles from my house, and started the process. Usually when someone orders business cards through them, they take the information and send it digitally to Miami to be printed and mailed back, but I was leaving the next day for Hudson. They had me "copy and paste" the pictures so I would have a whole page of cards. They then printed them on cardstock and cut them out. Before they were finished with the order, Ralph called me and had me order another 1,000. We were now going to have a total of 2,500-boat cards for the trip.

I drove over to Digit Tech just before they closed and picked up the cards. By the time I got home I had a message from Digit Tech. Somehow Tom, the owner, hadn't received the message from his secretary that Ralph had increased the order an additional 1,000. Tom discovered the mishap when going over the invoice. Tom printed them after hours and then drove to the halfway spot between his office and my house for the delivery. I thought that was really cool. In this day in age, a company went out of their way to help us on such a small order. Thanks Digit Tech!

Kevin, from Cape Surf, told me our trip sounded like a great project and he had been looking for something like this to give back to the community. He told me to come by just before they closed at seven that night. Kevin hooked me up with a double board surfboard bag to use as a sleeping bag, two rash guards, a bunch of T-shirts to give out to some of the Wounded Heroes who might go for rides on the boat, and some small surfshop stickers.

We already had an eight-foot old surfboard bag, which Steve Webster, a surf buddy, gave me. We needed two, yet the one Steve gave me was riddled with holes and was probably not very water resistant. We would be using his when we docked at the harbors and didn't have to worry about rolling, pitching, waves. The new bag would be for when we were underway and out at sea. Whoever wasn't driving might try to sleep, since the majority of our traveling would be during the night.

Bryan, my son, was on vacation from college, in Miami with his girlfriend. Her dad was taking them fishing offshore and Bryan needed to know the numbers on his fishing license which was somewhere in our house. I spent two hours looking everywhere for the seemingly nonexistent license. By then he had discovered all he had to do, if they got checked by the Marine Patrol, was to give his driver's license number which was linked to his fishing license. Good to know.

Jonathan, my other son, was at Doug Butler's summer running camp about thirty minutes away. Jill, my lovely wife, drove him there with our beautiful dog, Casey. Wickham Park was Casey's favorite place in the whole world to go for a walk. You can't beat Doug's running camp, everyone loves it. If my left knee, which has a torn meniscus, didn't; I'd probably be up there running with them too. If I run much more than a quarter-mile, my knee swells up and it is difficult to walk for a couple of days.

Most of the T-shirts were folded together in groups of five, all the same size. Whenever one was pulled out, the whole group was messed up. While Jill and Jonathan were gone, I individually folded all the shirts and stacked them by size and color.

I stayed up past two a.m. doing computer stuff and packing. My plan was to leave around 9:00 in the morning. I wasn't going to be able to drive myself, since Jill's car was in the shop and Bryan was going to use our PT Cruiser up at college over the summer term. Jill was going to drive me to Orlando where Hahns, my brother in-law, was going to drive me to Hudson. Hudson is a couple of towns north of Tampa where Ralph's boat shop is and where we'd be loading the boat.

Friday, June 26th

The morning was really hectic and I left much later than planned. Ralph called several times to try to speed things up. I wasted an hour looking for my safe boating book which I got from the safe boating class I took last year. I never found it. Jill drove me to Orlando, where we waited for Hahns. He had taken Aaron, his oldest son, to the dentist. When Hahns arrived home, he joked about the fact there was no actual checklist of safety items we needed to bring, not to mention a checklist of other items as well. Aaron cracked a joke about using the surfboard bag as a body bag to send us back home. We loaded everything from my PT Cruiser into his Mustang. Jill, not really a fan of this boating thing, wished me good luck and kissed me goodbye.

On the way over to Hudson, while making sarcastic comments about the likelihood of the trip's success without incident on my audio recorder, we almost got side swiped by another car. I don't know how they didn't see us as they tried to change lanes into us, oh wait, yes I do. They were on a cell phone! We commented about the ocean being safer than driving on the highway. Hahns and I finally found a Wachovia bank so I could cash a check. I wanted to have a couple of hundred dollars of my own money. I wasn't supposed to have to spend any of my own money on the trip as CrossTheAtlantic.com Corp. was footing the entire journey, but I still wanted some cash in my wallet.

When we were eleven minutes away from Ralph's boat shop, according to the car GPS, we started wondering how many people were going to be at the shop, or was it going to be just Ralph. I guessed the boat was ready and Ralph was just waiting for my stuff to finish packing up the boat. I was really looking forward to a relaxing break to get rested up for tomorrow's departure. A couple of days ago, Ralph and I had talked about going out for a media ride sometime before actually going to the send-off.

Surprise, surprise, the boat was a disaster, I guess Ralph's last couple of days were just like mine, so much to do and no time to do it. The boat had no T-top; no engine covers, no seats, only one of the gas tanks, wires hanging out of everywhere, and nothing was packed. The floor was just replaced during the week, with a stronger, three inch higher floor. All Ralph's new boats are made with the stronger, higher floor. We discovered on the Bermuda trip, when the boat was overloaded with fuel and stopped, there was a lot of water coming in the back scupper holes, used for draining water out of the boat while the boat is going forward. Ralph is always implementing new improvements whenever possible. There was fiberglass dust on everything and we still had to fiberglass in the back storage compartment. I was bummed, but I couldn't blame Ralph, as I knew how hard he worked to get to this point. He couldn't get anything done until he had the money to work with. The boat looked like it was still a few days away from being ready for departure, which was in about 25 hours.

When Ralph first suggested changing out the floor, I was against it, because of time and money, and the boat did so well on the last trip. But Ralph had reminded me that we would be even heavier than the last trip and the water temperature would be much colder. I remembered as if it were yesterday when we froze going from Bermuda to New York during the second night. I was so cold I could hardly stand it and this trip was expected to be much colder. I agreed. The dryer boat would be nicer.

Ralph had hired a professional graphic designer to really dress up the boat. The graphic tech was nearly finished putting on a full length decal or should I say wrap. It changed the hull of our bright yellow Intruder 21, the technical name of our boat, into the fluorescent green Interstate Battery color with yellow lightning bolts. The bold black letters *I Am Second* really made the boat look special. My surfboard had the same logo on the bottom which after we mounted it on the T-top, would stand out great for any aerial shots. The graphic wrap was really expensive and came directly out of our trip money. Ralph hoped that with our professional adventurer's look more companies would now take us seriously. The general consensus before had been that we weren't for real. They

Wounded Hero Voyage I

could join the team and their logos would be placed on the boat too.

We worked late into the evening with the help of Marino, John Carroll, Jeff, Ian, Hahns, and whoever else stopped by. Marino is a boat builder and helps Ralph build his boats. John Carroll is an investor with Ralph's boat company and wants to help out wherever he can. Jeff is John's son and Ian is a friend of theirs. Anne, Ralph's wife, came by with their kids and she insisted we take a break and go out to dinner. We went to Cracker Barrel. As we were waiting for our food Ralph did a telephone interview and I glanced around. That's when I noticed a *Wounded Warrior Project* brochure on the table. Wow. That's pretty cool. One of the Wounded Hero Foundation, which we were promoting, was right in front of us. Definitely a what are the odds kind of moment.

Nine days before departure, the day the trip was sponsored.

Lucky the First Time

In another of Ralph's many telephone interviews at his shop, he talked a lot about the NFL football players who drowned seventy-miles off of Tampa, Florida a few months before. Their V-bottom boat had capsized in heavy seas. Ralph had actually met Marquis Cooper, the player for the Tampa Bay Bucs, on two different occasions. The first time Marquis was with Dwayne White, also a Bucs player, and two other people. Somehow they had wrapped a fishing line around their propeller and Ralph offered to tow them in. Marquis said they would be fine, but Ralph stayed with them until they got their motor started and they motored in together. Salesman Ralph tried to talk them into buying one of his boats, explaining how his Intruder 21 was dryer and a lot more stable. Marquis and Dwayne actually autographed a ball cap for Anne while they were there. The second time Ralph met Marquis, the football player and another guy were heading out shark fishing and asked Ralph if he wanted to follow them. At first, Ralph said no, but his kids, who were with him, changed his mind... "They're famous professional football players dad! You have to!" During their fishing trip, Ralph gave Marquis another sales pitch, but couldn't close the deal. Ralph feels a little guilty sometimes, saying had he been a better salesman; they would all still be alive today. V-bottoms with the floatation below the deck often capsize easily once the boat fills with water. A safer V-bottom would also have floatation in the side walls and possibly some on the outside above the waterline like a Zodiac. Ralph told me his Intruder 21 got Runner-Up as the *Innovation of the Year Award* in the Miami Boat Show against the Everglade 21, the same type of boat which Marquis owned.

Wounded Hero Voyage I

After our voyage, while writing this book, I read *Not Without Hope* by Nick Schuyler. Nick was the only one of the four football players who was rescued. Marquis Cooper, Will Bleakley, and Corey Smith were the other guys that didn't make it. On Feb 28, 2009 they motored seventy miles out, to fish over a wreck, in a 21-foot open fishing boat (the same size as our boat). They planned to head back in early since there was a cold front coming in sometime during the evening and the seas were already in the seven-foot range. As they went to pull up their anchor, it snagged on something. They decided to try to rip the anchor off the sea bed by tying the anchor line to the back portside boat cleat (the left back bracket generally used for tying boats to docks). After several failed attempts at a gradual increase of speed, they slammed the throttle down to full power using their 200 horse power outboard engine. The boat's rear portside transom (left back corner of the boat) dipped low and a gush of water came over and filled up their boat. In one horrific motion, their boat flipped over. They had capsized seventy miles out to sea and were all by themselves. They tried everything they could think of to re-right the boat, but without leverage and because of the boat's slick bottom, there was nothing to grip onto. The four 200-plus-pounds of muscle-ripped guys were helpless to re-right their boat.

Lucky the First Time

Ralph wiring under the dash

Ralph and I stayed up working on the boat long after everyone else left. Hahns was tired so he went to the hotel earlier. Ralph would drop me off there when we were done. We finally were too exhausted to continue and since we still had a lot of supplies to buy for the trip, we decided we might as well go shopping. Two-hours later, around 2:00 a.m. we figured it would be a better use of our time for me to sleep at Ralph's house. This would save him from having to drive the extra miles to the hotel and then back to his house. We both needed the sleep.

Early the next morning, we were back working at the shop. I wasted another couple of hours on the Internet trying to send some pictures to some of our sponsors. The PC and Internet connections in Ralph's office needed something, exactly what, I know, but the thought of a slight tap with a sledge hammer definitely came to mind.

John Carroll, Jeff and Ian stored our gear into the hatches. The small boat had a lot of built in storage compartments, six on the front deck, a compartment above the steering wheel, a larger one below the steering wheel, three on the back deck, and one long one across the whole back. The T-top had zip-around storage bags hanging down from the front and back with a hard-glove box centered underneath with a Plexiglas window. We brought along two large coolers (used for our personal dry storage) strapped to the floor up front, my large blue duffel strapped on the left side of the center console, miscellaneous bags on the seat in front of the console, and two bags lashed on the back of the captain's seat. On the dash we placed a couple of plastic bins to hold the cameras and little things.

Between the two big dry-box coolers and in the space forward of the front metal seventy-gallon gas tank, which was up against the front seat, was where the seven portable five-gallon plastic jerry jugs were stored. On each side of the console, up against the rail on the floor, sat 2-fifty-gallon plastic semi transparent gas tanks placed end-to-end. This left no room for a walkway to the front other than walking on top of the tanks or the boat railing. The remaining 38-gallon plastic see through plastic tank was built in on the floor inside the lower console storage area. Also in the same cabinet were the two Interstate Batteries that we carried.

Lucky the First Time

Just hours before departure Bob, Ralph, John Carroll, and Jeff

Captain's seat still not in, but the sponsor's wrap is nearly done.

Wounded Hero Voyage I

I won't go into detail on all the little things that we brought since they come up in the story or have already been mentioned, but we brought along a yellow and white bean bag chair since Ralph was told that they absorb some of the pounding and can be easily moved anywhere on the boat. Ralph also brought along his good laptop and a smaller one for me to use. Whenever possible, we planned to get on the Internet to comment on the CrosstheAtlantic.com blog, do email, and try to find more sponsors.

The last of the wrap, seats going in, but still no propellers on the motors

Hahns and I were both starving and I also needed to go to a hardware store to purchase some stainless steel nuts and bolts. Ralph said we didn't have the time to pick up food; we were running too late. I made an executive decision; captain's orders are only good when out at sea, so Hahns and I took off to Burger King and

Lucky the First Time

the local hardware store. It's probably a good thing we did, everyone gobbled up the burgers, except Ralph. He only ate half of his but he never stopped working. Most of the bolts I bought were used up in a few minutes for things like bolting down the gas tanks and the captain's seat. Hours later, I threw out Ralph's half uneaten sandwich. During the next few hours we managed to locate the elusive spare propeller. We were ready to begin our journey just after 3:30 p.m.; leaving us little time to get to the Marriott Hotel Marina for our send off.

Ralph in boat and Bob on side, first start of the brand-new motors

I climbed into Hahns' showroom-clean Mustang and sat on a towel since my clothes were all sweaty. We followed the boat trailered by Don Brown, one of Ralph's investors, to the Marriott through the rain, and saw my straw hat fly out of the boat and land on the road. As Hahns and I stopped to recover the hat, we called

Ralph to tell them we were going to be slightly delayed and for them to drive a tad slower. We'd noticed that my two fourteen-foot windsurfer poles, strapped to the T-top, had spray-in-foam oozing out of them. I had earlier filled the ends of the poles with foam so they wouldn't sink if they ended up in the water. These poles were for mounting our cameras in filming our voyage and also leverage tools in the event we capsized.

After leaving the highway, both cars stopped to gas up the boat. We still hadn't had the chance to connect the non-stock gas tanks into the valve manifold system. This would allow us to drain the tanks in any order we thought the conditions warranted. As a matter of fact, we didn't even have enough gas line and clamps to make the manifold system operable. We'd worry about that later.

Hahns commented he heard Ralph complaining he didn't have enough time to adequately wax the motor and the T-top aluminum to protect them from the salt spray. Hahns had been looking at the portable propane gas grill and then glancing at the exteriorly mounted 4-fifty-gallon gas tanks and the 1-seventy-gallon among the seven loosely laid out five-gallon jerry cans, when he said, "I think you have more important things to worry about." Hahns still hadn't even considered the 27 gallons built into the console. I quickly added up the figures for Hahns, "Yep, 332 gallons of highly explosive fuel, I don't believe we'll be having any open flames on this trip."

We joked that there probably wasn't even a lighter or a match anywhere on the boat anyway. Me, being a wanna-be survivor-show-contestant, quickly pointed out we still had wires going to our Interstate Batteries and a four-inch magnifying glass to

Lucky the First Time

help us blind people see small print. If we wanted fire, that would not be a problem.

I began fueling the gas tanks, with the 75 gallons of gasoline needed for this first leg of the trip, Tampa to Fort Myers. We didn't need to carry too much extra fuel because the added weight of excess fuel would hinder our fuel economy and make the boat sluggish. I was about halfway done when a large man wearing a tux got out of a black limo and came up to inquire about being a sponsor. He took the information from Ralph and said he would get back with us. If someone wanted to become a sponsor, anyone could easily get into contact with us through Ralph's website and the use of cell phones, satellite phone, and messages left with people helping us. We would be able to have a company logo made and waiting for us at our next port of call.

Getting gasoline on the way to the send off

Tampa, Florida, Recovered Photographer

We arrived with the boat ramp at thirty seconds until five. We were supposed to be at the Marriott docks at 5:00 p.m. and we still had a ways to go by water. To compile our tardiness, it started to downpour and I had just changed into my brand new clean *I Am Second* button down Interstate Battery shirt. Needless to say, we were soaked by the time we got the boat into the water. As fast as the rain had started, it stopped. We quickly dried off places on the boat and plastered on our sponsors' stickers. We had to have them on before we arrived at the docks for the send-off pictures.

I was surprised at the turnout for the Bon Voyage Rally, as Ralph called it. There was a good size crowd, but not the numbers I was expecting, since Ralph had bought radio ads promoting our departure. It probably didn't help we were late and I'm sure the downpour must have chased away many of our supporters. The fact that hardly anybody actually thought we'd be able to complete our voyage didn't help either.

John Carroll, Jeff and Ian, our road support team selling T-shirts and helping where ever they could, brought T-shirts out to the boardwalk so Anne and her family could start selling them. Ralph and I met Jason Mckean, a Wounded Hero who was wounded on

Tampa, Florida, Recovered Photographer

September 13, 2003 in Baghdad, Iraq by an IED (improvised explosive device). He was on the back of an unarmored light mobile terrain vehicle when the IED went off near the front of it. It wounded Jason, the driver, and one of his buddies inside. He suffered a severed right achilles tendon, shrapnel in his right leg, mostly in his knee, shrapnel in his right arm, mostly in his elbow. He also suffered severe traumatic brain injury and lost the majority of his memory along with post traumatic distress syndrome from being in the war for nine months since the beginning. He has had over seven surgeries to remove over fifty pieces of shrapnel and to this day he still suffers memory loss and is still in pain all the time. Jason Mckean was in A Company 1-325 Airborne Infantry Regiment 82 Airborne Division. He was the first of several Wounded Heroes scheduled to ride a leg of our journey with us. Jason seemed so young compared to Ralph and I. His only concern was he didn't want to get sea sick.

> Excerpt Quote from Cross the Atlantic blog: "Well my name is Jason Mckean. I'm an Iraq Vet with a purple heart. I will be joining Ralph and Robert Brown on the start of their world record, going from Tampa Bay, Fl to Ft. Myers, Fl. I think this is a great way to show their support for Wounded Heroes. I'm glad to be a part of it. Thanks guys."

An employee from the Marriott served Jason, Ralph and me each a burger, fries, and soda. After the sky cleared, more and more people came out to watch and take pictures. A lady reached over a dock railing and put her hands on our heads saying a prayer for our safety and the success of our voyage. A guy named Kevin handed Ralph a big bag of coffee and Ralph replied with a big grin, "I'm a connoisseur of the bean." Ralph said he would find a way to brew it.

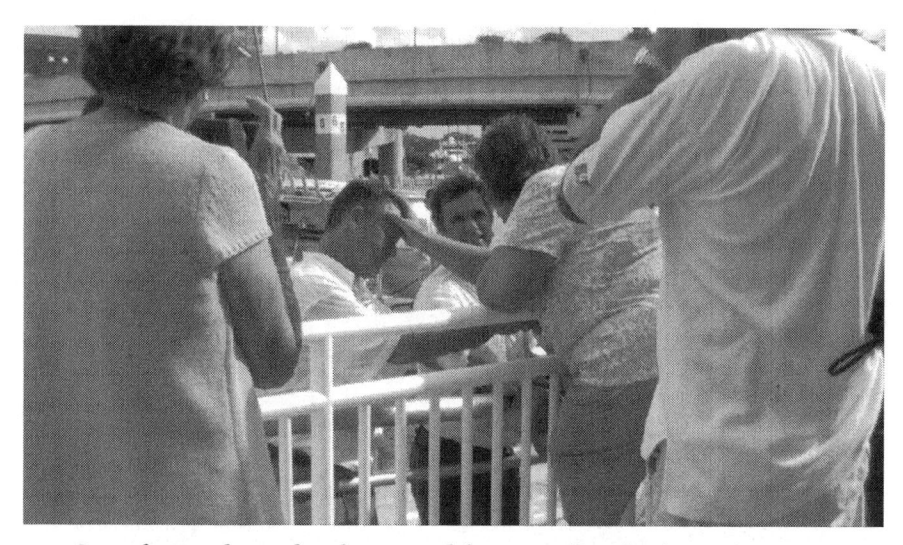

One of several people who prayed for our safety during our voyage

John McDaniel, from Wounded Warriors in Action, started the introduction speech to the crowd explaining how Jason and other heroes became part of this venture. Shawn, from Ralph's Friday morning prayer group, led the blessing for our epic journey. Saying things like; there is a certain degree of skepticism about our trip, but then went on to talk about Ralph's determination, perseverance, and tenacity. He explained how Ralph had met Norm Miller, founder of I Am Second organization and the Chairman of Interstate Battery, at a Christian organization. They became our major sponsor and were entitled to name the boat. Our Intruder 21 flats boat was named I Am Second spreading the idea that God should be first in everyone's life. "I am Second is a movement meant to inspire people of all kinds to live for God and for others," from IAmSecond.com.

Ralph jumped up on a cement retaining wall and with a bunch of enthusiasm gave a rather long speech touching many

Tampa, Florida, Recovered Photographer

aspects of his reasons for doing this unbelievable trip. Ralph saluted all the heroes who do their job and explained what happens when a soldier gets injured and is shipped to Landstuhl Medical Hospital in Germany, the main hospital for the war. In addition, the financial strain a family has to endure; often the spouse loses his or her job while taking time off to take care of our Wounded Hero. "Who Pays For That?" He went on to promote his slogan, "Do More Than Just Say Thanks."

Ralph, a former Marine, went into great depths about the 29-years ago when he thought he was going to be part of the Iran Hostage Rescue Mission, known as Operation Eagle Claw. Ralph explained that on August 24, 1980 a chopper came down in a dust storm on a C130 in the desert and eight members of the newly formed elite Delta Force died in the explosion. Our voyage across the Atlantic Ocean is dedicated to John Harvey, George Homes, and Dewy Johnson; the three Marines who died that day.

Ralph explaining why he had dedicated our voyage to Wounded Heroes like Jason on his right.

Wounded Hero Voyage I

Ralph yelled over to me, since I had wandered away over to the boat, "Did you want to say something?"

I answered back, "Let's Go!" The crowd wasn't going to let me get off that easy. I ended up talking about *The Bermuda Suicide Challenge*, the book I wrote about our first trip two years before. I said I was going to write a book about our voyage and one of my main goals was to get a picture of our boat with an iceberg in the back ground. Since we were going without an escort, one of us would have to get off the boat to take the pictures. That explained the purpose of the surfboard on the T-top above the boat. I briefly stated I wanted to get much better video footage on this trip so we could possibly make a documentary of the trip.

We spent a lot of time shaking hands, answering questions, signing a few autographs, posing for pictures, and doing an interview for the local news station. We probably overstayed our departure, since many of the people started to leave before we had cast off. We'd been scheduled to depart at 5:00 p.m., but we actually pulled away from the Marriott Waterside dock at exactly 7:11 p.m. Eastern Standard time on June 27, 2009.

Ralph's wife, Anne, selling "Do More" T-shirts

Tampa, Florida, Recovered Photographer

(<u>NOTE TO THE READER</u>: Since the trip involved thousands of miles over many days, I don't always mention when we change drivers or when someone wakes up, because it would sound really monotonous real fast, so the reader can assume if one of us was driving the other <u>could</u> be asleep or that we had already done a complete driving rotation. There was never a set schedule as the one that was the most alert operated the boat. Typically about every three hours we'd switch off. I also won't always report how much later or the distance traveled between paragraphs for the same reason.)

Jason had the helm as the three of us waved good bye. Hahns who had been video taping the send off for me had a great video angle from one of the upper floors of the hotel and filmed us going off without him. We had never discussed how he was going to get back to his car, a mile or so away and how I was going to get my camera back from him. We lowered our American flag before we passed under a low bridge. On the other side we immediately raised Old Glory back to her rightful place atop of one of our two 14-foot fiberglass poles. We had her flying over twenty foot above the water with the pole mounted in one of the roof fishing rod holders. Yes, this was a patriotic Wounded Hero Voyage and we wanted to fly her high.

We weren't much more than a half-mile away when we realized our missing Hahns. By use of cell phones, the plan became Hahns would get a ride with Jeff Denny, Miki Renner, and Don

Brown. They caught up to us in their bow rider powerboat and became our boat's entourage of one. Now with Hahns aboard they become our official camera boat for our departure. Hahns filmed as the four of them made humorous comments about our, in their minds, doomed voyage. Much to their entertainment, Ralph was busy wiring up the lights which we would be needing in the next couple of hours. Lucky for us there was no Coast Guard inspection, since lights aren't required for daytime use.

Motoring underneath the bridge in the slow speed zone

Wounded Hero Jason driving during our departure from Tampa

Tampa, Florida, Recovered Photographer

I spent the time as we motored in the long canal heading out toward the bay organizing the boat. I had to try and find a place for everything and there wasn't enough storage space to put everything away. We passed a lot of really nice boats, houses, and a big industrial area before eventually entering the bay. The bay had light chop and the sun was starting to dip in the sky, so it was time for our photography flotilla to pass us our cameras and leave us to our solo adventure. We now had our lights working and since we had forgotten to load the coolers with drinks, we were handed a couple of waters from our departing friends. Thanks guys, we were thirsty. Oops, I just remembered I left my straw hat in Hahns' car, oh well.

Later, Ralph told me a lot of the media who were supposed to be at our send off never showed up because they were covering the breaking story of US Airways flight 1241 at the Tampa International Airport. Upon landing, the 737 jet with 138 people and a crew of five had a front tire blow out which possibly caused the landing gear to collapse. Infomercial king, Billy Mays, famous for selling the OxiClean products on television, was on that flight. It was reported that luggage fell down from the overhead compartment and jolted him hard on the head. At that time, none of the passengers reported any serious injuries. But Billy Mays went to bed early that night, not feeling well and as we know now, he died during the night. He was pronounced dead at 7:45 a.m. on June 28th. A few days later at his autopsy, it was discovered he had died from a heart attack caused by his previous unknown heart disease.

To Fort Myers, Going Back in Time

We were busy trying to figure out the workings of our brand new Garmin chartplotter. It was different from the plotter we had on our Bermuda trip. The Garmin was mounted to the boat right out of the box and out on the water was where we figured out it didn't have a compass page. To make matters worse, our only compass was still on the workbench back in Ralph's shop. Oops, make note... purchase a compass ASAP. Jason was doing most of the driving, and since neither Ralph nor I were able to clearly see the fine print on the small plotter's viewing screen, Jason was the one who had to read. And you know what happens when you are on a moving boat, going up and down and you are looking down and not on the horizon. Well Jason was the first to get a little sea sick. After he discharged a little over the side and stopped trying to read the plotter, he was fine.

As the sun was starting to set, I took my first bath in a couple of days. I hadn't had one at Ralph's house; we had gotten home too late and left too early. I jumped into the water for a couple of minutes to try to rinse off the sweat and fiberglass dust, much of which had gotten into my skin and was making me itch.

To Fort Myers, Going Back in Time

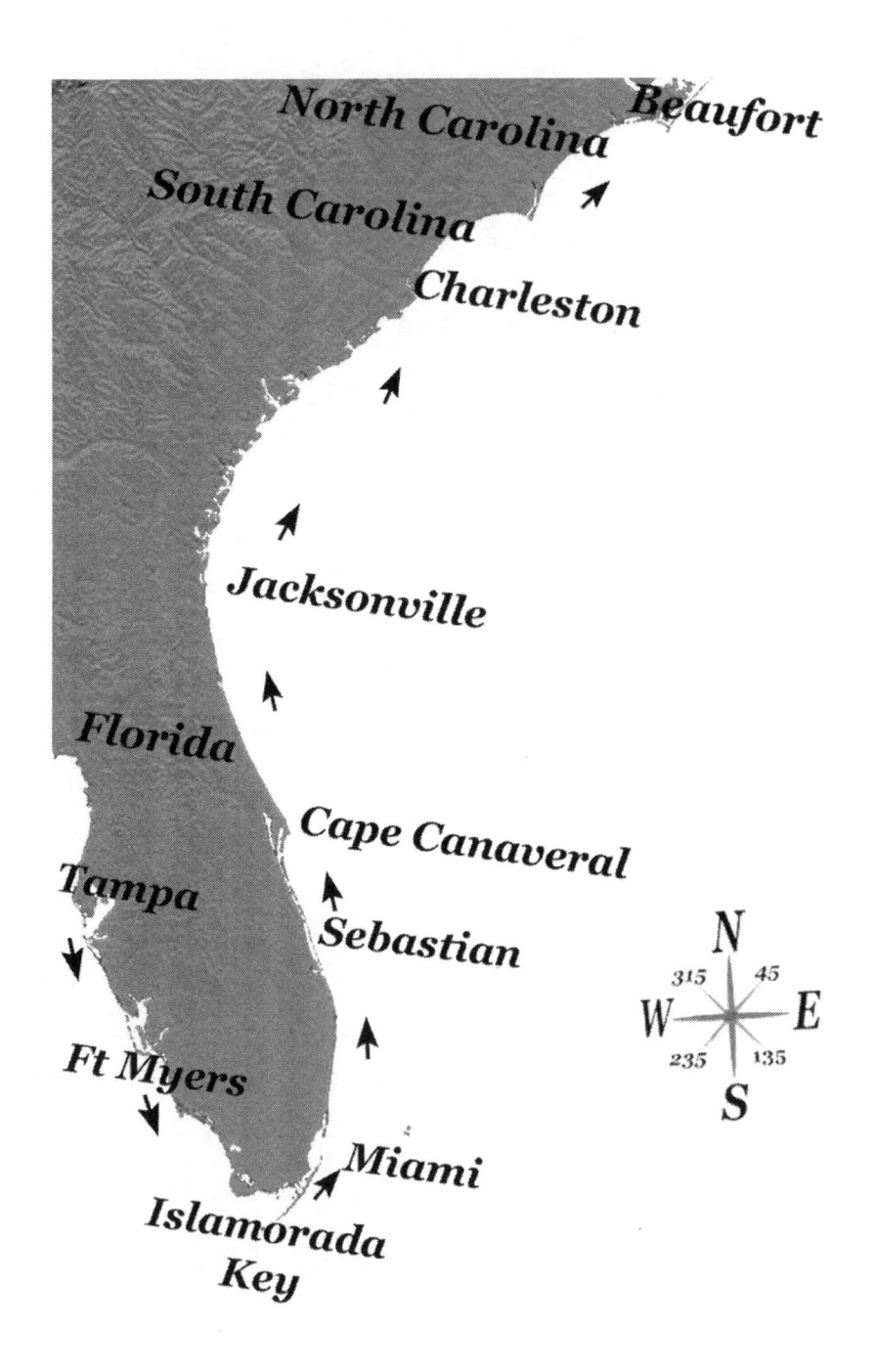

Wounded Hero Voyage I

In the dark and traveling along at a good clip we noticed floating crabs in the beam of our forward light. They were easy to see as the light reflected off their shells which made them appear white. Soon, a flock of seagulls joined us. They were flying right next to us and then they would dart in front of our bow and snatch the crabs right out of the water. Sometimes there would be as many as twenty birds just off our T-top and it amazed me we never hit any of them. The birds not only had to lookout for our forward movement, but also when we hit a wave, the bow would bounce off the wave and change directions rapidly. The birds flew just inches off our bow during their plunders, sometimes over or just under our bow. I took some video of them hoping they would be visible, but it was awfully dark out.

We stopped for a few minutes while Ralph readied the safety ropes. Just like in the beginning of our first voyage, we tied ourselves to the boat whenever it was dark and when we were out of the cockpit area. We joked the rope was just long enough for us to bounce around the back of the boat and get chewed up in the propeller.

The Skyway Bridge looked magnificent from the water with all its lights. It was 10:30 p.m. when we passed underneath it leaving Tampa Bay and heading out to sea. We stayed within the deeper water marked by red and green channel markers as the channel meandered between some small islands. Going out to sea, the red is on the left and green is on the right. My trick to remembering this is that there are five letters in both green and right.

To Fort Myers, Going Back in Time

Sunday, Jun 28th

The three of us motored all night and arrived at the Tarpon Lodge in Fort Myers. We had a little trouble finding the place, driving around in a bunch of channels. We spent most of the day at the lodge. John Carroll and his group met us there and got us a room by trading a couple of my books. The place was beautiful. The white multileveled lodge was separated from the water by a luscious green field of grass clustered with cocoanut palms and an array of Florida flowers. It looked like we had traveled back in time with a lot of white lacey curtains and things in the dining room, dark brown wooden floors and furniture, and light cream walls. I enjoyed inspecting all the mounted fish and their collection of photographs on the walls. The place had that comforting smell of a leathery book mixed with the fresh salt air. Someday I'd like to bring Jill out here for a weekend. I took a refreshing dip in the pool and ate inside the antique decorated dining room.

We were interviewed by two different news stations near the water, credit goes to John Carroll's phone calls, and we had a chance to sleep for a couple of hours. John McDaniel came by and picked up Jason. We'd be seeing John McDaniel again in the Keys; he had another Wounded Hero for that leg of the trip. I felt bad because of our inability to leave Tampa on time and all the things we had to do while motoring down to Fort Myers, we never had a chance to take Jason fishing. I feel we still owe him a day of fishing.

Ralph hooked up with the Pineland Marina next door while getting gas. The guys there took a case of shirts which they were going to sell for us; bought four or five of my *Bermuda Suicide Challenge* books, donated 75 gallons of gas, and then loaded us down with a bunch of delicious-junk food. They were extremely helpful and gave us a laminated local chart which advertised their marina. It wasn't far to walk between the lodge and the marina, but they still gave me a ride in their golf cart.

Ralph and I departed Ft. Myers late Sunday afternoon on June 28th. We headed out into seas over four-foot for the second leg of our trip. This part would take us along the west coast of Florida, into the Gulf of Mexico, and west of the Florida Everglades. As we were leaving we hit our first storm. We wanted pictures and video. So I went out on my surfboard to capture the action. It was just before dark when Ralph drove the boat in large circles around me, jumping the waves in the boat. I had a little trouble with the tiny waterproof GoPro camera. I forgot to change out the year-old batteries earlier and now the camera kept turning off because of low power. It was too dark to film so we decided we'd had enough and besides, we'd have plenty of time to film later during the trip.

Jason wasn't the only one to get sick on our little adventure. I woke up from lying on the aft section of the boat with a bad headache and feeling woozy. As soon as I sat up, I knew I was going to have to lean over the side; I was feeling sick. I tried to keep it down, because that is just what guys do as they never want to admit to getting sea sick. As it turned out, I blamed this one on gas fumes. When Ralph got fuel, he spilt some and it worked its way to the back. The gas had collected about a foot away from where my face was.

During the night, Ralph was driving when we were closing in on some type of ferry boat off in the distance, probably in route to the Florida Keys. We were gaining on it as it was at the one o'clock position in front of us. When we were about forty yards off to the side of the ferry it suddenly gained speed. I thought we should have probably given it a wider berth, but Ralph hadn't altered his course. It seemed the ferry wanted to race us. When it appeared we were going to pass the ferry its captain turned a large blinding spotlight on us. Ralph got on the radio and contacted the captain asking him why he was shining his light on us. The Captain said something to the effect we were driving too close.

The funny thing was, by this time it was obvious we were indeed passing the ferry on its left side. If the Captain had a problem with us; why was he increasing his speed when we were just about to pass him or why he didn't alter his course long before we got close to him? We had been on this path for a long time and steadily gaining on him. We were a much smaller boat and going at a much faster speed. The Captain then suddenly altered his course as if to get away from us. By this time, we were already out in front and leaving him in our wake.

The weather conditions had been steadily deteriorating. There was a small tropical storm heading towards us causing the seas to grow to five and six-foot swells and wind gusts were approaching 35 mph. It was a wet ride and a long time until morning. We talked about anchoring and waiting out in the storm, but we didn't have a working white anchor light and we were on a mission to get to Islamorada, so stopping was out of the question. By sunup, the storm had passed.

Ralph did all the driving early in the morning. I slept through several hours of him skimming across six inches of water, and in some cases less within the Florida Bay, the large basically unmarked shallow area located between mainland Florida and the Keys. We were lucky we weren't heavy with fuel. He told me at one time he almost ran into an island just before the sun came up and later the motor scraped the bottom a couple of times. When I got up, I witnessed an hour or two of it. It was a little scary because there was hardly any water under the boat. This would not be a good time to hit a rock or piece of coral.

Someone had to be the first.... Ralph wanted to try to use the radio and our radio antenna on top of the T-top was always falling down. As a matter of fact, we usually just left it down until we wanted to use it; seemed to be less trouble that way. It is held up by a turn handle similar to the quick release mechanism used for removing the wheel on a ten speed bike. I can't really be sure what happened, but after tightening the handle and possibly turning to climb off the gas tank I was standing on, I fell into the water. We weren't going very fast and no, I didn't have my safety rope on. Since the rail of the boat was only inches above the water, I had no problem climbing back in over the side. We planned to permanently fix our antenna when we had the time. We were going to change out our antenna with a taller one allowing us to transmit over longer distances. Our longer antenna was still in its cardboard tube strapped along side one of the long fiberglass poles on the T-top.

To Fort Myers, Going Back in Time

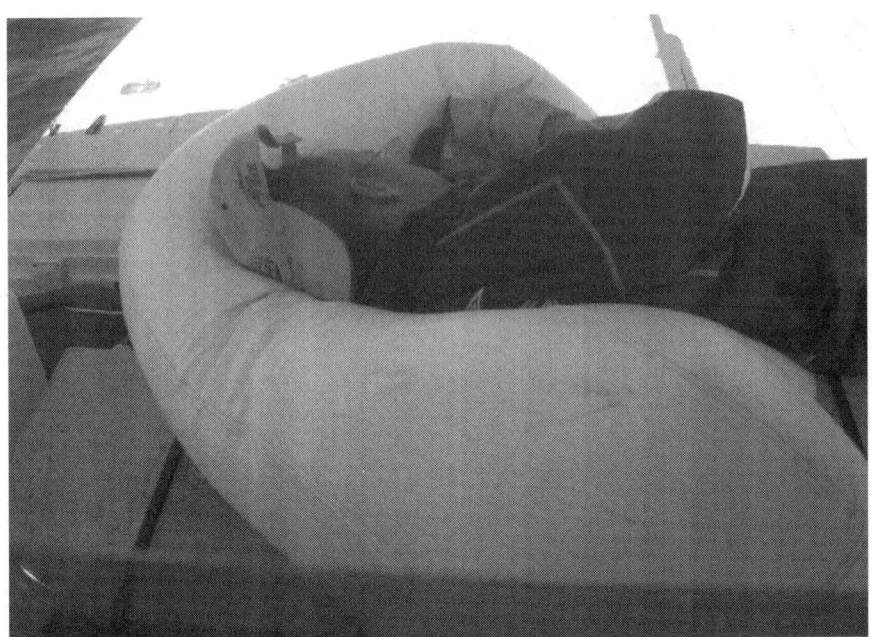

Ralph asleep on the bean bag on top of the seventy-gallon tank

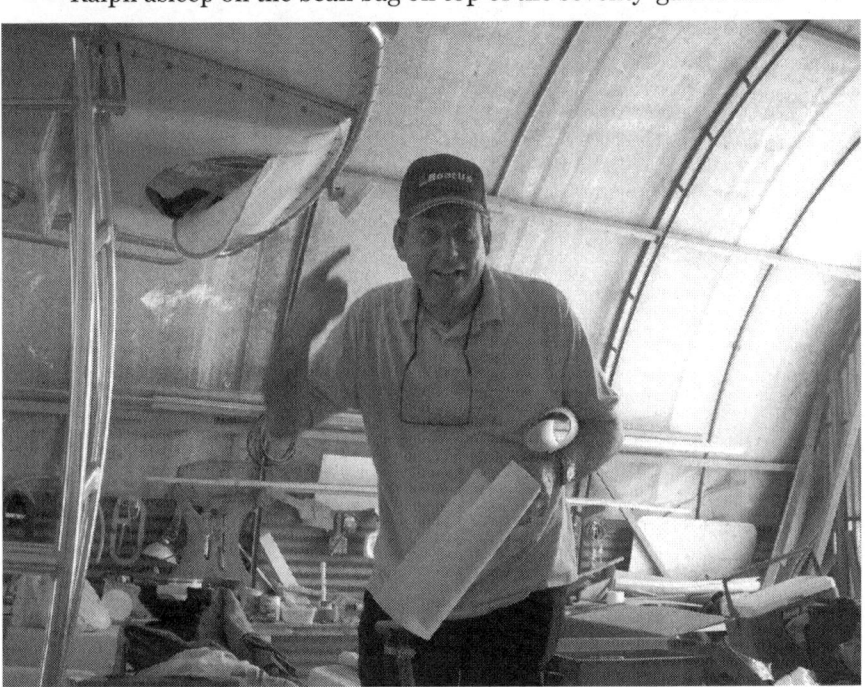

John Carroll, wearing a Boat US hat, is making a list of everything we had on the boat back at Ralph's shop the morning of our departure.

Islamorada, Florida Keys, the Lube Job

Monday, June 29th

We arrived at the World Wide Sportsman Bass Pro Shop in Islamorada Key in the morning where we had a prime dock location set up in advance for us. It was right next to the outdoor Polynesian looking restaurant in front of the waterside entrance to the store. The docks were long with a mixture of expensive yachts and little fishing boats tied up to them. The white painted bumper poles extended four-foot above the graying wood planked docks. The dock lead to the massive modern sportsman store and was lined with palm branch roofed outer buildings. I spent some time in the store looking at all the neat gear I wished we had on the boat.

John Carroll, Jeff and Ian had a room about a mile walk up the street. I took my time walking to their hotel and even stopped in an old book store to try to locate a book written by Hugo Vihlen, the guy who twice sailed across the Atlantic Ocean in the smallest sailboats. I found out about Hugo while I was cleaning out my closet at home a couple of months earlier. I ran into a photograph of Hugo, in his five-foot eleven-inch sailboat, *April Fool*. It was tied up to a submarine out at sea in 1968. The picture was autographed to my father and mother with a note saying he believed my parents beat him in a bath tub race on the TV game show *Treasure Island*.

Islamorada, Florida Keys, the Lube Job

That show had aired some thirty years earlier. What were the odds my parents would have a photograph of the guy who held the world record for crossing the Atlantic Ocean in the smallest sailboat and then without consciously knowing about it, my brother and I were attempting to break the world record for the smallest powerboat to ever cross the Atlantic Ocean? I read his first book, *April Fool,* and contacted him. He told me his second book, *The Stormy Voyage of Father's Day,* is much better than his first book. His second voyage was in 1993 in a five-foot four-inch sailboat. Several months later, Hugo emailed me and suggested we fasten hand holds on the bottom of the boat so we could hold onto the boat if we capsized. Unfortunately the book store didn't have either of Hugo's books.

Hugo, sailed the smallest sailboat across the Atlantic, signed this picture for our parents on a TV game show called Treasure Island.

Wounded Hero Voyage I

I made it to John Carroll's hotel room and slept on one of the soft non-moving beds for an hour or two and then took a dip in the pool before walking back to the Bass Pro Shop. John McDaniel, of Wounded Warriors in Action, introduced us to our second Wounded Warrior of the trip; Julio Salazar, 3rd Battalion, 1st Marine Division, who had served in Fallujah, Iraq.

When Julio had been on patrol he was hit by an IED (improvised explosive device). Julio's injuries included taking shrapnel to his left shoulder, a broken left shoulder, a collapsed left lung, five broken ribs and three others shattered, a broken ring finger and the explosive took a chunk out of his right thigh. He'd been flown to Landstuhl, Germany, for two weeks until he was stable enough to be moved to a hospital in San Diego, California. A year later, when he was discharged from the service, he moved to Florida and while working at the Veterans Administration (VA) he met John McDaniel. John through Wounded Warriors in Action took Julio hunting and fishing. Then one day Julio called John and during their conversation found out about our adventure and, wa-la, he became one of our co-adventurers.

I had a burger at the outdoor restaurant and met a trawler captain and his wife. They talked about how good their diesel fuel economy was in their slow moving trawler. They said they hardly ever went over eight knots (1kts = 1.15 mph so 8kts = 9.2 mph). They bought one of my books and gave us twenty dollars to help pay for a *must have* radar reflector. It's a small metal angled object designed to bounce radar waves from radars senders back to themselves so we'd show up on their monitors. He was concerned that our boat was so small and close to the water that without the reflector few boats would be able to see us, especially in fog. He

Islamorada, Florida Keys, the Lube Job

knew we'd be running into a lot of heavy fog in the Northeast. He also stressed the importance of getting radar for our boat. Although it seems like that's what he'd just helped us purchase, radar is different from a radar reflector. The reflector enables others to see us; the radar allows us to see boats, islands and icebergs at night or in the fog. I told them Ideal Image was looking into getting us a radar and might have one for us when we reached my hometown area and we'd get the radar reflector the first chance we could since one wasn't readily available at the Sportsman shop. It would have to be ordered and we couldn't wait around for it.

American flag flying high over head at dock in front of the pro shop

We spent the whole day with our boat tied up to the dock within throwing distance to the dock gas pumps. When we finally decided it was time to fuel up, the station had closed just fifteen minutes earlier. We had no idea that it closed so early. There was nobody at the marina who could turn the pumps on for us. John Carroll and his minivan came to our rescue. We loaded up all seven of our five-gallon plastic jerry cans and he drove us to the local gas station.

Before we left, we picked up a new white anchor light, an oil suction tube for when we needed to change the oil, another small waterproof duffel bag, and a compass. Ralph had to borrow my phone, as he seemed to have lost his.

It was close to 11:00 at night when we left the bass pro shop. We headed out idling and somehow found ourselves barely scraping in six inches of water. When idling, our draft (amount of boat underwater) was around eight inches without a heavy load. We weren't really heavy as we didn't fill up our major gas tanks, but we did have another body and his duffel bag along with all our supplies, so we weren't light either. We decided we weren't heading in the direction toward the channel and turned. Ralph kept talking about the need to change the oil, since this was a brand new engine just being broken in. So before we left the Gulf side of the Keys, we pulled up to a calm spot among the islands and pulled out our brand new oil siphon apparatus. We wouldn't be able to change the oil filter because it was located behind the motor cawling and was too low on the motor while over water. But we could at least change out the oil, or so we thought.... We removed the oil fill cap and inserted our rubber hose, which kept hitting something. Even when we used the smaller adaptor hose, we had trouble getting it past what had to be some type of blocking pin partway down in the fill tube. We were attempting to reclaim the oil in our old drink bottles and after about ten minutes only managed to drain about two-thirds of a quart. We gave up, determined to change our oil at our next stop.

Islamorada, Florida Keys, the Lube Job

Bob trying to change the oil with a suction tube

Ralph and I had developed a nasty-itchy rash around our wrists. I had taken off my shirt the first night after leaving Tampa, so I also had the rash down my sides and under my armpits. We were so hurried in rebuilding the inside of the boat before we left Ralph's shop that we never had the time to rinse the fiberglass dust out or even take showers before we loaded it. The whole inside of the boat had been covered in a fine layer of an almost invisible fiberglass dust and now it was affecting us. There wasn't much we could do about it until we sweated it out of our pores and rinsed out the boat.

Tuesday, June 30th

We slept in the boat anchored close to a small island, from about 3:00 a.m. to 8:00 in the morning legally using our new clip-on white anchor light. Our next stop was Miami and we didn't want to get there in the middle of the night. I slept in my blue hammock strung up below the T-top. I tied it to both ends of one of our windsurf poles that extended out from the front and back of the T-top. Julio slept in the front on the bean bag while Ralph slept on the aft on top of our kid-sized pool air mattress. I woke up to their conversation about belching and drinking Red Bull. We also found my fishing lure that I didn't know was lost. It had been banging around earlier and must have broken free from my fishing rod up on the T-top and landed on the floor.

Just south of Miami we saw some stilt houses. Something I didn't expect. Julio said they'd been there a long time. At one time they were considered luxury houses, back in the 80's and 90's, but they'd been condemned after hurricane Andrew, and abandoned. For a long time kids used them for partying and others used them as a place for drug deals, but that was all stopped. Now they are just good places to fish.

We arrived in Key Biscayne, Miami around 11:00 am in a wind driven salt haze, to get fuel. We bought some food and Julio picked out some bait for later. The next couple of hours were spent waiting for the media to show up at the Miami Marina, a private marina. The sky was starting to cloud up, so Julio and I took the boat to a public marina where his friend worked. We needed to change the oil. Ralph stayed to talk to the media when they showed up.

Alex, Julio's friend, worked a deal for the oil change with his boss. The marina using a really big fork lift capable of lifting boats fifty foot onto racks to pull *I Am Second* out of the water and carried it to the lower section of a huge boat rack. Alex had a tough time removing the lower cowling which covered the oil filter on the Suzuki 115. One of the bolts was stuck so tight he had to use an

Islamorada, Florida Keys, the Lube Job

impact screwdriver to get it off. But before he was able to finish removing it, the whole sky opened up and we were in the middle of a torrential downpour. Luckily I had just climbed up into the boat and removed my handycam. While sitting out the storm underneath another boat, I started to wonder if our oil filter they left on the back deck of *I Am Second*, which was out in the rain, was still in its cardboard container, and whether it was right side up and full of water.

During a short lull in the storm, I made it over to the office where Julio and all the mechanics were waiting out the storm. From there I called Kevin, the guy I bought my handycam from in Merritt Island, to find out what had happened to my underwater camera case for my handycam. Ralph's wife, Anne, had never received it. He checked and found out Sony had never sent it. He also worked in an Orlando store and said he would personally transfer one from there and I could pick it up at the store in Merritt Island. We would be stopping at the nearby town of Cape Canaveral in a few days. Ralph called me. There was a reporter with him waiting to get some footage of the boat and we needed to get back ASAP.

By the time Julio and I got back to the Miami Marina, the guy I'll call Media Bill because I'm not positive of his name, had been waiting more than an hour and a half in his car. We finished the interview, bought some more waterproof dry bags, some sandwiches, and made a deal with the Miami Marina to sell a box of shirts for us.

It was getting late, and since we blew the fishing earlier with Jason, we took, or should I say Julio took us, fishing underneath a nearby bridge. Just as we were almost there, I was fooling around with a bungee on top of the T-top and my florescent green Interstate

Wounded Hero Voyage I

Battery hat blew off. We immediately whipped the boat around to get it as it should have been an easy find, but it was gone. As we went under the bridge we heard a loud clack, clack, clack! Our flag pole was higher than the cement beams of the overhead bridge, but just low enough to bend, slip under and smack the next beam as we moved forward. It hit about ten beams until we popped out the other side of the bridge. It didn't do any damage so it gave us confidence the pole would hold up in the rough seas and not break off.

    Julio and I had our fishing licenses so we started fishing while Ralph tried to contact the license department over the phone to renew his. While Ralph was on the phone, I started using Ralph's fishing rod since my reel had popped off during the early morning drive. We didn't lose it, it fell into the boat. I just lost the tiny screws to the "C" clamp which held it on; a new item for our store wish list. Julio was the man. He caught eight or nine mango snappers in the ten or so minutes while I caught only two fish, a snapper and a grouper. Ralph got his license just as we had to leave. The rain was here again.

    We raced in the leading edge of the storm as the sun dropped out of the sky. We alternated in and out of the rain. Ralph decided this was a good time to stop the boat and rig up the safety ropes. There were lightning strikes all around and it was getting scary. Julio and I wanted to keep going, but Ralph was more concerned the concussion from a lightning strike could disorient us and someone could fall off the boat. Julio and I just wanted to get moving and put on the ropes while fleeing.

    We fought with the storm, neck and neck, up the coast. The lightning wasn't as bad now, but struck often enough to keep us on

Islamorada, Florida Keys, the Lube Job

our toes. I felt like I was on the old TV show *Miami Vice*, just flying along on a speed boat, jumping swells out in the ocean. The ocean was a rolling white carpet of sea spray. We must have looked pretty cool. We still had our big American flag flying twenty foot above the water (not a good idea in a lightning storm). We should have taken it down before the storm got bad back at the bridge, but the storm rolled in so fast we just wanted to get out of there. The Miami shoreline looked really impressive from our vantage point. The lights were twinkling from all the condos, with the lightning and rain flipping between foreground and background.

We had to stop to fool around with the small motor bracket. It had slipped down because the part of the bracket that the motor was attached to, which pivoted up from the back of the boat, wouldn't stay up. This was causing part of the lift handle, which we already hack sawed shorter, to jam into the back edge of the deck. Our kicker motor was dragging in the water and throwing water everywhere. It still hung down after several attempts to tie it tight to the deck cleats, so we added a heavy rope from around the top of the kicker directly up to the back of the T-top. We were off again.

Wednesday, July 1st

It was nearly 2:00 in the morning, about a mile offshore from Jupiter Beach, when a blue and white Coast Guard cutter snuck up behind us. It stopped just off our right side, about forty-foot away. I felt like we were doing something wrong and quickly told Ralph to get on the radio to see what they wanted. Hugo Vihlen, the small sailboat guy, on his last crossing, was stopped 26 miles off the coast of New England, where the Coast Guard deemed his vessel *manifestly unsafe* to make a trans-Atlantic crossing.

Hugo then had to transport his boat up to St. John's, Newfoundland, Canada, where he departed in his five-foot four-inch sailboat. Robert Manry, a small boat sailor, had to sneak off shore in 1965 in his thirteen-foot five-inch sailboat to cross from Massachusetts to England, afraid someone would try to stop him. So here we were, with everyone telling us it was impossible to take a flats boat across to Europe, especially without a cabin or a keel, getting stopped by the Coast Guard. They didn't so much as check anything on our boat as soon as they radioed in and confirmed our trip. Ralph had previously made a bunch of phone calls telling everyone what we had planned to do. We weren't hiding anything. The Coast Guard crew gave us an okay to continue, but we could see it in their facial expressions and their mannerisms that they thought we had absolutely no chance of completing our task. The look was kind of hard to describe, they nodded their head up and down and kind of overly smiled with a slight smirk and were really polite. I think they weren't too worried about our safety as we skirted the coast, figuring that would be enough to scare us into quitting on our own.

We traveled up the coast during most of the night and entered Sebastian Inlet before the sun came up. Sebastian Inlet could be a dangerous place to enter the Indian River if you didn't hit it just right with the tide and the currents. I once broke a windshield out of my Bayliner bow rider motorboat by going through Port St. Lucie Inlet, a similar Florida inlet. The impact of my boat hitting the jacked up waves (waves made higher because they are pushed up by an outgoing tide), caused my boat to flex which crushed the walk-through windshield door leading to the bow. For boat safety, tempered glass windshields are used in many boats. There had been tempered pebble sized glass all over my boat.

Islamorada, Florida Keys, the Lube Job

Ralphs Intruders (our type of boat) are made with Lexan windshields, a much stronger material than Plexiglas.

We were looking for Captain Hiram's, a restaurant where we were scheduled to exchange Julio for another Wounded Hero. Because it was predawn, we had trouble finding Capt Hiram's in the dark. We knew it was near the inlet and soon realized it wasn't really near the ocean side of the river, since there wasn't a building big enough to be a restaurant. Ralph decided to check the other side, a mile or so just opposite the inlet. There it was, an easy find, but since we weren't sure if we were allowed to tie up to the dock, we anchored near a buoy with a few other boats.

When the sun came up, we motored over to the docks. I recognized a guy on the docks as one of the guys who used to work at Ron Jon surf shop when it was still a small shop. Eric Olson was a friend of a friend, Guy Camilleri. Guy used to be one of my best surfing buddies back in the seventies. I asked Eric if he still kept in touch with Guy. He said he'd lost Guy's number years ago so I gave it to him off my cell phone.

The restaurant was closed, but the cleaning crew was there. They let me recharge my phone and handycam while we walked up to the closest open restaurant in walking distance. We went to a biker bar named Earl's. They served large egg biscuits which were great. While we were there, the *Coastal Angler Magazine* was delivered and they had done a story about our trip. I thought that was really cool; now we had another piece of tangible proof of our voyage to go with the collection of papers Ralph had in his pile of stuff.

As we walked back along the dock to our boat, I notice my yellow T-shirt was no longer hanging up where I had left it. I'd

Wounded Hero Voyage I

washed it earlier with one of the dock hoses and hung it from the bottom of the T-top. For a split second I was really mad thinking someone stole it. But then I looked in the direction of the wind, 75 yards away, I noticed it drifting away on its wooden hanger (one should not jump to conclusions). We motored over and rescued it.

The Wounded Hero that was supposed to swap out with Julio on the next leg of our journey wasn't going to be able to go on the trip, so Julio volunteered to ride up to our home town area, the next stop on our trip. As we were departing through the Inlet, we came up on some guys jumping waves with jet skis. We found out they were filming a commercial for Red Bull. We gave them one of our two Go Pro cameras to shoot some video of us as we were leaving. Because of the way they filmed, I figured the video would be worthless. I expected it to be really blurry since we were going almost full throttle and they were really bouncing around and way too close. They drove alongside of us about five foot off the side of our boat.

After rounding the rock jetties (barrier extending out into the ocean to prevent beach sand from filling up the channel as it commonly shifts along the coast with the tide), we passed Florida's most famous surf spot. Sebastian Inlet is one of the locations on the surf pro circuit where several world famous surfers were discovered. Kelly Slater, from our home town of Cocoa Beach, where Ralph and I also grew up and went to school, is now one of the most famous athletes in the world. At the time of our voyage, he was the all time world record holder of nine world championships (at the time of this publication he was the eleven-time-world champion.) Way to go Kelly, congrats! Kelly is by no way the only recognized surfer from these parts. The Hobgood brothers, CJ and Damien, both lived in

Islamorada, Florida Keys, the Lube Job

the neighboring town of Satellite Beach and the list of famous surfers from these parts is long... Bruce Valluzzi, Claude Codgen, Dick Catri, Mike Crawford, Gary Propper, Mike Tabeling, Sean Slater, Todd Holland, Rich and Phil Salick, Greg Loehr, Pat Mulhern, Murph the Surf, Matt Kechele, Charlie Kuhn, Frieda Zamba, Lisa Anderson (four time Women's World Champion), and that is just the beginning....

Since we'd left with so many tasks undone, it didn't take me long to realize we didn't have our website *CrossTheAtlantic.com* blatantly obvious on the boat, so we agreed to call Lickity Split signs and have them make a couple of banners for the top of our gas tanks. Our trip was still relatively unknown, and we debated whether we should ride offshore a mile or so, or ride close to the breakers so the boat could be seen by the beachgoers. We never really decided. It depended on who was driving and what time of day it was. I usually drove close as Ralph tended to hang offshore. As we were coming up on Cocoa Beach, we tried to get John Carroll to get out to the end of the Cocoa Beach Pier and get some shots as we drove by but he didn't have time. We would be passing it before he could get there. Ralph tried to call the pier's manager, but he couldn't get him on the phone. Our destination was Rusty's Seafood Restaurant in the Cove at Port Canaveral. We were supposed to have a small send off party from there since Ralph and I both grew up in the area.

Turning westward, we passed the green entrance buoy as we traveled down the channel, staying clear of all the fishermen casting off the rock jetty. We saw several cruise ships with a graying sky behind. Rusty's was on the south side of the harbor, a little ways down. Years ago, I worked for Rusty Fisher while in high school.

Wounded Hero Voyage I

Rusty used to own the Cocoa Beach landmark restaurant, Bernard's Surf, where many of the pioneering astronauts used to eat and party. I was employed as a busboy, salad maker and sometimes as a dishwasher. His son, Rhett, now ran the port restaurant, Rusty's. Rhett has had other world-record parties at Rusty's. I went to Justin DeBree's party when he had it there. Justin was the standup paddle boarder who stopped there on route to southern Georgia.

Dan Shoemaker, a friend, offered to take me on all the errands I still needed to do. We stopped at the camera shop at the Merritt Square Mall to pick up my waterproof camera case, a small inverter for charging things off the boat battery, more SD cards (digital memory cards for cameras) since we still hadn't located the four we bought the night before we left. We went to Lickity Split Signs for the *CrossTheAtlantic.com* banners. And finally to my house to get a cordless drill and other miscellaneous tools, bungee straps, email addresses, but most important, my heavy duty tripod so I could get video of both Ralph and myself together. I could not find it. I felt really rushed to get back to Rusty's as people were starting to show up. I got to say hi and goodbye to Casey, my Golden Retriever, since she was the only member of my family home at the time.

By five o'clock, Ralph's wife, Anne, and extended family, along with our mom, who wanted to stay anonymous because of reporters, Jill and my youngest son Jonathan, along with a lot of our friends were at Rusty's. Some came from several hours away by car. Anne gave Ralph a new cell phone to replace the one lost in the Keys. Minutes later, we found his lost cell phone inside my handycam bag in the glove box up above the dash. A friend of Julio's came by and picked him up. He said goodbye and good luck. Julio

Islamorada, Florida Keys, the Lube Job

was one of the few, and I am including most of my friends, who gave me the impression that we would successfully make it to Europe.

Ralph spent much of the time at Rusty's on his old cell phone doing interviews and trying to drum up more media. In one of the interviews he explained how he got into the boat building business. A long time ago, he was out boating and ran over a rock in shallow water. The collision caused him to damage the lower unit on his engine. He thought there had to be a better way and started fooling around designing boat hulls which would allow the motor to operate in shallower water. His first boat design was called the DreamSurfer 230 (www.dreamboats.net), a much bigger boat than the Intruder 21 we were taking to Europe.

Bob, Wounded Hero Julio, and Ralph at Rusty's restaurant dock

I didn't want another gas fiasco like the one we had in the Keys and so I made some calls. I found out the gas pumps were only open until 6:00 p.m. which only left us a few minutes to fuel up. I took the boat up to the station but nobody was there. I found a sign stating we had to go to the marina across the street to get help. I ran over there and the line to the register was exceptionally long. I worried I wouldn't make it in time. When I finally got to the checkout, the guy said I didn't call him, but he would sell me the gas. His pumps were open until 9:00 p.m. His competitor closed at 6:00. Because I spent so much time there, I was hardly at our sendoff party.

We gave my handycam to a friend to get some video with both of us on the boat going fast over some waves near the jetties. The learning curve with my handycam proved to burn someone other than me. This time the handycam wasn't turned on when he thought it was. In his defense, it was almost dark and he had never used this type of camera before. His wife, on the other hand, learned from his mistake and took some great video of a beautiful sunset with us slowly motoring back to Rusty's. In the video Marcie is telling my wife, "That boat will make it through everything."

We were told multiple times we weren't pushing the "'Spot" button, and people were having a tough time following us. According to the directions, we were spotting right, but for some reason it wasn't registering our locations. The Spot is a navigational tool which is linked to a website. Our webmaster should have been able to capture it on our website to show viewers of our location supposedly every time we pushed the button. It was satellite linked and should have worked as long as we held the Spot out from underneath any metal when we pushed the button. We always held it in our hand extended out into the open air outside of the T-top. When we first arrived at the port, our website's Spotter page said we

Islamorada, Florida Keys, the Lube Job

were in Sebastian, even though we had spotted several times along our route.

We left much later than we had planned; it was after 9:00 p.m. We kissed our wives goodbye and headed out to sea, again, after dark. If I could do it all over again, I'd have chosen to spend the night at Cape Canaveral and left late the next day with the boat set up to video. We needed a tripod, attach something with a swivel on the long poles to make it easily and quickly attach my handycam to, to add more locations on the boat to attach the long poles for better angles, and to get a kite setup for getting some aerial shots. I wanted to be able to make a quality documentary after the trip was over.

Bob and his wife, Jill, standing on the deck of the *I Am Second*

Wounded Hero Voyage I

We hadn't gone much more than a mile or so when we heard a bang, swoosh, and then a splash. We had taken down our American flag while motoring out of the port, because it was going to be a long ride and since it would be dark, nobody would see it anyway. We stowed the pole on top of the T-top with the other one. Only somehow we never finished strapping them down properly. As soon as we realized what had happened, we turned an about-face, but in the choppy seas the poles had vanished. These poles had a duel purpose. One was for taking pictures of us in the boat from as far away as the pole would reach, and the other was for re-righting the boat in the event of a capsize. We figured, without ever actually putting it into practice, these poles would be a lifesaver in the event of an emergency. By using the poles as leverage and using the swells with the proper timing, we'd be able to re-right the boat. If we were to capsize the boat hundreds of miles from shore, nobody would be around to rescue us. We had to be self sufficient. So it was critical that we find the poles. The poles were capped off with foam at both ends; one was a dark green and the other sort of a grayish color. After about twenty minutes of driving around in larger and larger circles, we finally spotted the glow of something white... our poles, our possible lifesavers. I had glued and foamed white PVC pipes into the bottom ends of the poles so they could be inserted into the fishing rod holders.

Growing up in the area, I knew there was a three-mile perimeter around the Cape Kennedy beaches. It was a security issue with the rocket launches. We had to go out around the buoys identifying the area. On our Garmin GPS, the area showed up as a shaded area with red and blue stripes. The seas were one to three foot and before we had a chance to get somewhat waterproof, we hit

Islamorada, Florida Keys, the Lube Job

a wave just right and got soaked with at least a five-gallon bucket of water. Yep, that's a good way to start off a night leg of the trip. (While writing this book, I found out the three-mile stay-away zone was only in effect when a rocket was on the launch pad.)

Thursday, July 2

After we passed the no-trespass zone of the Cape, we again motored fairly close to the beach. It was interesting to watch the shoreline with all the different lights and condos. As we clocked off the miles, we eventually passed places like Daytona and Flagler. We passed their piers jetting way out into the water. We stayed close to shore and the surface of the ocean became almost as smooth as glass. I was having a lot of trouble staying awake. I caught myself dozing off quite a few times and would turn a little more seaward for fear of running ashore. Somewhere near St. Augustine I came out of a doze just in time to see the beach coming up quickly. I turned really hard and missed the beach by not much more than ten foot. My heart pounded against my chest and now I was shocked wide awake. I turned more seaward. I laughed; Ralph never even woke up. I guess we were now even for the island he almost ran into going across the Florida Bay on route to the Keys.

It was so black out when I looked eastward, I couldn't even see the water. The cloud cover blocked out all the stars. It was 3:00 a.m. Boy was I getting sleepy. I continued steering the boat and it seemed to take many hours before it was 4:30. I blinked the sleep from my eyes and that's when I could have sworn there was a bridge out there, but that was impossible, we were over a mile out to sea. It turned out to be a low fog band right down next to the water, looking solid and ominous. Looking eastward there was nothing, but looking westward toward shore, there was just enough light from the cities to expose the fog band, which gave it the appearance of a bridge. Because I was moving, the stationary lights looked like moving cars on the bridge.

After I woke Ralph up and went to sleep, I was so tired I never even woke up during our entrance into Jacksonville's harbor. Ralph told me I slept through the first two times he moved the boat to a new location. The third time we docked in front of a Hooters restaurant on the boardwalk. Jim Suber, Jacksonville Dock Master who Ralph talked with, thought it would be a good location because there was a political convention right next door. The Tea Party was having a gathering later in the day and there would be crowds of people swarming all around the docks all day. Someone from the crowd invited us to take showers at the nearby Gold Gym. We readily accepted.

Bob is asleep on the air mattress raft with his eye patch.

Islamorada, Florida Keys, the Lube Job

John Carroll arrived shortly after we docked. He met two girls, Feebee and Holley, on the boardwalk who wanted to help him sell the shirts. They were both from Florida, not too far away from where John lived in Satellite Beach. One or both of them were at one time in the military and they both loved the idea of the Wounded Hero Voyage and wanted to do what they could to help out. The girls bought shirts and one of them bought my Bermuda book.

We were interviewed by a Jacksonville news station. Rick, the cameraman, decided to change the shoot from a position by the boat to under the overhang because it was so bright out. He let us know that in the final piece he was going to show the boat with us as a silhouette or make it semi-transparent using some shots he would get later. Rick came back several hours later so he could go with me when I went to fuel the boat at the gas station across the harbor. It often seemed the guys working the pumps were never close by when we needed them. It took me about ten minutes of walking around and asking people to find the guy whose job was to work the pumps. I found him working on another dock talking on a cell phone. Rick walked back to Hooters because he wanted to get some shots from on top of a bridge. He wanted me to motor under the bridge, so they could use the shot as if we were leaving Jacksonville.

Ralph asked the guy, who seemed to be in charge, if he could talk at the Tea Party Rally Convention to promote our trip. The guy said he would love to have him make a small presentation and that Ralph would be up soon. Hours later when many of the people had already left, they finally let Ralph talk. When he was done, we probably sold more shirts in fifteen minutes than we had previously to date. I think if they had let Ralph talk earlier we would have sold out. The guy who had let Ralph speak asked if we would stay until Saturday (the day after tomorrow). They were having another patriotic convention and he wanted Ralph to speak. My brother apologized letting him know we would be long gone by then. The guy also wanted a bunch of shirts to sell on consignment. He ended up with a whole bag of them including the waterproof bag which Anne had bought to store them in on the boat.

We were then invited to make a small presentation at the Power Squadron meeting held in a room above the shops surrounding the Tea Party meeting area. We spent about an hour there. The members seemed excited to talk about our trip. Again, there was considerable doubt we could make it. The reoccurring phrase I was noticing was *good luck*, but it wasn't the kind of good luck you tell your kid when he was about to go to the plate during a baseball game. It was more like; you're going to need a lot of luck.

One of the guys in the Power Squadron taught a class in navigation using a sextant. Before the trip I'd thought of buying a sextant and learning how to find my position out at sea using the sun and stars. I have always been fascinated by how people can do that. It became a passing thought after I found out how much a sextant cost. As we headed back to the boat, we walked down the outside stairs, which were tiled. One of my Flip-Flops slipped and I did one of those flailing arms you-had-to-see saves. One (me) could easily get hurt on land just as easily as on the open ocean!

The Power Squadron people came outside and waved goodbye from their harbor porch balcony as we motored away. The sky was starting to look ominous with light rain and dark gray clouds all around. There was a little lightning off in the distance,

Islamorada, Florida Keys, the Lube Job

and as usual, the sun was again setting as we were leaving. It was too dark to video the harbor, but there were a lot of big ships, cool sites, and images I wanted to capture. I still hadn't put my handycam into its protective case so even if had been light enough, I wouldn't have risked exposing the camera to the elements.

Ralph waiting to speak about our voyage during a Tea Party

In Route to South Carolina, Duck!

Our throttle had been giving us grief since we left Tampa. For some reason the dang thing was too loose. As soon as we took our hand off the control, it slowly started to drift backwards, slowing the boat down. I wasn't sure if it would slip under normal river conditions but all the ocean pounding was definitely not helping. We were on a heading of sixty degrees going to South Carolina, the seas were about two to three foot, a little choppy but no white caps, not much wind; good ocean conditions. It was dark out and we just passed a cruise ship about a mile east of us. If it had been during the daytime, we probably would have ventured a little closer. Ralph really wanted a picture of our little boat next to a huge cruise ship out at sea.

I didn't know why the thought hadn't hit me earlier, but I was standing on a section of rubber mat which was made to piece together with other mats. Along the edges were little fingers of mat which interlock with other pieces. I bent over with my knife and sliced one of the mat fingers off and crammed it between the throttle handle and its bracket. The throttle was finally fixed! There was just enough friction to keep the throttle from slipping. Every once in a while, the finger had to be shoved back in or replaced with a new non-compressed piece. But it was such a relief to only have to fool with the throttle a couple of times a day instead of constantly

In Route to South Carolina, Duck!

holding it. It held so well I often drove with my feet, sitting way back in the chair, with my arms spread out on top of the bench seat.

Now that the shore wasn't anywhere in view and with no stars visible, traveling in a straight line was very difficult. If we took our eyes off the chartplotter the boat would gravitate away from its heading. Twice during the night, I went so far off track; it was easier to continue around in a circle to get back on course because I had gone more than 180 degrees around.

We basically used the same set up Ralph used on our first trip to Bermuda to keep our forward light from glaring off the white deck. The pilot always needs to see forward of the boat and this reflected light blinded him. Ralph used a piece of the floor mat. We brought a lot of them with us as they proved on the Bermuda trip to be very valuable out at sea in a variety of circumstances. The situation required the mat to be cut in half since one full piece proved to be too flimsy. The doubled up mat was held tight under the light with other invaluable items, wire ties. We often took the light block down whenever we were in port because we couldn't hang our front Wounded Hero banner straight with the mat in the way.

Almost all of the junk food given to us from Pine Island Marine was gone. We ate it to help keep awake during the nights. The remaining M & M candies had lost their color and were white. The yellow candy bags that we tried to keep dry had been drenched many times as with everything else on board.

I've been a house painter/builder for over thirty years. I have done a lot of ceiling work and looking up, doing everything from painting to skip trowel. So I'd say I have a rather sensitive neck. Normally, going over a big wave and bouncing didn't bother me, but every now and then if I had my head and neck turned at a bad angle and I didn't see the bounce coming, I could get a sudden jarring. The impact sent a nerve spike down my spine, which was really painful.

We hadn't had a Wounded Hero with us since Julio left us in Cape Canaveral. It was probably a safety issue, since during most of the earlier trip; we were usually within five miles from shore. Now we were taking the shortest distance routes. This leg from Jacksonville to Charleston, South Carolina was close to 200 miles as a bird flies. At some point, we would be about 35 miles from the nearest point to land and it would be during the night on a boat with less than a foot of free board (the distance from the water level outside the boat to the top edge of the side of the boat).

The seas were getting into the three to five-foot range, and we were going pretty much the same direction. We were now able to catch some waves and surf them with the boat. It was starting to come back to me, from all the boat surfing we did going to Bermuda in 2007. The faces of the waves were nearly invisible, everything was black. As the boat went down the face of the wave, the front T-top light exposed the bottom of the trough or the back of the wave in front. It looked like the bow of the boat was going to pierce the sea. The water was just about an inch from coming over the front deck and then the boat would suddenly pop up. I remembered from the last trip, the first time it happened, I thought we were going to pearl, a surf term for the nose going underwater.

The wind was beginning to pick up and we were starting to see a little white cap on some of the chop. The red moon had risen and was behind us now, making navigation at night fairly easy by looking behind.

In Route to South Carolina, Duck!

The little motor was starting to really bounce around now, but there wasn't much we could do about it. The bracket needed to be replaced and we didn't have any extras with us. I was a bit concerned about the gas line going to the motor. The deck around the motor was being chaffed by the bracket hitting the deck. Because of the angle the gas line goes into the motor, the line can rub against the chaffed deck. Sometimes I got a whiff of gas but that could easily have been from any of the thirteen gas tanks we had onboard. Oops, the moon is now off to my side, I better get back on course and keep it behind me!

The temperature was starting to drop. Earlier I was wearing my yellow Mustang Survivor jacket but I had gotten too hot and started to sweat. I'd taken it off and it was now hanging from the T-top with Bungees, blowing in the wind. So now I was wearing a pair of Flip Flops, baggies, shirt, and the light weight Interstate Battery windbreaker without its inside liner. It was time to put the Mustang jacket back on.

The Garmin chartplotter was a little hard to read as its screen was only about three by four inches. I didn't know why Ralph had such a small one... well I did know, cash was tight and the bigger ones were a lot more money. This one was now covered in a light salt coating and I was using a magnifying glass to see some of the towns we were even with written in white. We were now even with Mud River, halfway up the coast of Georgia, and I guessed we were about 25 to thirty-miles off the coast. I am the curious sort, so I decided to play around with the Garmin to see what some of the other functions did. Next thing I knew the screen went black. It took me about ten-minutes of pushing buttons to get it back to where it was before I screwed with it.

Wounded Hero Voyage I

Ralph is using the magnifying glass to see the small print on the small screen of the Garmin chartplotter

Friday, July 3rd

It was about 3:30 a.m. and there were a couple of other boats out that night. Off in the distance all I could see was a blinking light. I changed my direction just slightly so we didn't cross paths. The little motor was really eating up the back of Ralph's boat, so we were going to have to stop and tighten some ropes. As soon as we idled the 115 horsepower Suzuki, about ten flying fish flew into the boat; something big must have been chasing them. One of the biggest ones hit me right in a very sensitive-inappropriate spot causing me to double over for a few minutes! Although we really wanted to throw out a flying fish on a line, we didn't as we were on an extremely tight time schedule. There would be plenty of time for

In Route to South Carolina, Duck!

fishing later.

While fooling around with the Garmin, I zoomed in to make the boat on the Garmin screen bigger. That's when I noticed the boat was sitting in the dead center of a dark purple line. I zoomed out a little and it showed we were sitting right in the center of a no-trespass danger zone. We figured it must be a practice bombing area and continued through it. We weren't sure where they practiced, but we knew they had some spots somewhere out here. Thinking back on it, I remembered the waves were a little bigger there, but we didn't notice the depth. Perhaps we had been traveling over a shallow shoal or a wreck.

One of the side banners that made it easy to start up a conversation while in port. We were often asked about "I Am Second" easy to answer, "God is first." Wounded Hero Voyage is about promoting Wounded Hero Foundations. Crossing the Atlantic was to honor the memory of John Harvey, George Holmes, and Dewey Johnson.

Wounded Hero Voyage I

Charleston, South Carolina, for Old Glory

We entered the Charleston Harbor after going around the jetties; they extended far out to sea. We first passed a huge cargo freighter and then tons of people out in day boats, fishing and sailing. As we went past the Armory on the right, Ralph was in communication by cell phone with Bernie, an entrepreneur who Ralph met at CEO Space in California. Bernie Heckmann was with his wife, Barbara, and their son Christian; all three were scanning the horizon looking for us while Ralph was trying to give them our position based on the landmarks and other boats out on the water. We spotted Christian's yellow shirt as soon as we passed the breakwater. They were on the edge of the outer dock waving to us. They directed us to a premium docking spot, close to the office, right off the boardwalk courtesy of Garrison Rudisill. They greeted us each with a good luck necklace which was supposed to give us positive energy.

Ralph was able to get his shower right away while I was going to figure out how to hook up my handycam in its waterproof case. I was hesitant because I wasn't sure how the handycam was going to be able to be operated inside the case. It had one of those flip-out doors on the side which turned it on automatically. The

Charleston, South Carolina, for Old Glory

cardboard box, which I still hadn't opened, had a bunch of lose parts rattling around inside.

I barely sat down in the shade to start figuring out the case when it was time to go and check out a location to display the boat. There was going to be a big grand opening ceremony for a new park opening later that evening. Bernie said a crowd of 30,000 to 100,000 people were expected to attend. The town had recently built a new suspension bridge across the bay. The park was the grounds around the new bridge and a refurbished section of what was left of the old bridge. Everything looked brand new; green grass, new roads and sidewalks, several new buildings and venders setting up everywhere. Bernie was still trying to get through the red tape so *I Am Second* could be put on display there.

We all went to borrow a truck from one of Bernie's friends. From there it was decided Barbara and I would go and get the trailer, we were borrowing from another of Bernie's friends, to pull the boat out of the water. Ralph, Christian, and Bernie went to get a new heavier replacement bracket for our kicker, along with other things like another dry bag and a new water container which didn't have a hole in it. We had completed this last crossing with just a couple of small water bottles. It wasn't until we'd arrived that we found out our big plastic water container had split on the bottom. That was probably not the smartest thing to do; the last leg was a couple of hundred miles with a current going north east out to sea. If the motors broke down in deep water, we might have been stuck drifting out to sea until we were rescued.

At the trailer place, there were a bunch to choose from, and because Ralph's boat was a mono-cat and not a "V" bottom, I wasn't sure which one to get. To be on the safe side we decided, by cell phone, to all meet for lunch at a Subway and then go get the trailer together. Ralph checked a couple trailers with a tape measure and picked the closest one to the measurements off the top of his head. They left to finish shopping and we agreed to meet back at the boat for some scheduled interviews.

While parking the trailer in a tightly packed, overcrowded, dirt overflow parking lot at the yacht club, I bumped the trailer's fender during a tight turn into the step bumper of a parked work van. The damage was minimal on both. The van's bumper had no dents, just a small scratch about an inch long, barely identifiable amongst the flat black bumper speckled with paint and other small scratches. The trailer had a small dimple on the bottom edge of the fender and a small wrinkle on the top. I left one of our boat business cards, along with my cell phone number, on the windshield of the van, and continued to park the trailer.

Barbara and I, running late, ran through high brush taking a shortcut to the crowd of reporters around the boat. Ralph did most of the talking while I readied the boat. It seems reporters like having movement on the boat during most of our video interviews. After all but one reporter left, this guy knowing what pictures the others had taken, wanted something unique. He had us raise the American flag attached to our long pole. We had to stretch tip toed on the rails of the boat to lift the end of the pole high enough to insert the end into the fishing rod holder on the T-top. We had to stop multiple times so he could get the pictures and angles he wanted. I think he was trying for an Iwo Jima flag type picture. The article was going to run in the paper the following day, July 4th.

The reporter left and Ralph motored the boat to Boat Ramp Park while I met him there with the truck and trailer. He almost had the boat up on the trailer when it was stopped by the fenders. We took the fenders off. One was going to have to come off anyway, to pound out the earlier damage. By the time we got the fender off, Bernie, Barbara, and Christian arrived with the bad news.

Bernie wasn't able to get permission for us to put the boat on display, something to do with not enough notice and the fire marshal. Since we weren't going to display the boat, we worked on it long after dark, using Bernie's headlights and the overhead boat light along with our plug in floodlight. It would have gone much faster if we had a half-inch deep well socket. Much of the work was completed inside an eight-inch access hole from the topside of the deck. Bernie made several trips to the local store buying bolts and scrounging tools. One of his friends stopped by with a full tool box; of course the elusive half-inch deep well socket was not there.

Ralph met his wife and family at a hotel; they had driven up in a rented car. This was as far north as they planned to go. After Charleston, John Carroll would be our only Florida road support, for selling shirts and taking care of anything else we might need. We didn't want to take a chance on something happening to the boat. So I spent the night in my hammock on the boat wearing my bug suit and black eye mask to block out the all-night security lights. We'd brought along two mosquito net suits because we were warned of black flies and mosquitoes up north. I didn't get much sleep because of all the noise. I was amazed at how many people came to launch their boats in the middle of the night.

Saturday, July 4th

In the morning on July 4th, using the cordless drill, we finished mounting the kicker's bracket. We had to do some drill wobbling since we didn't have a big enough drill bit to make the right size hole. We had to use the heavy mount base from the old bracket as a spacer for the new bracket otherwise the new bracket would hit the protruding rail around the boat. Of course, now that we were using longer and bigger bolts, we needed the 9/16 deep well socket which we didn't have either. While Ralph finished bolting, I started logging the location of everything in the boat on the back of my books "for sale" sign. There was so much small stuff in so many different locations we wasted a lot of time just trying to find things. John made a similar list in Tampa which was probably left in Tampa or else his car.

Sandi and Hannah, friends from my home town of Merritt Island, were in Charleston visiting family. They found out about our arrival and came out to visit us. They caught up with us through cell phones and met us at the Boat Ramp Park. It was kind of neat seeing people from home this far away. I received a call from Guy Camilleri, my surfer friend from Cocoa Beach. Eric Olson from Captain Hiram's restaurant in Sebastian Inlet hooked up with him, so Guy called to say good luck on the voyage and also thank me for reconnecting him with his old friend, Eric.

We wanted to give Christian a boat ride to our new display location for the *I Am Second* boat. Bernie had somehow gotten permission for us to dock about fifty foot behind the aircraft carrier, Yorktown. I thought: How cool was that? We would be tied up to the floating dock where the water taxi parked. On the other side of the dock were another four huge Navy gun ships. It cost twenty five dollars for spectators to walk on the boardwalk to view all the military ships. Too expensive for many families, but after 5:00 p.m. it was going to be dropped to just five dollars. They were expecting a

Charleston, South Carolina, for Old Glory

few thousand people to be milling around.

During Christian's ride over to the *Yorktown*, I zigzagged all over the bay boat jumping every boat wake I could find. Climbing out of the boat I noticed our fourteen foot flag pole was missing. I knew it hadn't been stolen since I had just added four smaller flags to it; one for the Marines, Navy, Army and Coast Guard. I spent most of the remainder of my time in Charleston driving around the bay looking for our lost flag pole. It crossed my mind, that earlier in the morning our missing American flag could have been on just about everyone's breakfast table in Charleston, because of our articles in the newspapers with the photo of us raising Old Glory.

As long as we were losing things to the Atlantic Ocean, we might as well donate my book for sale sign. After spending hours going through the whole boat, cataloging everything and listing it on the back of the sign, something bad happened. Yep, just after Heath, Ralph's youngest son, helped me figure out the camera case, he tossed me the sign and either a gust of wind or an unlucky throw caused it to zing between the dock and the boat. That plastic sign disappeared beneath the surface as if it were made of lead!

Oh, the handycam case was easy. There are buttons on the outside of the case which regulate the handycam via a plugged-in cable. The viewing monitor is turned around and closed so the screen is facing outward. There is a flip-out mirror on the outside of the case for viewing from behind the handycam. All the little pieces inside are for different mounting conditions using different size cameras. The only problem was the wide angle lens and the extra thick ten-hour battery lengthened the camera so none of the mounting adaptors worked without the lens touching the front glass piece. I was forced to go to a piece of floor mat to rig it so it would work. At least now we could film our adventures.

Now that it was 5:00 p.m. on July 4th, and all the tourists were going to start milling around the docks waiting for the fireworks. Thus, making it easier to sell shirts and get some exposure for our trip. We were leaving. I tried to persuade Ralph to delay our departure for at least a couple of hours, but we had media lined up at locations further up the coast. We left and made a big loop around the shoreline just incase the flagpole had drifted up onshore. No luck. We left disappointed. We went to the gas station and then put out to sea, heading for Beaufort, North Carolina. Ralph said we had to be there by 11:00 a.m. the next morning.

After dark, we watched fireworks almost continuously for a couple of hours. From several-miles offshore, we saw small clusters of fireworks all along the coast. We were usually so far out they looked like they were only going up a couple of inches.

The seas were one to three foot and we were going over them about one every second. I felt like I was riding a horse at a canter. We went up down *tish*, up down *tish*. *Tish* is the sound the boat made as the front of the boat came down. Every once in a while the front of the boat would drop down just so... and the spray, or what some people refer to as spitting, would occur. With our added weight and the mono-cat bottom, if the boat came down evenly the twin hulls could trap water inside and because of the curvature of the boat, water is forced forward. It looked kind of cool. In surfing, sometimes the tube of a breaking wave would collapse inside and squeeze out a hydrated fog mist. In the right conditions and if the surfer is good enough, he or she is assisted out of the tube along with the mist. When that is caught on film it really looks spectacular. I sometimes thought of the boat as the closing wave

Charleston, South Carolina, for Old Glory

spitting out the water mist out front.

Around midnight, when we were close to shore, we came up on an anchored unlit dark barge. It was just north of one of the green channel markers sitting all by itself. When I first noticed it, with the water mist in the air, it looked like a large ominous shadow from some sort of abandoned boat-ghost movie. I could easily picture it in a Scooby Do cartoon or an Alfred Hitchcock movie. It must have been used earlier to launch offshore fireworks but there was no excuse for not having some type of anchor light on it.

Sunday, July 5th

Ralph woke up as it was getting rough offshore so he suggested I drive closer to the coast thinking it would be calmer. He was right and since I was wide awake I got really close. I was having a lot of fun and Ralph was asleep. I had been driving inshore for quite a while when out of nowhere I came across a lone green marker. I looked toward shore in the dark looking for a harbor or something, but didn't see any openings, and thought to myself, that was a weird spot for a marker. I didn't slow down and was going pretty fast, but luckily I stood up and leaned forward to scan the ocean in front. A few seconds later I noticed what looked like small breakers. I squinted my eyes and thought, why are those waves breaking in that direction? For a split second I considered running straight through them since this was a flats boat and they were pretty small and I would be hitting them straight on.... It suddenly occurred to me, something wasn't right... a feeling. They weren't breakers. I was heading for a rock jetty. Instinctively I cranked on the wheel and pulled back on the throttle. The boat swung a hard right about thirty foot from the rocks and I headed straight out to sea. Again, a close call in the middle of the night and Ralph was sound asleep. We were near Murrells Inlet in South Carolina.

Our sleeping accommodations at sea were usually one of two places. The best place in my opinion was the bean bag up front, but the conditions were almost never favorable. For the front to be good, the sun should be out, because there was nothing to block the cool breeze and it could get cold. It had to be calm, since the boat moved up and down like a hinge. Think of the water behind the boat as half the hinge, the motor area as the pin or pivot area, and the boat as the other half. The front of the boat goes higher than the back. The front was often dropped several feet and smacked down hard which caused for an extremely jarring ride. It was infrequent that the motor came completely out of the water. The back was still bumpy but considerably calmer than the front. Both places were wet when going out to sea unless it was calm. Ralph was asleep in the back, on top of the air mattress, underneath one of our most treasured boat items, the colorful extremely soft vinyl waterproof banner from Suzuki. They gave it to us to advertise their motor, but we also used it as a blanket. Ralph was tucked in wearing his yellow raincoat and his green ball cap.

Even though I was standing on rubber mats, my heels were becoming really sensitive. I think it was because my feet were always wet and salty. Upon closer inspection, I noticed my heels were starting to develop large vertical cracks in them. To give them a break I spent more time sitting back against the backrest and driving with my feet.

Charleston, South Carolina, for Old Glory

Monday, July 6th

At four in the morning, several-miles from shore, nearing Cape Fear, South Carolina, there were a lot of rock islands. As we came up on them, we could see waves breaking on them. Many of them were barely above the surface and close together. We broke out the spotlight, fooled with the connection to get it to work and picked our way through the islands at idle speed. We changed our heading a little more northeast to get further from shore. This area would be even more dangerous in completely calm seas as we needed the swells to help identify near surface obstructions.

I decided to try out the surfboard bag my friend Steve Webster gave me. We were planning to use it for sleeping. It proved to be utterly a failure. It was eight-foot long, so one end was always hanging over and getting wet. It was riddled with holes and the fabric so worn out which made it impossible to be water-resistant. The inside had a fine layer of sand, salt, and wax, making it sticky. It was too confining, so narrow I couldn't even turn over inside it. I couldn't use the safety rope around my waist, so I had it around one arm and my neck. The whole experience was miserably uncomfortable. So I made a mental note to test out the new-double-board bag from Cape Surf the next night.

Near Moorhead, North Carolina, Ralph needed to make some phone calls. He normally called Anne almost everyday along with several of the behind-the-scenes people that tracked us and some of the local media in the area. Whenever we were close to shore, we turned our cell phones on, but after about three-miles offshore, we turned them off so we wouldn't get stuck with some sort of roaming charge. Both of our cell services were for within the United States only. Ralph couldn't get any reception on his, but my

Verizon phone was working fine. So, while he made his calls I decided to make some cell phone commercials showing how Verizon was better than T-Mobile. In the event we ever got someone important enough to really consider sponsoring our trip and/or the documentary about our voyage, I wanted to have something to show them. After all, against popular belief, in my heart I knew we were going to make it. As Ralph had said many times, "Quitting is not an option." We both had to sign documents for at least one of our sponsors which stated that if one of us got hurt or even died, the other would continue the mission.

Many times the shoreline was dotted with rows of what had to be rental beach shacks. If that was what they were, these beaches would make a great place to have a family reunion. They didn't appear to be very big, but since we were out so far, I could've been wrong.

A while further up the coast, we were quickly loosing our peaceful morning sky. The graying bombers were moving in and were bringing their buddies. The whole sky in front of us was covered. It looked like they were daring us to pass underneath... yeah that lightning bolt was a nice touch, so we put away the bag of chips we were nibbling on. Ralph buttoned the top button on his rain coat and I reached for the now waterproof handycam. The question nobody had ever answered for me, and kept popping into my head was... what happened if our boat got struck by a lightning bolt? *I Am Second* was the tallest thing on the water for miles around. I've been told my whole life not to be on the water in boats during a lightning storm. Would a bolt hitting the aluminum T-top, follow the wet outside of the boat and disperse in the ocean or just zap us dead? Would it be a good idea to attach a big grounding wire

Charleston, South Carolina, for Old Glory

to the T-top and direct the current down below the waterline outside the boat? Would the gas tanks blow up? Should I be wearing rubber gloves and boots while holding the metal T-top and standing in water? Not that I'm worried... "Whatever happens, happens!"

We stopped for fuel when we arrived at the Portside Marina in Beaufort, North Carolina. When we docked, we must have ticked the guy off because he seemed irritated about something, almost like he didn't want to wait on us. A few minutes later he was our best friend. We thought he must have just read our banners and realized we were traveling from Florida in a flats boat by way of the Atlantic Ocean. They let us use their small outdoor shower building to get cleaned up. I sucked down a Coke while the clerk went over a local water chart and then checked the weather report for us.

Around one o'clock in the afternoon we went wide around Cape Hatteras because of all the outer islands. We'd planned to go east before heading north anyway so it wasn't that big a deal. For something to do, I dug through our medical kit to find a needle. I found a cheap plastic pair of tweezers, but I really needed a needle. In Charleston, I picked up a small metal shard while working on the kicker bracket. My hand was becoming infected. I had a half-inch diameter red pus-filled blister with a little swelling. After ripping a piece of dead skin off with the tweezers, I pushed and squeezed the area trying to force the metal out, no luck. If I had a needle, I could easily dig it out. Once the liquid was forced out, I rinsed it in the ocean then put some Neosporin on it. That should take care of my infection. If the metal didn't work itself out, I'd deal with it later. (It never occurred to me to use a fish hook as a needle, as we had plenty onboard.

Boston, Mass

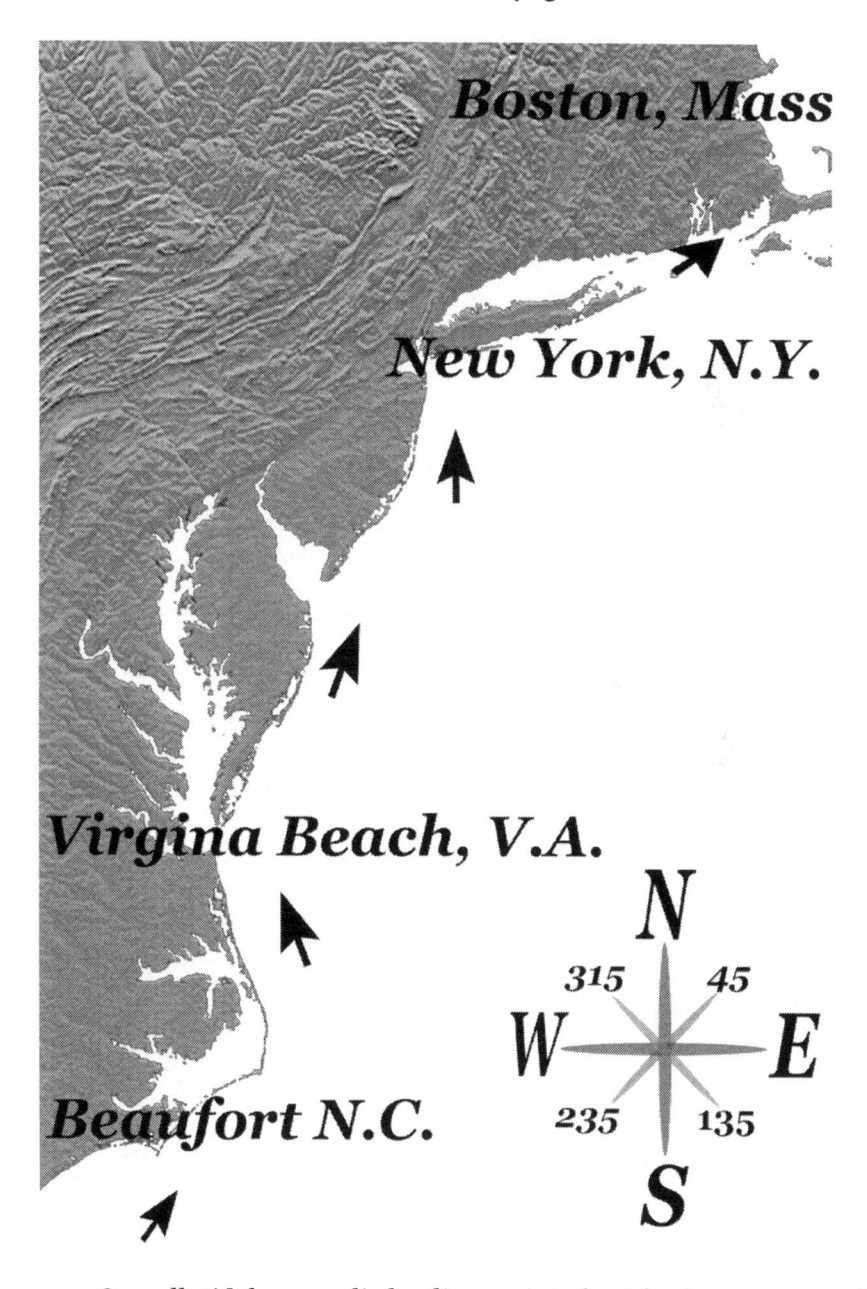

New York, N.Y.

Virgina Beach, V.A.

Beaufort N.C.

N
315 | 45
W — E
235 | 135
S

Overall I'd been a little disappointed with the amount of wildlife we were seeing. That day so far was pretty good. It consisted of two pods of dolphins. The first pod of five were charcoal gray and the second eight were a bluish gray; other than the color they looked about the same. Both pods swam close to the boat for a few minutes while I filmed them. We slowed down hoping they would swarm around and under the boat like the big pod of white-sided dolphin did on our Bermuda trip. The first group was working together rounding up fish, but when we came by they stopped to investigate us before turning back. The second group stayed with us a little longer. Ralph was sitting on the front deck while I filmed from the captain's seat. This time we didn't slow down and they split up a few on both sides of the boat. There was also a bunch of flying fish, a few birds, and a large sea turtle.

I mounted one of our two GoPro cameras to the end of one of the long poles. I wanted to extend the pole out and video back toward the boat. GoPro gave us a bag full of clamp-type adaptors and quick mounts that attached with a special double stick tape. I was a little leery of trusting the double stick tape mounts under those conditions so I used the clamp type. We didn't have a swivel mount which would have been great for quick positioning. It was hard to point the camera where we wanted it using only the fishing rod holders on the sides of the T-top. When I made the PVC inserts for the two poles, I only checked one rod holder on the T-top. I wasn't aware that there were different sizes; all the other rod holders were too small. The pole was vibrating way too much to expect quality video. Next time, I'll attach a string or bungee to limit the pole's upswing.

The conditions for surfboard surfing were getting better; we were riding just outside the breaking swells. The beaches had been empty of people for miles and miles. The swells were heading northwest and the breaking waves peeled off to the north. For surfing I prefer lefts since I'm goofy footed (right foot is out in front) and would rather face the waves, but I'd still jump on these if I could get Ralph to stop. It would take a while and be a pain to pull the surfboard down from the T-top since we'd strapped it to the long pole and extra antenna, and then multi-bungeed, tied, and shimmed the board with pool noodles to keep it from being bashed on the metal framework of the T-top. There was nothing within the five-foot roof span, no center running bar on which to get a downward hold on the inside of the surfboard. We should have mounted a real surfboard rack on top of the T-top so it would only take seconds to get down. Then we could space out some of the media stops for some quick impromptu surfing. This beach was pristine and equipped with a free roaming porpoise. Ralph reminded me this wasn't a vacation; we had to find sponsors and the later in the season we made our actual crossing, the worse the weather was likely to be.

We arrived at the Virginia Beach Fishing Center so late everything was closed. We debated whether to stay there overnight and head to New York in the morning or just leave. We were tired and low on gas. We met some people on the dock who knew the guy who operated the fuel dock. Ralph called the man, we got our fuel, and our decision was made. We decided to tough it out and headed for New York; Fox News had an interview set up with us for the next afternoon and we still had a lot of ocean miles to go.

The landscape of the immense shoreline was incredible. Sometimes the evergreen woods went almost all the way to the beach; there were big white sand dunes, magnificent rock boulders, luscious green grass.... I even saw two horses and a colt all by themselves just hanging out on the beach. Later, we passed two guys with a lean-to as a tent, then a couple of groups camping, some

Charleston, South Carolina, for Old Glory

people sitting around a campfire, some kids playing with their golden retriever, which reminded me of Casey, my dog at home. It seemed the big pass-time around these parts was to ride on the beach in long caravans of SUVs, Jeeps, and black or white Hummers. We saw literally hundreds of these vehicles over the last ten or fifteen-miles.

Ralph lost his Interstate Battery hat along the coast. He got up yelling, "Hat! Hat! Hat!" and I thought he'd said, "land, land, land!" By the time we turned around it was gone. To date, the Atlantic had taken two of our Interstate hats, my books for sale sign, and our tall flag pole.

Mid-morning, when I woke up, Ralph told me about how great the conditions had been all morning. The ocean was like a sheet of glass with rolling one footers. While he was telling me this, he slowed the boat to make a bunch of phone calls. He did this because it was hard to hear when the boat was moving fast with all the wind, water, and engine noises. We found out our Fox interview was rescheduled to the following day. We were idling for quite some time before Ralph was finally ready to go, and by then the wind had picked up considerably. I told him God gave us a gift of perfect driving conditions and since Ralph abused them by talking on the phone, God took the gift away and put a little wind on it.

I was talking with Jill on the phone when we rounded the corner and New York City came into view. This was a neat feeling since we'd been here before in this same boat. The last time was our Bermuda trip that landed us in the 2009 Guinness World Record book; 774 miles from Bermuda to New York, a record we planned to break during this voyage as we cruised from Iceland to England in the next couple of weeks.

New York, We Need That

We'd traveled 1,600 and some odd miles from Tampa, Florida and passed under the Verrazano Narrows Bridge, the ocean entrance to New York Harbor. We couldn't see the Statue of Liberty... yet. It would come into view in a few minutes. We passed a bunch of boats including a big freighter Ralph believed was transferring something to a smaller vessel. It was also discharging seawater out of its hull into the harbor. Ralph said it was a common practice. I thought it must be because of the need for extra ballast when out at sea.

When we arrived at the statue we took a few pictures, but we also wanted photos of us in the boat, with Lady Liberty in the background. There were a couple of guys close by in a sailboat, so we persuaded them to take some still shots. They ran aground outside the channel as soon as they were done, probably because they were distracted talking to us. We used our boat to pull them off. Because of their long-heavy keel, we had to slowly pull their sailboat at a slight angle so it gradually rotated toward deeper water. Then we could pull it straight with more power. We exchanged business cards and they said they'd follow our trip. Before we left Liberty, we took turns posing for pictures wearing our sponsors' T-shirts so we'd have some photos to email to them.

New York, We Need That

Bob and Ralph idling in front of the Statue of Liberty in New York

Towing the sailboat which ran aground while taking our picture

Wounded Hero Voyage I

Ralph made call after call now that we were in calm water protected from most of the wind by the cement buildings; that was until his cell kept dropping calls. I loaned him mine again, as soon as I finished talking to Dayton, a sailor, I met over the Internet about a year ago. Dayton found out about our Bermuda trip, something he's been planning to do in a 19-foot sailboat, but had to put it off because of mechanical problems with his boat. He'd called me to find out if we had left on our Atlantic crossing yet. I felt bad because I was supposed to have contacted him before we left Tampa. He'd offered us a place to stay and the possibility of doing some promotions for us when we arrived in North Carolina. The last time I talked with Dayton was weeks before we were funded and I was so busy the last days before we left that I never contacted him.

We cruised several miles up the Hudson River looking for the West 79th Street Yacht Basin. We passed some *No Wake* signs wondering how all the big ships going by were supposed to cancel out their wakes. Many of the wakes we were going over were close to two-foot high. We tied our boat in one of the open slots among one of the many wooden docks. We did the minimum amount of unloading and paper work at the office before going to the restaurant 200-foot from our boat and just feet from the chain link security gate around the yacht basin. We both wolfed down a burger, some fries, and a Coke.

Soon after leaving the restaurant, I saved Ralph's life as he was about to walk out in front of a car. He stepped off a curb as a car rounded a corner and I put my arm out in front of him and pointed to the car. Yep, boating is sooooo dangerous! We walked to the Rockefeller Center Building to look for the FedEx building; Interstate Battery had sent us a couple of new shirts. They had

New York, We Need That

correctly assumed the ones we were wearing would be pretty nasty and smelly by this time. Since they had set up a live interview with us for the next day, they wanted us to look good. Also, I also wanted to hit some of the morning television shows so I could hang out front in the audience with our banner. We were going to bring along a lot of items from our trip to increase our chances of getting spotted. We would be hard to miss if we could get there early enough with our green hats, yellow jackets, shirts, fishing rods, and our six-foot website banner. Out of the three television morning shows; *Today, The Early Show*, and *Good Morning America*, we hoped to be interviewed by at least one of them.

Ralph is going to deny it, but I saved him again. He better snap out of those zombie thought modes and get tuned into real life. Cars weighing tons will always flatten a middle-aged man in a green hat. I wanted a New York hotdog with all the condiments from one of the street venders. Ralph debated whether he should get one or not. I told him I didn't want to write in my book we went to New York and didn't have a hot dog so he got one as well.

A year ago, when we were supposed to have gone on this trip, Ralph was in contact with someone from *The Early Show*. Supposedly, they were interested in interviewing us from our boat and going for a short ride. We hadn't heard a thing all year, so while we were in New York, we stopped by *The Early Show*. The receptionist wouldn't talk to us and told us the only communication that they would accept would have to be packaged up and left with the people in the mail room. We left the packaged information with a girl in the mail room.

We found out where the *Today Show* with Matt Lauer was and decided we would start there in the morning. We'd probably hang around after and try to get on the *Regis Show* next. I didn't really think we'd get on, but it wouldn't hurt to try.

There was a big Apple Computer store close by, so we went in and tried to get on some of the computers available for the tourists. After a while, a couple of people left and we were both able to spend sometime on the Internet. I also wanted to learn how to use or download my handycam videos. Like I said before I am not a computer person. I wasn't even on Facebook during our voyage. The people working there said I would have to download a program and have a hard drive to store the video on. I'd work on getting some type of hard drive later. I wasn't sure of the time, since my watch kept stopping, but we thought it was after 11:00 when we started to walk back to the boat. I retired my watch in the trashcan as I could no longer depend on it.

I grossed Ralph out when we stopped at a vendor cooking chicken and beef kabobs on a stick. As I was pulling the stick out from the bun, one of the beef chucks dropped to the asphalt road. As everyone knows, there is a three-second rule which states when something falls on the ground; it is not contaminated within the first three seconds, no matter what it is. I'm pretty fast when it has to do with food. I had that chunk up and in my mouth within two seconds. Ralph tried to give me some crap about the sanity of eating food off the ground especially in New York. I politely told him, I didn't make up the three-second rule. It has been in effect as long as anyone could remember.

We were almost back to the boat when we had the bright idea to take a shortcut based on Ralph's navigational skills. It seemed logical at the time. But we became lost and our short hike back to the boat was extended. We also realized walking for hours

New York, We Need That

in New York in Flip Flops and Gator Crocs was probably not the best idea. Both of our feet were sore.

Tuesday, July 7th

Our second morning in New York started by cleaning up the boat and airing out as much stuff out as possible. Ralph decided we shouldn't go to the morning shows because we were going to be interviewed for an article in Newsweek and we didn't want to miss it. Lisa Miller, a religious editor who writes a column on things related to religion, spent over an hour with us. Ralph was a little concerned when she appeared to be looking for negative things about our voyage named *I Am Second*. I thought nothing of it, she seemed nice enough....

Walking toward the heart of the city we passed a construction dock and asked the guys out front if we could have some scrap aluminum from a pile that looked like trash. We still needed a piece for a brace for our kicker, which was still giving us grief. Our stronger, bigger bracket was still way undersized for all the pounding the boat was taking. We told them about our voyage and why we needed it. They said all their aluminum had a purpose and we could dig through the big trash dumpster if we wanted to. They were all laughing at us, saying if we were really on this trip, then why didn't our sponsors pay for the things we needed? (That's not the way it worked. Our sponsors had agreed to give us a certain amount, and if it wasn't enough, then it was our job to find additional sponsors. Thus Ralph was on the phone every chance he could contacting businesses and media outlets.) We found a piece of wood measuring 2-inches x 12-inches x 18 inches and figured we could make it work. A couple of blocks up the road we hid the wood in a flower bed to be picked up that night on the way home.

Wounded Hero Voyage I

I left my red backpack at a soup-type restaurant where we had been unsuccessfully trying to get on the Internet with our laptops while eating lunch. I didn't realize it was missing until we got to a Star Bucks a few blocks away. Ralph ran back to look for it as he is better with directions than I am. It surprised me when he returned with it. I thought it was gone for sure. Star Bucks was a hot spot where we were able to get on the Internet for the first time since leaving Ralph's shop in Tampa. We backed up our SD cards from the GoPro cameras and looked at some of our videos taken by them. For some reason we weren't getting any audio; we were hoping it was an issue with the settings on the computer and not the cameras. Our Sebastian Inlet video taken by the jet skiers was worthless as I expected. It looked like they were zoomed in and the image was all over the place. I knew I should have told them to back off about fifteen foot. Ralph also did some calculations; it looked like we might only have enough money to get to Iceland. It was extremely critical we get a lot of media attention in New York so we could get additional sponsors. Ralph asked a girl what the monthly rent of a typical, nothing fancy, studio apartment in New York went for. She said they start at $1,800!

Our National Fox interview set up by Interstate Battery turned out to be a live chat with Rick Leventhal on the *Strategy Room*, an Internet show on Fox. They were a great bunch of guys and admitted Michael Jackson's funeral that week was killing any hopes of getting any exposure in New York. Every news media outlet had Michael Jackson on the brain and didn't seem to want to cover anything else. Interstate Battery wanted us both to wear their shirts and hats on all of our interviews, but since we had a responsibility to the Wounded Hero Foundations and we were

New York, We Need That

trying to sell shirts for their causes, we agreed that at least one of us should wear one of our wounded hero shirts. Rick aired some video clips that he somehow got from our Jacksonville interview. The video, which was shot from the bridge I drove under, looked pretty. After the interview, we gave Rick a Bermuda book. Ralph talked so passionately about the trip that even after they turned the lights off to leave; he was still talking and signing the book. Rick commented he'd look into getting us some funding for the trip. I hoped they might want *Fox Strategy Room* written somewhere on our boat.

    Oh, I forgot to mention, while we were in the waiting room to go in for the interview, Geraldo Rivera slipped out of a door down the hallway after his part in another show was over. I mentioned to Ralph that I had tried to contact Geraldo about the trip last year, before it was cancelled, to invite him for lunch with us out at sea. Someone on his team had emailed me back and asked for more information. Ralph shot out of the room like he was on fire. He caught up to Geraldo, who didn't seem to know anything about the trip, but still gave Ralph a few minutes of his time and took a business card. Geraldo looked at the card and said, "You are going to cross the ocean in that?" Then he said he was in a hurry and left. I had to admire Ralph's tenacity. I was still standing there with a soda in one hand and a cookie in the other.

> Quote from Cross the Atlantic blog: Lou Belcher said, "I'm following every step. I just tweeted on Twitter about your Fox interview. Hope it helps. I'll be watching."

    We were standing on the steps of the News Corporation Building when a really polite security guard, dressed in a black suit, stopped us from taking the picture we wanted. I thought it was funny that in New York we could step off their property, turn around and get the picture and there were many people doing just that, but we could not take it from their front steps. I opted not take the picture.

In Times Square, as I was walking across the street at an intersection (nobody seems to J-walk in New York), I was next to a guy talking on a cell phone. He leaned over and whispered in my ear, "It's amazing cocaine." I think I was just solicited to buy some cocaine. Since I don't do drugs and never have, it was a waste of his efforts. I just kept walking, ignored him, and thought... welcome to New York.

Wednesday, July 8th

Ralph changed his mind and decided not to do the morning shows. He was concerned it would make us look cheesy, desperate, and hurt our credibility. I disagreed, but gave in since it would be a lot of work to get there before the crowd. People arrived there before the crack of dawn. We would have to be close to the front to get noticed.

While walking on the Hudson Bay River Walk toward the city, Ralph was starting to show some signs of depression. He was moving slower, didn't want to talk, kept to himself, and wasn't smiling. After asking him repeatedly what was wrong, he confessed our kitty for the trip was now down to 6,000 dollars. That wasn't even enough gas money to get to Europe, let along airfare for the trip back. He said getting the boat back to the United States wasn't figured in either. We had left on faith believing more sponsors would join us.

New York, We Need That

He asked me if I still wanted to press forward with all this uncertainty, because if he had to. He would go it alone. He admitted that he spent too much money on advertising and the boat's *Interstate I Am Second* green wrap. He thought by now we'd have more sponsors and money wouldn't have been an issue. Ralph debated about removing some of the green wrap so it would be obvious there was still room for more sponsors. Interstate Battery really only paid for a portion of the advertising space. Not all of both sides. Ralph and Charlie Brim, the liaison for Interstate Battery, had several heated discussions about how the press releases should read. Ralph believed they should be more about the adventure and the military foundations.

Shirt sales were so low the cost of the shirts weren't even close to being paid off. If the shirts sales would improve, Ralph could use that money to pay for the trip. When we acquired more sponsors, we would reimburse the shirt sale fund (which is how typical fundraising is done). Ralph's goal was not to use one penny of the profit from the shirt sales. Somehow, we needed to get more sponsors. Surely there had to be more American companies that wanted to help our soldiers. Even though the shirt sales were small, our trip still brought a lot of attention to the Wounded Hero Foundations. Hopefully a lot of people would donate money directly to them after hearing about our trip. If nothing else, our voyage should make other wounded hero foundation signs on other fundraising programs more readily recognizable just like I did at the Cracker Barrel in Tampa.

We stopped at a public library because Ralph needed to have some Dreamboat business documents copied. During our two-plus hours there, we copied and labeled pictures onto flash drives, and sent some emails. I also spent sometime looking for Hugo's second book (the small sailboat sailor). The library didn't have it on the shelf, but it was at one of the other libraries in the city. The card catalog had a price tag of $16.95 for the book. I wasn't exactly sure what that meant. Was this book for sale at the library or was that the replacement cost if the book was lost?

While walking in front of the famous Trump Towers, Ralph was handing out boat cards when all of a sudden everyone started whipping out their cameras. A limo was pulling up. Everyone crowded around and we never got to see the person drawing all the attention. Being a handyman, I'm always noticing things which don't seem right. On the ground in front of many buildings, including the Trump Towers, were sidewalks with metal grates. I watched a girl walk by and almost lose a heel in one. If I were the code inspector, something that dangerous wouldn't be allowed anywhere near an entrance to a building. Afterwards, I started to notice quite a few women wearing high heels and many of the sidewalks were in bad shape. I guessed they just had to be careful.

We passed a hot dog vender and Ralph wanted to see if he could talk the guy down fifty cents per hotdog. Ralph was purchasing a total of four. After the guy agreed and we finished eating, Ralph gave the guy a two dollar tip. This meant we broke even on the original price. I was a bit confused so I asked Ralph why he did that after working so hard to bring the cost down. He said the guy had to make a living too.

The New York streets were crawling with yellow cabs. It amazed me that the one movie I was hoping to see in England was advertised so heavily here. Harry Potter signs dominated the taxi roof signs. Later I stopped and had Ralph take a picture of me in

New York, We Need That

front of a big Harry Potter billboard.

We developed some pictures and put them together with the documents Ralph had printed earlier at the library. This took us a while as it seemed all the photo printers in the area were out of commission. Anyway, after getting directions from several people, including a UPS driver, we finally found the mail room for the CBS Prod Casting Center. As we left and walked along the street next to the building, I saw Katie Couric, the anchor woman for CBS News. She walked by with a group of about eight people. They passed just inches away from us. I stopped and told Ralph I thought she was Katie Couric. He asked me if I was sure. All I had to say was, "I think so," before he was off chasing her down.

Ralph started his conversation off by saying, "I know that this is tacky, but I need your help." He gave the short version, which if you know Ralph that alone was an amazing thing. He told her about the 29 years ago when he was in the Marines... up to the part where we were sleeping on the boat in New York. She politely excluded herself out of the conversation and had Ralph talk with Bill Peterson, someone who she worked with. I wanted to take some photos, but I didn't desire to be one of those obnoxious camera people. I was a little embarrassed, but that didn't stop me from sneaking off a picture as she was walking away. When Ralph came back to where I was standing, I asked if he had given them any of our newly printed photographs. Ralph hadn't, but waited until Katie and her crew were finished with their quick meeting sitting on the concrete steps leading up to Jake's Fine Food and Ale before he ran back and handed Bill some photos. I was amazed nobody but me recognized Katie. I guess in New York celebs blend in pretty well among all the people.

Wounded Hero Voyage I

On our first trip from Bermuda to New York, we got a boat ticket for being behind the Statue of Liberty. Peter Mithelson found out about it and sent Ralph the money to pay for the ticket. Peter emailed Ralph and wanted to meet with us while we were still in New York. Peter and a friend of his, Kevin Lonergan, came by the dock to see the boat. They were riding motorcycles. They visited for about an hour. As it turned out, Peter had some connections with the media and set up a local interview for us the next morning. We had walked all the way back to their motorcycles when I realized we didn't get their pictures with us on the boat. We got the pictures.

Ralph, Bob, Peter, and Kevin posing on the *I Am Second*

Up to this time, we hadn't been doing any cooking or heating of any food along the way. Several months before, I purchased two 12-volt lighter plug-in thermoses for this purpose. One of the two never made it on the trip because it was still at Ralph's shop. We

New York, We Need That

spent about 45 minutes warming up one can of stew, so at least we knew we could warm up things for the colder waters coming soon.

Thursday, July 9th

I woke up and looked over the edge of my hammock to see a whole slue of police and ambulances. They were all busy doing something in the park right next to and below the restaurant that we ate at our first night in New York. The restaurant was up on the street elevation while the park and river walk were about ten-foot lower. The green grass was all torn up from the vehicles driving across it. We found out later there was a fight between a few of the homeless people earlier in the morning.

Bob in his hammock, the street level restaurant is just off the dock.

We did our laundry in the walk-through room going to the dock office. The bathroom and showers were also off the laundry room. I pulled all our wet-rusty-stained white towels out from the bottom of all the hatches. We should have never lumped the towels into hatches with anything metal inside. The two-cleanest towels I cut into a stack of wash-cloth size towels and threw the rest away. Regular sized towels took up too much room and because of their size, and being on a boat, once wet, always wet. Not long after doing all our whites, I put on a fresh white shirt and then immediately dripped a couple drops of soup right down the front while eating lunch.

Bad news! We got a call from Interstate Battery saying they would not be able to donate anymore money for our trip. We would have to find additional sponsors.

To keep myself busy, I installed the two-12-volt lighter plugs in the cockpit area that we never got around to in Tampa. They would make it easier to use the thermos, recharge our cell phones and camera batteries, and use our spotlight. On our Bermuda trip, lighter plugs were out in the weather where salt water could seep in and they rusted and corroded within hours. They were a constant pain in the neck. I mounted one under the dash and left it hanging upside down on its own wire. The second one was outside the dash. I ran the wire through one of the old lighter holes and also left it hanging upside down so the water wouldn't collect inside. I wondered how long these were going to last.

Ralph was busy trying to get the jack plate motor to work properly. It is used to raise and lower the Suzuki 115 engine. The jack plate would go down, but not up. It was under the back deck inside the gas filter and battery switch compartment. It was

New York, We Need That

mounted on the inside back wall, so it was a long stretch to work on. His pride and joy Blackberry cell phone took that moment to tumble out of his top pocket, land, and splash inside the little bit of water residing there.

During our morning walk along the river walk heading to the city, Ralph stopped to call in his radio interview, using my phone. Lucky for us he'd stored his numbers in more places than just his Blackberry. He also had them written down in his don't-go-anywhere-without-notebook. After Ralph was finished talking to his interviewer, they said they wanted to talk to me. I usually try to let Ralph do all the talking. He's better at it than I am, and besides, this was his trip. I was there for support, to help, to document everything, and of course for the excitement.

I explained during the interview that Ralph planned to be in England on my birthday, August 8th, a total of 48 days for the trip. Storms generally traveled in the same direction as we were going, so if we could get a day or two-head start on them, we should be fine. Most of our crossings are expected be less than sixty hours except for the big one from Iceland to England. We planned on using a sea anchor on any seas breaking bigger than 15 foot and just ride it out. The sea anchor is a parachute which drags in the water, in our situation from the bow. The wind pushes the boat around so it faces into the oncoming waves. Our small boat, with the sea anchor, will rise up over each swell like a cork while a larger boat, because of its length, will angle downward on the backside of a large swell and then get pounded by the following wave coming over its bow. No, we don't think people should try to copy us. It might look like we just climbed into a boat and took off, well we sort of did because of last minute funding, but we did a lot of homework before taking off on this trip. I took a safe boating class, read a bunch of books, looked at a lot of weather charts, and talked to a lot of knowledgeable people. I'm a surfer and not afraid of big waves and I've been around the water my whole life. To me this was just a long outrageous boat ride and I am thankful Ralph had invited me to go. I wrote a book on the last trip and plan on writing one on this one too. If people don't buy the shirts, then this is really just an adventure. Without the sale of shirts, we lose the real purpose of the trip. Which was to show the world that America cares and wants to honor the three Marines: John Harvey, George Holmes and Dewey Johnson and to say thanks to all the people in uniform who risk their lives daily.

Lisa Miller's Newsweek article came out and Ralph was upset because she seemed to miss the whole point of the trip. Her article was basically slamming us as a couple of idiots going out for a joyride, pretending to be religious. She concluded that because we hadn't even brought a Bible onboard a boat named *I Am Second* which meant *God is First*. Once she pointed out that bit of information, Ralph who'd graduated from Hyles-Anderson Bible College with a Masters Degree (something Lisa was not aware of) admitted she was right on one point. He should have brought along a Bible; something at home he reads almost daily. Ralph went out and purchased one hoping it wouldn't get too wet.

During my time in New York City, there were things I didn't expect to see. Women were jogging everywhere, often by themselves. Dog parks were everywhere. Pay phones were still plentiful. Location signs to get you to your destination were missing but advertisements were literally everywhere. Most of the locals were friendly. Many New Yorkers dressed like it was Halloween. A guy

New York, We Need That

was weaving in and out of people passing them on an incredibly crowded sidewalk while reading a three-inch thick book with his face buried deep inside. A blind lady, with a white cane, walked as fast as if she could see, maneuvering through dense crowds of people without a problem. Bathrooms seemed to exist only in restaurants and purchases were required to use them. Some places we passed by smelled of urine so strongly I had to hold my breath and pick up my pace. Many buildings had TVs erected on the outside of them which were bigger than any moving truck I'd ever seen. Almost half of the people I saw walking around were talking on their cell phones. Ralph pulled his cup, which he had just thrown away; back out of a trash can because he thought he might use it on the boat. My list could go on and on.

We spent some time in Starbuck's trying to get video off my handycam. After a couple of hours, Ralph was able to copy part of it onto a flash drive which we'd then convert to discs to send out to certain people.

Ralph in New York at night

Wounded Hero Voyage I

My feet were starting to burn from all the walking. I wasn't sure if it was because my socks might be sliding around, because my feet were sore from being in all the salt water, or from too much walking by a middle-aged overweight man.

Friday, July 10th

We rigged up our "props" before we went to sleep at 12:58 in the morning and planned on getting up at 4:30 to finally go stand in front of Matt Lauer and then *The Early Show*. Ralph had changed his mind about the shows, since nothing else seemed to be working. We couldn't compete with Michael Jackson's funeral.

We got up as planned and headed to the *Good Morning America* show. We missed the turn and walked too far because we weren't paying attention, just walking and talking. I was dying from the heat as I was wearing my yellow survivor jacket and black insulated pants. When we finally arrived at the plaza, we realized it was Friday, concert day. The line was backed up around the building and then went on for several blocks. We knew there was no chance of being seen with that crowd so we left and headed for *The Early Show* and never even found out who or what band was playing.

We were surprised to find out we were the first people to arrive at *The Early Show*. They had us wait off to the side where we talked to some of the camera crew. They thought we were a shoo-in for sure. They even helped us get a good spot around the large fountain pool, but when the mob arrived, we were bumped around to probably the worse spot to be noticed. The camera guys tried to move us over, but the guy in charge, who hadn't at the time heard our story, kept moving us around to the end. We ended up being

New York, We Need That

behind some people probably because the guy didn't want all our signage to block the camera's view of the crowd. Our white-main banner was six-foot long with the red-lettered CrossTheAtlantic.com logo. We tied it to two fishing poles and hung a smaller green Interstate Wounded Hero banner across the bottom and our Wounded Hero T-shirts on the sides, and my *Bermuda Suicide Challenge* book was each hanging from one of the fishing poles, plus we were both wearing our thick yellow jackets. We weren't the only ones in costume. There was a whole heard of Chick-fil-A cows, pink hat ladies, and a decked-out rock band.... *The Early Show* filmed mainly inside the building and would break to the fountain area every ten minutes or so for a few seconds. While they filmed inside, we talked to several people from the show, including the weather man. He asked us a lot of questions and we fully expected to be mentioned on the show, but later, when I talked with Jill, she said she saw us several times as the camera panned the crowd, but they didn't have any footage of us being interviewed.

Bob and Ralph out in front of *The Early Show* with their garb

Wounded Hero Voyage I

After everything was over, we hung around out front and talked to people while we rolled up our banners. Ralph was the only one to recognize Chris Wragge, the anchor of *The Early Show* that day. He looked a little different out of his impressive suit which was in his hand on a hanger. I thought he was about to go workout, judging from the clothes he was wearing. Ralph went over and talked with him. He hadn't heard about our story but seemed to be impressed. He was waiting for someone to pick him up so he spent some time talking to us. He gave us his email and phone number so we could keep him posted during the trip. Ralph wrote it down in his notebook. I gave Chris my Bermuda Suicide Challenge book.

Ralph and Chris Wragge near the fountain of *The Early Show*.

Chris' ride arrived so he left. We were walking when Ralph stopped to study this guy off at a distance. We assumed he was

New York, We Need That

homeless, judging from his clothes and the fact he was digging through trashcans eating and looking for food. Ralph said no one should have to survive by digging through trash so we went over and introduced ourselves. Jordon explained he was looking for food and didn't have any money. That about broke our hearts and Ralph invited him to go with us to Food Express. The three of us went there and sat down and had breakfast together. We had an interesting discussion about how he would go back to Yugoslavia, his former country, if he could get there. He said something about not being able to muddle through the paperwork and didn't have any money.

We stopped at a Kinko's to have the information on the flash drive turned into a DVD. Interstate Battery wanted some trip footage to make a television commercial. I waited outside with all our stuff. I must have looked homeless myself, a guy with a couple of fishing rods, holding some winter-looking jackets, in the middle of July, in New York City. A family walked by and one of their kids wore a Cocoa Beach T-shirt, my hometown growing up. I spoke up and told them I was from Cocoa Beach. The mom gave me a nervous glance, pulled her kid closer, and kept walking. When they got to the intersection I heard the kid ask his mom how I knew he was from Cocoa Beach. She stretched the bottom on his T-shirt out so he could read it upside down. I don't really think she believed I was from Cocoa Beach after all, this was New York City.

Wounded Hero Voyage I

Leaving New York, with Unsecured Possessions

It was just a little after 2:00 in the afternoon when we said goodbye to the people at the West 79th Street Yacht Basin. We were heading to the Statue of Liberty to take more pictures and then off to the fuel dock before heading out to sea toward upstate New York. We came across a really nice yacht which was anchored out in the middle of the harbor. Ralph asked if they would video us driving around. We didn't find out until later that almost all the video was worthless; out in the bright sunlight it was nearly impossible to see the reflection of the viewing screen and what was being taped. The little red light that says record was also nearly impossible to see. Many times I did the same thing. When I thought I was recording, I wasn't and vice versa. We got some really good footage of their boat's deck and their feet.

The first gas station we came to on the New Jersey side had gas for $3.89 per gallon. Since we had bought fuel for less than three dollars elsewhere on the trip, we decided to check out the other station. The other station was a little different. The fuel was in big tanks on the deck of a barge. Its gas was ten cents cheaper per gallon. We did some quick calculations and decided an additional thirty gallons would be enough to get us to Hampton Bay, New York.

We were about 200 yards away from the fuel barge, heading

out for our next leg. Ralph steered while I video-taped the New York skyline. All of a sudden Ralph yelled, "The door... my notebook!" The overhead glove-box door was normally held shut with the two springs which also allows it to stay open. I know it sounds weird, but the springs don't let the door stay partially open. It is either open or shut.

On our Bermuda trip we learned that when in seas, with all the junk we'd cram into it, if we had a heavy impact, like going over swells, it was possible for the door to get knocked open by the stuff inside. To remedy this problem, it was a must that we put a bungee, sometimes two, to guarantee it didn't pop open. The security bungees were still hanging, by only one hook, below the cabinet when the door flew open and out flew Ralph's never-go-anywhere-without-notebook. It was in the drink. Business card, papers, pencils, photos, press releases, and receipts floated everywhere. We turned around and picked up anything we found on the surface of the water. We spent another ten minutes looking and sweeping back and forth, but Ralph's precious notebook with all his contacts and plans for the trip was on the way to Davy Jones's Locker. He was devastated. Add Ralph's notebook to the list of articles claimed by the Atlantic.

After leaving New York, we had planned on visiting our Uncle David and Aunt Barbara who lived on Long Island. Uncle David was the guy who met us in New York on our Bermuda trip. He took the photograph, which I used in my Bermuda book, of the Harbor Patrol giving us the ticket around Statue of Liberty. Ralph said we were running so late that we could only spend about fifteen minutes with them if we stopped. We had to get up the coast for a really important interview. About an hour later, Ralph suggested that instead of stopping then when we were really in a big hurry, we'd rent a car later, after the interview and drive back to Long Island to visit.

The conditions for making up time were terrible. The winds were kicking up to between fifteen and twenty-miles per hour and the white-capped seas were growing to four and five foot. Ralph was trying to make time and it was going to be a rough ride. Since I needed to be fresh when it was my time to drive, I climbed into our Cape Surf board bag. I needed to try to get some sleep.

No such luck. We'd hit a bump about every second or so. And pretty much, about once a minute, most, if not my whole body, would be bounced up off the back deck for a split second. Even though there were a couple of rubber floor mats and a two-thirds filled air mattress underneath, often the landings sent vibrations through the mattress and into me. Depending on how I laid, sometimes it really hurt. If I crossed my legs, the impact was localized to the places on my body supporting my weight. It was better to spread out and have more points of contact to absorb the impact. The mattress, sleeping bag, and I were tied to the boat with individual lines. When it was rough, like now, I would usually hold onto one of the ropes with one hand so I could pull myself forward to minimize my back slide. I had to resituate everything about every thirty minutes as something was always sliding somewhere.

Looking around from the board-bag perspective, I could look up at the T-top and watch the end of the long pole vibrate up and down about a foot. Our anchor light stuck out of a rod holder and would shoot upward until it was stopped by its tie-down string. The banners shook wildly, jerking back and forth, even though we had bungees holding the lower corners tight. Sleep was impossible.

Leaving New York, with Unsecured Possessions

Instead of logging all this in the voice recorder, I asked Ralph to hand me the handycam and I videotaped for a while. Looking off the side of the boat, I was lying about six inches above the deck, which was below the top of the swells that the boat cut through. Every second or two a thin sheet of white water blasted upwards off the edges of the back third of our boat. Near its bottom and the leading edge were solid white, but the rest was semi-transparent. Looking forward I could watch drops of water come together, forming mini streams that flowed down the fifty-gallon gas tanks. The wind that rushed alongside the fifties blew the mini streams backwards at an irregular, downward angle until they were below my line of sight.

Ralph had two meetings scheduled, and it was quickly becoming evident there was no way we were going to make the first meeting at 5:00 p.m. He was busy on the phone trying to get in touch with our contacts. Eventually Ralph called the restaurant and found out it closed at 5:00, not 6:00 like he thought he was told. Nobody was waiting there for us... Ralph was really upset! He didn't understand why they didn't have their cell phones on. If any of them had checked the weather, they would have known it was going to be hard for us to be on time. Well, so much for meeting number one, now we'd just concentrate on getting to the next one.

We arrived at Oakland's Restaurant and Marina in Hampton Bay. We docked the boat and while I tied it up, Ralph jumped off and ran in to see about the meeting. Again we missed our meeting and we were going as fast as possible. While Ralph was inside a teenager came over to me at the end of the dock. He was fascinated we had come into the harbor at night in such a little boat, especially since it had been so rough out there that day. His jaw dropped when I told him we had come here from Florida and planned to cross the

Atlantic. Impossible, he said, nobody can take a little boat like ours that far out in the open ocean. He said we'd get swamped! I told him we already owned a world record for going to Bermuda in this same boat. Since he didn't believe me, I showed him my book. He got real excited and bought it on the spot then wanted me to autograph it for him. I asked him his name and was surprised he spelled his the same way as my son, Bryan with a "y" instead of an "i".

I guess after all that I was kind of in la-la land and I accidentally put too much gas in the back two-fifty-gallon tanks. Up to then, they'd both been empty. I was only supposed to put in a couple of gallons for emergencies, but instead I put about twenty gallons in each one. Because we wanted the boat to get up on plane, we preferred to be a little front heavy when the boat was loaded. Ralph and Marino, the boat builder who helps Ralph build his boats back at the shop, rigged up the same elaborated gas valve system we used on the Bermuda trip. The object was to feed our engine from any tank with the turn of a couple of valves, but we were still missing some of our gas lines. Now, we'd have to unclamp the lines from the front tanks and attach them to the back ones to burn off the wrongly filled back tanks.

The Shinnecock Marlin and Tuna Club was having a shark fishing tournament the next day and were just finishing up with their Captain's Feast on the back deck at Oakland's. Ralph went over there and tried to buy a plate, thinking it would be a lot cheaper than the fancy restaurant. They said they weren't allowed to sell dinners. So we opted to go back to the boat and heat up a can of soup, but we did manage to pass out some boat cards at the event. Ralph went in to apologize to management for missing our

Leaving New York, with Unsecured Possessions

appointment, and then we took off. It was too late in the day to try to rent a car and go see our uncle and aunt. We'd have to catch up with them later. This was a decision I regretted later as Aunt Barbara died within a few months of our return and the bummer was, I hadn't seen her in years. We should have made time for them.

The wind had stopped completely and the ocean had glassed off, leaving just good sized swells. The moon was almost full and just coming up, which made for a gorgeous night. I was driving and almost hit an unlit buoy so I leaned forward looking for more. I plugged in our spotlight but it wouldn't come on. The salt-spray corrosion problem had come back to haunt those lighter plug-ins again.

Our Suzuki motor shut down and I didn't want to wake Ralph up so I just sat there for a minute or so, verified there was gas in the tank and tried to start it again. It fired right up. Water sprayed out the back of the motor like normal, which proved the water pump was working. I shrugged my shoulders, checked my heading, and proceeded forward. I began to wonder if maybe we had water in the gas. A few minutes later, she shut down again. It was time to wake up Ralph and drain the water separator located under the back deck. This involved moving the air mattress and boardbag, and then lifting the hinged storage compartment door which spans across the whole back. We used an empty soup can which we held underneath a bleeder valve beneath the water separator canister. The separator was mounted against the forward wall inside of the compartment. I couldn't get the bleeder valve to turn using just my bare hands so I initially thought of using a wrench, but because everything is made of plastic, I decided to use a cloth towel instead. I was able to loosen it up. I pumped the inline fuel ball valve a few times to force the fluid through and then screwed the bleeder valve tight. I poured the two inches of cloudy fuel (because of the water in it) into the ocean and put the can back into the trash. I always felt bad whenever I did that, but the floating fuel quickly evaporates and I didn't know what else to do with it. Our Suzuki started right up.

A couple of hours later the Suzuki shut down again. The boat came to a complete stop and as I was grumbling under my breath and started to turn around to inspect the motor, I noticed something big in the water about twenty-foot straight ahead; a big metal buoy, about three foot in diameter. I looked to the right and left and saw there were at least thirty of these buoys in the water, spaced about ten foot apart. It looked like they were holding up some sort of heavy net. If the motor hadn't shut down when it did, we'd have gotten tangled up in the whole mess.

So, after thanking God, we went to work to try to figure out why the engine had died. We discovered that we'd forgotten to turn one of the many gas valves into the correct position, so when we thought we were draining the right back tank, we were really draining the front left tank. This time it wasn't water that killed the engine, we had run out of gas. A turn of a valve, a couple pumps of the fuel ball, and we were back underway. God had saved us again! The first couple times I almost ran into the beach and jetties, and Ralph almost hit the island, now me again with the string of buoys. All these close calls were at night. We navigated our way around all the buoys when all of a sudden the oil light came on. I figured the computer was telling us it was time to change the oil again.

Saturday, July 11th

Around 3:30 in the morning, we were beat and decided to

Leaving New York, with Unsecured Possessions

take a break and anchored on the downwind, or in nautical terms, leeward side, of an island. I spent about half an hour looking for my little blue nylon hammock which I used to sleep in every time we stopped the boat and couldn't find it. I ended up using the beanbag out on the front deck. I wore my two piece Interstate jacket with its removable liner, and my Mustang jacket; it was that cold. Ralph was completely zipped inside the board bag. About 6:30 in the morning we awoke as the sun came up and witnessed one of the most beautiful places we'd ever seen. The island looked like a chunk of Ireland off of Massachusetts. It was mountainous, with bright green grass, small cottages, and sheep. There was even a small red sailboat beached on the sandy shore with a couple more boats anchored near some little buoys. The water was completely flat and several fishermen were off in the distance in their small red and white open fishing boats. Of all the places I wanted to stop and fish, Nantucket Sound was it. But, this was not a vacation. We were on a mission....

We headed up Buzzard's Bay towards the Cape Cod Channel in the vicinity of Nantucket Sound. The channel provides the shortcut through the 65-mile long peninsula of Massachusetts. The place was riddled with crab traps and fishermen.

My right knee had a weird pain in it. Normally it was my left knee that was always a little sore. I think yesterday in Ralph's mad ocean racing I was brutally pounded as we jumped wave after wave. I'd ridden for a while laying on my stomach, down on the back deck, and my knees had gotten a good jarring through the mats. Now that the water was calm, I hoped it would work itself out.

The opening to the Cod Channel was decorated with a huge metal framed entrance. From off in the distance, I mistook it for a suspension bridge. On both sides were buildings and windmills. We passed a big cargo ship, tied up to a dock on the south shore, before going under the fancy header. Inside the channel the grass was manicured beyond the high seawalls and I felt like we were in Switzerland. I had been there years ago. We soon passed under the real expansion bridge. People were fishing, there was a guy in a row boat, and just before departing the channel, we saw a huge green power plant.

We stopped at 9:30 a.m. and just drifted around so Ralph could do a planned radio interview with Captain Wade Osborne on Afishionado Radio, an outdoor talk show broadcasting from Clearwater, Florida. I pulled out a fishing rod in anticipation of landing "the big one." We were approximately a mile and a half from shore when off in the distance, we could see a caravan of boats heading our way in single file. Using a shiner (chrome lure), I made multiple casts as I stood on the back deck of the boat. While I still had the fishing line in the water, the twenty to thirty boats came within thirty foot of us. I guess the lead boat wanted to either read our banners or wanted to give us a private showing of their beautiful boats. Most, if not all, of the vessels looked brand new. Either way, with all the commotion they were stirring up in the water, I wasn't going to catch any fish.

For miles and miles we passed lobster or maybe crab traps. I couldn't tell the difference just looking at all the small buoys everywhere. There were thousands of them. We came upon a boat named *Happy Days*. We stopped and talked to the skipper. He was pulling up some lobster traps. When we asked if we could video tape him, he did better than that. He gave us an education on lobsters. He pulled one out of a trap and told us she was pregnant

Leaving New York, with Unsecured Possessions

then explained the rules of keeping a bug (the slang term for a lobster). She had eggs, which he showed us, and said he couldn't keep her, so he threw her back into the water. He told us how lobsters molt like snakes when they grow. During this phase they hide because their new shell is soft so they are hard to catch. He told us most lobsters are caught in 25 foot of water. Right now, the fisherman was pulling up traps from fifty foot. He said they can't put all the traps in shallow water and lobsters travel a lot. As he threw the trap back into the deep water, he said right now they are in shallow water. As we drove off I commented to Ralph for every buoy our friend snagged there were at least three lobster pots down below.

Learning about lobsters

While shoveling a handful of dry cereal down my throat, I made the mistake of leaning my head back too far and my hat blew off. This time we didn't have to turn the boat around because our Suzuki motor caught it. We talked about it, and on our Bermuda trips, we did it. Yep, it was time to stop losing hats. I scrounged a light weight strap off of a waterproof bag and tied my hat to the good luck necklace Barbara and Bernie gave me in South Carolina.

Boston, Massachusetts, Counter Clockwise

As we were closing in on Boston, our last stop in the United States, we started to notice a lot of rocks and small islands sticking up out of nowhere and we were miles from the coast. For the first time on the trip, I noticed the sweet smell of seaweed. It was a good ocean smell. A couple of windmills stood out among the buildings near the entrance to the harbor. Many of the old gunneries were still preserved from the days when Boston had to protect itself, although the cannons were missing.

We hugged the left side at the mouth of the Boston Harbor and stopped to clean up the boat and straighten up our banners. Before leaving New York, we moved our CrossTheAtlantic.com banners from the top of the gas tanks and hung them from the sides of the T-top where they could be seen easier. We had also taken down the front I Am Second Wounded Hero banner because it was flapping and obstructing my view when filming over the windshield. I had put it away and couldn't remember where causing me to waste twenty minutes looking for the darn thing. Everything should have a place and everything should be in its place.

The harbor waters were teaming with boats. All I could think about was the movie *Caddyshack* as we entered heavy hectic

Boston, Massachusetts, Counter Clockwise

boat traffic. In the movie Rodney Dangerfield's character was driving a yacht amuck in the congested harbor and just about plowed over every boat. The deeper into the harbor we traveled the worse it became. Sailboats were tacking from side to side against the wind, crossing in front of motorboats, in what was starting to look like a huge boat parade. There was a mixture of all kinds of boats, from little skiffs to full blown luxury yachts. We started to notice the majority of boats were going in a definite counterclockwise loop with a lot of boats, including ours, going the wrong way. We followed a sailboat going on a long tack across the harbor to get with the flow of traffic. A fire boat made a tremendous display of spraying its many water hoses, looking like a moving water fountain. Ralph said all the commotion reminded him of the movie *Jaws* when all the boaters took off in a wild frenzy to hunt down the shark. It was mayhem with small boats going over huge wakes.

We were looking for dock number seven and the marina named Shipyard Quarters. We asked for directions from one of the many Coast Guard and Harbor Patrol boats. They all had on their blue lights flashing. The patrol guy wasn't too sure, but sent us in what he thought was the general direction. Ralph turned on the radio and tuned in Channel 16 to ask for Shipyard Quarters. Someone told Ralph to switch to Channel 71 where we were directed to the fueling dock. Patrick, the son of the owner of Shipyard Quarters, and another guy came over to us in a boat and had us follow them.

We were both extremely tired and groggy. I was near the front, but not all the way forward. Too much frontal weight would cause the motor to rise up and it would becomes harder for the captain to maneuver the boat (the propeller needs water). We could have lowered the motor, but because the jack plate didn't work properly, it would be a pain to get back into position. Ralph thought the boat was in neutral as we came in a little too hot. He shoved the controls in reverse as he had misjudged the distance and speed, so even after I ran forward to push off, we still managed to bump into Patrick's workboat dinghy. No damage, but we were both a little embarrassed. Here we were... supposedly seasoned boaters and couldn't even dock our boat. Patrick gave us an excellent location right in front of the restaurant, Tavern on the Green, not far from the boardwalk. Later he moved us to an even better display spot. Patrick cut away a chain used to keep boaters out of a private dock rented by one of his special customers, so we'd be closer to the public boardwalk along a busy street.

Patrick had been in the Coast Guard for about six-years and was excited to be part of our adventure. He loved the idea of our trip and our cause to promote Wounded Heroes. We gave him a rundown of the whole trip to date and he said he was going to find us a big US flag to replace the one we lost in Charleston. He was also going to look into getting us a small Coast Guard flag.

We had a pretty decent lunch on the upstairs outdoor section of Tavern on the Green. We both were surprised when our bag lunch hamburger, which came with an apple and chips for ten dollars, was actually a thick steak burger.

Patrick explained that there was a fleet of reconditioned sailing ships which sailed from one harbor to another on exhibition tours usually lasting three days. Everybody loved these tall ships and the towns along their route organized boat parades to honor them. There was a continuous mob of spectators walking along the

Boston, Massachusetts, Counter Clockwise

boardwalks going from ship to ship. Many of the ships were open to the public. The harbor was sprinkled with probably about twenty of these historic tall ships. Some of our military and Coast Guard ships were also open during this event. Ralph and I spent several hours driving around in the boat parade so that all the people that came to see the tall ships could also see us and find out about our voyage through our website banners.

Every so often people took pictures of us. We were never sure if they knew about our trip or just thought our boat looked interesting. For a short time we followed a boat of seven people all sucking back beer after beer. As we trailed them down a short canal with five or six tall ships docked, one of the guys, with a big beer belly, started talking to us about our trip. In the end he said he wanted to help us and all American servicemen. He offered us ten dollars for four of our *Do More* shirts. Since each one sold for $25.00, we didn't sell him any.

On our first loop going around the harbor, Ralph wanted me to drive out of our single file position and go down into a turning basin where no other paraders were going. There was a military and a Coast Guard ship docked there. He said he wanted a better look at the vessels, but I think he wanted their crew to start up a conversation with us. I told him to drive since I didn't want to get yelled at for doing something I knew I wasn't supposed to do. I had to apologize to Ralph after we switched positions and he drove past a police patrol boat directing the flow of boats, without anybody stopping us. I was reminded of the time we got the ticket around the Statue of Liberty, when from the view from the patrol boat looking down into our boat; we must have looked like a bomb. The surprising thing was it didn't seem to concern anybody in New York in 2007 or in Boston in 2009. Many of our gas tanks stuck-up higher than our boat gunnels. During the second loop, Ralph tried the same thing and over a loud speaker we heard, "*I Am Second* boat, *I Am Second* boat, you need to get out of there and continue in formation with the rest of the boats." I didn't get my apology back from Ralph.

US Coast Guard tall ship was among the many tall ships on display

My right knee cap was starting to become more and more painful. It was beginning to swell and felt warm to the touch. After our second-complete loop, I was ready to get off the boat away from all the bouncing. I'd been babying my knee, not knowing exactly how I hurt it, but I told Ralph I thought it might have happened yesterday during our ocean racing to get to our missed meetings. I could barely move as I got off the boat as the knee had become painfully stiff. I hobbled around the dock while Ralph rummaged though all the stuff in one of the front deck hatches and found my missing hammock. He tied it up using a rope since the Atlantic had

Boston, Massachusetts, Counter Clockwise

gotten one of the two straps which originally came with it. I spent the next couple of hours trying to get comfortable peacefully swinging above the starboard side fuel tanks.

Ralph was worried about my knee almost as much as I was. He wanted to know if I'd be able to finish the trip and said if I couldn't continue, he'd look into getting an auto pilot and go by himself. (An auto pilot is an expensive piece of navigation equipment that works with a chartplotter to mechanically pilot the boat.) I assured him I'd be okay and would definitely be finishing the trip but I did have some concerns. I called my son Bryan, who just recently finished a paper on knee injuries since he had plans to go to medical school in a few years. He agreed with me thinking I bruised it on the back deck. His recommendation as a college kid and not a doctor was to ice it, twenty minutes on, twenty minutes off, repeated three times, and then elevate it above my heart as much as I could. He felt this would help the swelling go down considerably. I used an ice-cold soda donated from the guy on the next dock. He also bought two *Do More* shirts.

Allen, my cousin Jackie's boyfriend, called me. We met a few months before when he and Jackie were on vacation in Florida. Allen offered to bring his car so we could do whatever shopping we had to do, but I knew my cousin Terry was coming the next day, so we'd do our shopping then. Allen drove his car into town and then rode his bicycle to the docks. He wore his red *Do More* shirt and I was in my bright yellow *Do More* shirt so it'd be easier to find each other in front of the restaurant. Allen brought his laptop in his backpack so he could make copies of my videos. I wanted to back them up. I was worried if the handycam's memory filled up or the handycam got wet, we'd lose all the video we'd taken so far. Ralph wanted to find an Internet connection so he could work while Allen transferred the video files. We went upstairs to the back deck of a neighboring hotel and found a hotspot and a power outlet. But since it was so windy, almost dark, and concern over salt air getting into the computers, we decided to go to Allen's house.

Allen and Ralph set up the computers to copy the video from my handycam and then went out to get some sub sandwiches while I stayed behind to okay, through email to my publisher, the final approval for the *Running for Fun* book which my son Jonathan and I had written together. It was supposed to be a surprise for Jonathan, and I thought if it became available during the voyage, our chances of selling it would go up. When Allen and Ralph got back and checked on the video, it became obvious this was going to take a long time. Allen gave me a muscle relaxer for my knee and I was about to get my first night away from the boat in fifteen days. Hopefully that would help the injury. After Ralph spent a couple of hours on the Internet, Allen drove him back to the boat. Ralph didn't stay with us since he was worried about the boat and its electronics. Ralph got to enjoy a night by himself sleeping on the boat in the pouring rain. He said he pulled his jacket over his head and slept like a baby.

Sunday, July 12th

The next morning I had to use two hands to lift my leg from the bed onto the floor. After hobbling down the hallway, it loosened up fairly fast and felt much better than the night before. The video was finished by morning and since Allen was going out of town on business and had all the video on his spare external hard drive, he made only one test disc of the beginning of the trip. He'd make the

Boston, Massachusetts, Counter Clockwise

rest later and mail them to my house if I needed them after our voyage was over. We picked up some Dunkin Donuts and coffee for Ralph which he really appreciated.

Ralph and I set off walking up Bunker Hill Road looking for a church to go to. All we had to do was look at the skyline and we could see a bunch of steeples. We had already passed two Catholic churches but Ralph wanted to try to find a Baptist or a Methodist church. We both grew up Catholic, but I married into a Presbyterian faith and then became Methodist, since they had a youth group for our kids. Ralph drifted over to the Baptist side. Neither of us really cared as long as it was a Bible-believing church. A guy sitting on his front steps, reading the paper, told us there was another Catholic church on top of the hill. By the time we arrived it was 9:30 and church had started at 9:00. We decided to continue walking in the same direction, since there was a Walmart a mile or so up the street, and figured we could make the 11:00 a.m. service on our way back.

We stopped at a fire station where they were flying a POW flag just below an American flag. Ralph asked if they had either a spare POW, or more importantly, a spare American flag. They were out of both as far as the big flags, but they did have a 12 by 18-inch American we could have. So Fire Station 32 Ladder Company 9 of Boston gets credit for supplying us with our much-needed American flag.

We came across a Home Depot and went in and purchased a big American flag, rope, a rain coat for me since I needed something to block the wind coming between my jacket and pants while I slept in the hammock. We also bought metal brackets, two different diameter 10-foot PVC pipes, two-small wooden flag poles, three-more 5-gallon jerry cans, and two-meatball subs with Cokes. While we were in the store, Ralph got a call about an interview at the boat scheduled for 11:30. We'd have to miss the 11:00 church service and book it back to the boat. Maybe we'd be able to pickup a 5:00 service later in the day.

Ralph wanted to run to the Walmart across the street but since we'd missed too many interviews, we decided we really needed to be at this one. We inserted the two-PVC poles together and then put the two-wooden flag poles into the ends. Next, we hung the three gas cans and bags of supplies on the pole and started walking with our sandwiches in hand. I hadn't made two steps when out sloshed a bunch of tomato sauce which landed on my ankle and foot. We must have been a sight, two-overweight old guys, one hobbling as he tried to hustle it down the road, toting all this stuff as if we were carrying an animal back from a hunt.

Bruce Schulman, our main man behind the scenes, found us just by chance. I say chance because neither Ralph nor I had actually met him. Bruce had somehow gotten a hold of one of Ralph's press releases and decided it needed some polish. A couple of phone calls to Ralph, and Bruce became our logistic manager. He lived in the Boston area and was our go-to-guy. Whenever Ralph called, which could be anytime of the day or night, Bruce was there. He'd brought along his son, Noah, for this first meeting. They were on the dock, next to the boat, waiting for us. We managed to beat the news team to the boat.

Cousin Terry Gorman, his wife Sue, and two of their friends, Wayne and Priscilla, also came out to meet us. They brought a bunch of tuna wraps and bottled water for a little dock-side picnic which we decided to have after our interview with local Fox 25 News. Ralph still had Internet work to do so he went over to the

Boston, Massachusetts, Counter Clockwise

dock office while I got ready to take everyone for a ride on the last day of the boat parade. We had to borrow three life preservers from one of the boaters docked across from us so we'd have a total of seven. (The law required that the boat had to have a life jacket for everybody on the boat.) We pulled out into parade formation. I did very little of the driving. Sue wanted to pilot except for when we crossed over the bigger wakes. Sometimes many boats had to stop, constantly going into and out of gear trying to keep from drifting into the growing numbers of boats piling up around. The hold up was usually caused by a string of boats that came out of a side canal. It became a traffic jam as they tried to funnel themselves back into the main artery flow. The whole loop was several miles around with the congested area bottled up near the tall ships. Several police boats were directing to keep the flow going. Other areas had boats five wide operating at near full throttle. The parade wasn't nearly as congested as the day before and I thought everyone had a good time.

The tall ships were magnificent to see especially from the water. Their many multi-sized masts loomed way overhead as we approached close to their sides. Every boat looked unique as they hadn't come off of an assembly line. They came in a wide range of colors from bright yellow to flat black. I especially liked the ones that had their trimmings varnished in a high gloss coating showing off all the wood's natural grains. I would love to have the opportunity to sail aboard one of the antique ships someday.

Our parade group had a tough time getting Ralph away from all the work he had to do. He was constantly sending out press releases, calling companies, and making media phone calls. I had to call him multiple times before he met us at the Tavern on the Green for dinner. Everybody stayed for the dinner and I passed a copy of my *Running for Fun* manuscript around. The food was great and as soon as everyone was done, Ralph buzzed back to Patrick's office to finish his work. But when he got there, it was locked up for the night with all his stuff inside. Bruce and Noah were still around, so they drove Ralph over to a Walmart to do more shopping.

Bob, Bruce, Noah, Sue, Terry, Ralph, Priscilla, and Wayne

Because of all the people around, Tavern on the Green had four outdoor Porta Potties upstairs on the back deck. These were the cleanest I had ever seen or smelled. The attendant opened the door for each person as they entered and after each use he went inside and wiped everything down. I had never seen toilets that were flushable by use of a foot pump. The Porta Potty also had a small sink inside, also controlled by a foot pedal. The attendant gave each person a drop of sanitary cream and a paper towel as they came out.

Boston, Massachusetts, Counter Clockwise

My knee would loosen up when I was walking, but if I sat for any length of time, it became stiff and especially hurt when climbing up and down stairs. To get to the boat from the street required walking down a couple of sections of stairs leading down to the stationary dock and then there was a long ramp going down to the actual floating dock. Every time I had to lift my leg up it was really painful especially when going over larger items such as gas tanks or the sides of our boat. I got some ice from the outdoor bar and iced my leg while trying to sleep in my hammock. The outdoor music from the bar was enjoyable while resting under the stars.

Monday, July 13th

We woke with Ralph's phone ringing. We had set our cell-alarms to go off at 5:00 a.m. because we had several interviews to do that morning. But as he fumbled around trying to shut it off, he realized it was an actual call instead of the alarm. Armed Forces Radio Europe was calling us. I guess they thought we were out at sea and one of us would be awake, driving. Ralph rescheduled the telephone interview for later in the morning.

A taxi met us in front of the neighboring hotel and took us to a Dunkin Donuts so Ralph could get a coffee. From there we walked up the hill to the Fox 25 News building. We were about an hour early, so while Ralph went downstairs to make two of his three morning radio interviews, I sat and watched the news guys do the morning news. It seemed like they worked really well together as they were always joking and cutting up. Later, on live TV during our outside interview, with the traffic going by, my knees would not stop shaking. I don't think I was all that nervous but I was still freezing from sleeping on the boat and hadn't warmed up yet. Doug Goudie, nicknamed VB, was the commentator and he had a lot of fun teasing us and made me feel at ease. We liked his commentary so much Ralph used it on the front page of his website.

Ralph, VB, and Bob at the Fox 25 News interview

I talked with Joe, the cameraman, about what he liked to do when he's not at work and discovered he was a barefoot runner who liked to do mountain runs and triathlons. He talked about how he preferred to run without shoes and has a pair of running shoes with individual toes. I signed a Bermuda book for Joe, after offering it to VB, who said he wouldn't have time to read it. I think Joe would have liked Jonathan's *Running for Fun* book but it wasn't published yet. Before we left, VB wanted to buy us breakfast at one of his local favorites, the Fill-a-Buster. He gave us twenty dollars towards our western omelets and orange juices. He said he would have liked to have gone with us but he still had to work.

The omelets were great. While sitting there we met Timothy F. Cullen Esquire from the Commonwealth Military Division of

Massachusetts. He wanted to hear all about our voyage and gave us his card before he left. Ralph had another radio interview set up. This one was with Michael Harrington of SRN Radio, so he made the call. Ralph told me that Michael said 1,200 stations were supposed to pick up his interview. The employees of Fill-a-Buster worked as quietly as possible and shushed everyone coming into the restaurant while Ralph was on his cell interview in the corner.

We went into a government building, across the street, to use the bathroom because the restaurant's bathroom was temporarily out of order. Everyone entering the building had to go through an X-ray machine after unloading all their pockets. I felt like we were in a court house and maybe we were. I left a couple of business cards on one of their message boards on the way out. We came up to a Rite-Aid store so we stopped to print some pictures off of the SD card out of my camera.

Ralph proposed we cut out 600 miles of our northern Canada run because of our budget crunch. Our initial reason for going so far north was to get away from the area were the two ocean currents met... the Gulf Stream and the Labrador Current. This would change our angle when crossing the Labrador Current. Its current was generally heading in a southwest direction. By traveling further north we would be angling across it instead of hitting it head on. We agreed to make our decision later.

We met locals who were standing above our boat on the boardwalk which was about forty foot out from and about fifteen-foot higher than our boat. Ralph baited them into a conversation about the stupidity of people crossing the Atlantic in a boat with almost no sides. To have some fun with these guys I got in on their conversation. I agreed with them that a boat with sides less than a foot high, like that boat(nodding towards the *I Am Second*), would capsize if it was hit by a big wake. After a few minutes one of them realized I was wearing a green Interstate Battery hat and then suddenly looked back at the boat. They had a good laugh. One guy's name was Wayne and the other was John. They said they were best friends. John was in construction and Wayne was a painter and collectively called themselves "John Wayne." They were going to buy a boat together and of course the boat's name was to be *John Wayne*. John has some friends with the tall ships and was going to try to organize some kind of sendoff when we left on Wednesday at 11:00 a.m.

Ralph and I spent a couple of hours in the Shipyard Quarter's office to try to send some pictures to René, Ralph's webmaster for the trip. Their Internet connection was so slow and my knowledge of computers made for an incredibly bad relationship. Then I remembered Jill, my wife, had told me my Bermuda book was no longer on the front page of Ralph's Cross the Atlantic website. Before the trip, Ralph and I had agreed to put my book on the cover and donate ten percent of the profits of the book to the foundations. Having the book also let our present sponsors know that we would be promoting a book about this trip in the future and their logos would get additional exposure. I also needed to get some sales because I hadn't even paid off the original cost of printing the book, and now I had a second book, *Running for Fun*, coming out soon, which is not and wasn't going to be on the CrossTheAtlantic.com website. After our trip, I will be spending hundreds of hours writing the book of which I was taking audio notes and collecting videos for. I will again have a bunch of printing and editing cost. Of which I had no money to do it. I personally checked and Jill was right, no *Bermuda Suicide Challenge* book on the front page. It didn't take too long for me to become so worked up; I had to get out of there.

I looked unsuccessfully around the boat for about half an hour for the bottle of Ibuprofen which Allen had given me. My right knee, which now was a third bigger than my left, was killing me. It was well past dark and I wanted to go to sleep. That's when I remembered I had seen a CVS store close by when Allen dropped us off. I decided to go and get another bottle. I hadn't been paying close attention and must have missed it, so I kept walking. My knee was feeling better, it must have loosed up. I crossed a metal bridge and headed towards some tall buildings off in the distance. It was a nice night for a long walk. I ended up at a hole in the wall drug store close to the Fox 25 News building where we'd taken a cab to early that morning. I bought a can of stew for Ralph a pack of two individual Advil pills to hold me over until I found the bottle, and then went into a pub for a soda and a hamburger. I enjoyed watching a slow-pitch home run batting contest even though the volume was turned down before continuing my three-ish-mile walk back to the boat.

When I got back to the boat, Ralph used the twelve-volt thermos to warm up the can of stew. He was wondering where I had gone and said they would fix the website so the book could be back on the front page. He asked me about my knee. I said I was good referring to the book, my knee, and the trip.

Tuesday, July 14th

The cracks in my heels had multiplied and many had opened up to about an eighth of an inch. I've been filling the cracks with

Neosporin. Ralph lost his blue jeans and a red shirt to the Atlantic. He had them drying out on the pole and sometime during the night they must have fallen into the harbor.

Patrick dropped off some pastries given to him by his brother-in-law, Timmy. Paula, Patrick's wife, made them working at Sugar Plum Pastry in Kingston. Patrick said, after checking their boat trailers for one which would fit our boat, that they didn't have a match. We needed to pull the boat out of the water for an oil change. We were going to have to go back to what I had suggested, drive to the leeward side of an island and back the boat in and by using our jack plate we could lift the motor out of the water. We'd have to use a big trash bag (in case of spillage) and put a 5-gallon bucket under the motor to drain it. Ralph said he'd have to think about it. Our Suzuki 115 was brand new out of the box when we left Tampa. The manufacturer recommends that the oil be changed within the first 25 hours of operation, then at the next 50 hours, and then once every hundred hours.

We didn't think our compass was very accurate; most likely something metal, like the GPS was affecting it. So I remounted the compass in a different position on the dash. By walking around the other boats and by comparing their external dash mounted compasses to ours, I concluded ours was still off. I then relocated it to our windshield by use of E6000 glue and duct tape and it appeared to be right on. We were two thousand miles into the trip and now we finally had an accurate compass. I also mounted our ski mirror below the overhead glove box in case we decided to do any wake boarding (skiing with a surfboard instead of skis behind a boat). I wanted to be ready and legal, since the use of a mirror is required with only one person in a boat.

Boston, Massachusetts, Counter Clockwise

We still hadn't mounted our longer antenna and since Ralph was busy in the office and I was bored, I decided to take the project on. I had to cut the old cable, tie a string to it, and pull it out leaving the string inside the metal framework of the T-top. I didn't want to, but the only way to feed the new coaxial cable through the framework was to cut the factory end off and tape it to the string. By pulling the string, the cable was pulled through. Patrick said he'd take me to a marine store the next day to get the proper fitting to reconnect the cable. I found the big bottle of Ibuprofen behind the radio up in the glove box when I unconnected the old antenna cable.

I brought Ralph a sandwich at a sandwich shop along the boardwalk. He'd been in the office the whole morning trying to get more sponsors and talking to his webmaster. He told me René accidentally lost my book from the front page when she was making some updates; she apologized for the mistake. Ralph stayed to continue working while I walked back to the boat. I passed a couple of local guys fishing for stripers. I began to talk with them and one of men told me a story about when he was scammed on a deep sea fishing trip. He caught a big Mahi Mahi, one of the best eating fish in the world, and the captain said it was worthless and they'd save it for shark bait. Later on back in town, the local discovered the fish was Mahi Mahi and he'd have to pay a lot for a plate of it in a fancy restaurant.

Later in the afternoon, Ralph took a break and came out by the restaurant. Ralph watched me hobble down the gang plank after I'd been sitting for a while. I was going down to the boat and again he asked me if I would be able to go out to sea the next day. My knee was still shot and now both my heels were split big time. Every step hurt.

Leaving Boston, Wiped Clean

Wednesday, July 15th (day 19 since Tampa)

Patrick came by with more pastries and drove me around shopping for some bolts, the cable connection, fishing planers, a dry bag, squid line of eight-fake squids, and oil for Suzuki. They didn't have an oil filter or a radar reflector, they were both order items. On our next leg, we planned to do some fishing for some huge Tunas. A small one we'd eat according to Ralph, we still hadn't finished discussing an open fire on the boat, and anything big we'd take video and pictures before releasing.

I finished the antenna and we pulled out of Shipyard Quarters about 1:15 p.m. We headed across the harbor to meet up with some people from Suzuki. They offered, over some phone calls with Ralph, to change our oil and go over the big engine. That day was the start of what I considered the real trip. Everything up to this point was just publicity. Granted, our ocean mileage in a flats boat on this trip was already a new world record, we knew this since we had the old one.

It was a blustery day heading across the bay. We came up on the backside of a few mansions. We were driving pretty fast through a minimum-wake zone without knowing it, because we hadn't seen the sign. Another boater motioned for us to slow down and when we did our wake got even bigger. You see wake has a direct relationship

Leaving Boston, Wiped Clean

to water displacement and speed does come into the equation. The faster we go, the smaller wake, because more of the boat is out of the water, which is what is really pushing the water and to make the wake. We slowed down and noticed the bay wind swells hitting the shore were still bigger than our wake.

We met Bruce, our logistic manager, at the public boat ramp where we transferred all our pictures to his laptop. He was going to send them to Bernie (the guy who helped us in Charleston, SC), who was going to take over the CrossTheAtlantic.com website. When Ralph and René talked earlier she'd let him know that she didn't have enough time to dedicate to the website and do it justice. Since everyone who helped us was a volunteer, we always appreciated what time they did give. Ralph thanked her for the time she had donated to our project and said that he'd stay in touch.

Bill from R N R Marina and a guy from Suzuki also met us at the ramp. We loaded the boat on their trailer and they drove it over to R N R. I rode with Bruce, and Ralph went with them in their truck. The Suzuki representative gave the motor the once over including a computer hookup. Everything checked out. Jim, the mechanic, was surprised they had trouble getting cawling bolts lose since it was only two weeks since the last oil change in Miami. He had to use an impact driver to loosen them. Ralph gave Jim a Do More shirt and I bought the needed six foot of fuel line and clamps, but they didn't have the radar reflector in stock. Ralph stayed with the boat while I walked across the highway to get food for the next couple of days. One of the main questions we've been asked about our trips, is, what we eat when we're out at sea. So I asked a customer to video me while I shopped for oranges, carrots, spaghetti (cans), soup, three jugs of punch, a loaf of bread, peanut butter and jelly, and fruit cocktail (our standard). I would use the video in the documentary, later.

Ralph and I climbed into Bill's truck and we trailered the boat over to a gas station located next to a McDonalds. We fueled up with about 135 gallons. It was at least fifty cents a gallon cheaper than if we had filled up on the water. Thank you R N R. This gave us a total of 190 gallon of gas; if we wanted to completely fill up we had room for 347 gallons, including the three jerry jugs we bought on Sunday. After I wiped some of the New York harbor grit off the sides of the boat, Boston was comparably clean; I bought us a couple of Quarter Pounders with cheese, fries, and Cokes for our departure. Ralph realized he had forgotten to pick up the extra oil filter to go with the oil we had just bought for the next oil change. So we went back to R N R before being dropped off at the boat ramp. We weren't sure how easy a filter would be to find in another country.

Bob is wiping off the slime from New York Harbor while Ralph is refueling. The motor was just checked out at the dealer.

Leaving Boston, Wiped Clean

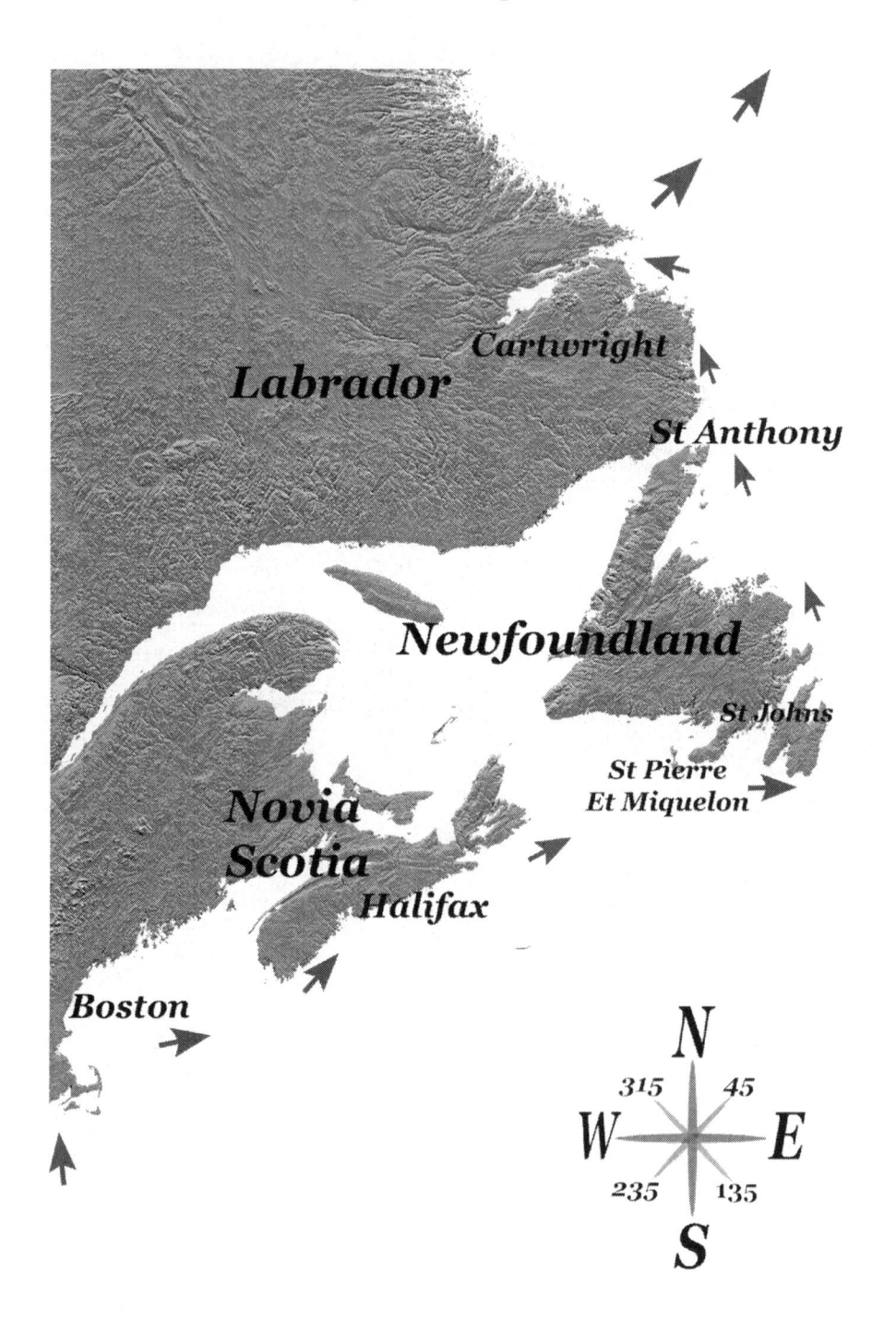

Wounded Hero Voyage I

It was 7:15 p.m. EST when we pushed off for Halifax, Nova Scotia, Canada about six hours later than planned; approximately 440 miles away as the crow flies. It had just donned on me that we had never tested our new antenna. I hoped it would work. As we organized the fishing rods I noticed we had lost the special lure Paul Koralewicz, a big time fisherman from my hometown, had given me. The "You'll catch fish with this lure," must have been banging around on a rod and finally broke off. I was bummed. I expected great things from that lure.

I Am Second throttling up leaving

Pouring fruit punch into a cup while moving was difficult; easy to miss and spill. The ice left over from my McDonald's Coke helped the drink from sloshing, but once it melted it was as if someone was tapping my elbow as I drank. I tried folding the lip of the cup; to make a sort of sippy cup, but still I'd have punch dripping off my chin and down my shirt. Since we didn't have straws, we decided to drink right out of the jugs.

We got to test out our radio when we were stopped by *Safeway Endeavor*, a patrol boat with flashing lights. It was as big as a sixty-foot trawler. They seemed surprised we were heading out to sea in such a small boat shortly before sundown. After they heard our plans they suggested we vector to a more northeast direction for about three miles and then pick up our normal course. They mentioned something about underwater obstructions up ahead. They waved goodbye and wished us luck. At least we knew our antenna was working.

The conditions were nearly perfect for our crossing. Our original plan was to head out to the spot Patrick, from Boston, had suggested for Tuna fishing. The spot was about twenty miles out of our way, but since we'd left so late and it was almost dark, we'd keep to our heading and fish in the morning. We wanted to be able to video tape whatever we caught. Ralph called his wife and described the beautiful sunset to her and told her that he wished she was here with him to snuggle with as it set.

Stopped and warned of underwater obstructions ahead.

While Ralph slept I was cooking canned spaghetti with meat sauce for dinner. We'd learned not to put the whole can into the

Wounded Hero Voyage I

thermos because it would take too long, if ever, to heat up. We would rarely wait more than 45 minutes for it to do its thing (become lukewarm) before we'd give up and eat it. While I waited patiently for my supper I polished off some of Patrick's pastries and played around with trying to see how long I could drive without touching the steering wheel. Not long, as the boat seemed to drift slowly to a southward course.

While I looked at the spotlight in one of the two plastic bins on the dash it donned on me I didn't even know how to send an SOS by flashlight. It was probably in the safe boating class I took a year ago, but I couldn't remember. I sure wish I'd have found that safe boating book I was looking for before we departed Florida. Ralph probably knows anyway, he is a Marine.

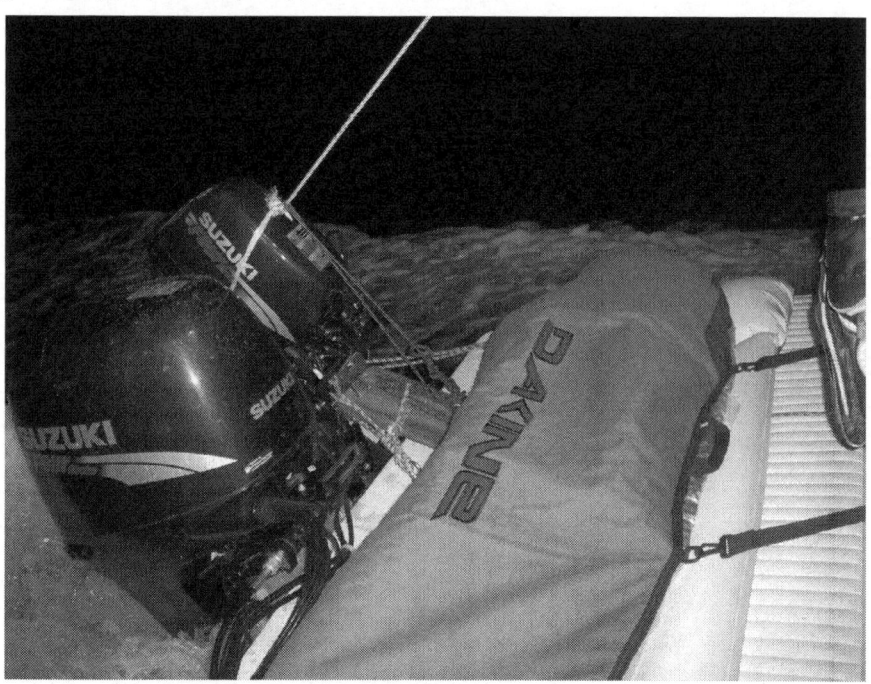

Ralph asleep inside the board bag which was clipped to the seat, notice the wooden brace angled under the kicker from New York.

Leaving Boston, Wiped Clean

Ralph was completely zipped up inside the board bag sound asleep, but he'd mistakenly left his blue Crocs on the back deck. I saved them before the Atlantic noticed they were there, easy for the taking. We needed to be more conscience of the little things as we had little to spare.

I spent a lot of time just looking at the wake, noticing the water looked completely black under the few visible stars out that night. The water which churned up around the motor was pearl white, a reflection off of the back spotlight. About eight foot up from the back of the boat was where the water started spraying out in little droplets. Most of the droplets traveled about eight or nine foot, mostly behind the boat, but some were going sideways. The rooster tail that formed from the twin hulls' wakes came together about twelve foot behind the motor. The water which churned around the motor was higher than the rooster tail and then it dropped down before it rose back up into part of the rooster tail. The rooster tail was the center of the hour glass shape of the inner wake. The inner wake appeared to crisscross at the rooster tail and then continued outward until in found its place among the wakes going outward from the back edges of the boat. Our 9.9 kicker was actually above the surface of the water, but its lower third was sprayed continuously.

Wounded Hero Voyage I

Wake off the back of the boat just before sunset

Thursday, July 16th

When I steered by using the compass, the direction or heading I was traveling was facing me. It was the back most (closets to the driver), reading spot on the floating wheel inside the compass. When the number, a nominal degree, or the letter, say "E" for EAST, drifted away from center (meaning the boat was changing direction); I imagined a rope going from the top center of my steering wheel over to the escaping "E" and then by turning the wheel away from that "E", I could pull it back to center of the compass (to get back on course).

When I'm navigating by the Garmin, I usually have it on the map function. I liked to watch the shape of the coastline when close to shore. We could set it up so there was a purple line going from our last plotted position and leading to a new point which I could lock onto. I didn't usually want that line to go across land, so I'd have to plot spots around land masses. Our current position in real time was depicted by a really small boat with a pointed front on the Garmin screen. My goal was to keep the boat on the purple line and facing forward. Sounds easy... yeah right... sure in the daytime it is easy, but at night without stars or without something in the horizon to focus on, I was all over the map. Because our boat was so small, there was a delayed reaction for the direction we were going to show up on the Garmin, thus the constant battle with over steering. If I stared at the screen, my vision quickly became blurry and when I took my eyes off of it, by the time I checked it again, it had drifted away from our purple imaginary road. Sometime during this crossing, Boston to Halifax, we lost our detailed maps. The Garmin came equipped with only the United State map detailed. We would have to find computer chips for the individual countries and load them on the Garmin if we wanted any type of accuracy in our maps.

Wow, that was really weird. I don't know if I was so tired I was hallucinating or what. I'd been heading east after dark like I'd been doing for a long time and then I noticed a red buoy out in the middle of the ocean about a hundred yards away. I turned the wheel a little to the left to go north around it. It seemed to be moving and then it suddenly disappeared and then reappeared. Whenever I turned east to go around it, it was there, so I again had to turn north. I did this for a while until the buoy started to rise out of the water. (This is the time to play the Twilight Zone theme music *dedede daa dedede daa*.) I should have realized the moon was playing peek-a-boo with the clouds on the horizon and the fog was disguising it. I figured it out when I had to turn south to get back on my original course and the buoy was on the east above the water where the moon should have been rising. I'm glad no one was watching. Imagine how stupid I felt after I realized I'd been trying to drive around the moon in a boat. The good news was now I had the moon to follow. It would be easier to stay on course.

Navigating by the golden trail reflection of the moon in the water was great, that was, until I fell asleep and woke up with its reflection on a swell in front of me. I swung the boat in a sharp turn trying to avoid what I mistook for an island (the swell lit up by the moon light looked like an island). Had it been an island, I'd be Gilligan and we'd have been dry docked. Another one of my hallucinatory moments while driving was when I came out of a doze facing to the right and saw the end of the long pole which was tied to the T-top out of my peripheral. What I thought I saw, towards the back of the boat, was a boat riding along side of us about to run us over. I shook my head thinking, "I've got to wake up...."

When I stopped the boat to take a pee break over the side, I asked Ralph if we should switch the fuel tanks. If we ran a tank dry, we'd have to turn a valve and then pump the ball valve to force fuel into the engine. The ball valve was hard to get to; it required the person sleeping to get up, since the valve was in the hatch underneath the back deck. Ralph, who was trying to sleep, said no, we'd be fine. Twenty minutes passed and big Suzuki shut down. Boats don't usually coast very far like a car does when they run out of fuel. Instead, they stop rather abrupt, especially when they are heavily loaded. Ralph got soaked by a quick dose of backwash coming over the back. He was suddenly woken up and became irritable rather fast. I tried to start the engine twice without pumping the ball and failed. Ralph had to get up.... All this could have been avoided by rotating a valve while the engine was running.

At about 150 miles from shore, I wasn't paying too close

Leaving Boston, Wiped Clean

attention, not expecting to see anything and almost ran into a big three foot in diameter red buoy. There was also a blue one close by. These must be used for some type of fishing, but there were no boats anywhere as far as I could see. We double checked our dept and the Garmin said we were in 650 foot of water. We kept the Garmin on the dept scale and it quickly jumped up to 35 foot and then dropped back down to 650 foot. We now thought the buoys must have been a marker for an underwater mountain. If it had been closer to morning, we'd have stopped to fish, since we were no longer rushing for media stops. I was still curious so I pulled out the magnifying glass to get a good look at the three by four-inch screen and discovered in fact it was labeled. *Obstruction, unexploded ordinance*, perhaps we had just gone over a sunken war ship or something.

 Ralph drove from about two in the morning to sunrise. At first light I got out the fishing gear and put fresh line on the reel I was going to troll with. I didn't want to lose the big one because my line was old and frayed. I also dropped in the squid line and let it drag back about fifty foot. Its purpose was to attract fish up from the deep. I wasn't too sure how close to the boat I should drag it, so I just looked at the picture on the package. We were driving right into the sun, heading east. Ralph went back to sleep while I went a-head-slow only a few miles per hour. A small flock of birds appeared and didn't attack our trolling squid line. I wasn't sure if that was a good thing or not. If the birds didn't recognize it as something to eat, I wasn't sure what the fish would think about it.

 I put on some Ocean Potion Suncare, it was a sunscreen extreme sun block of SPF 30. It was given to us along with other products in Cape Canaveral directly from the manager of the Merritt

Island Oceans Potion factory during our sendoff party. I put it on often as I was already a victim of sun damage and have to visit a dermatologist yearly.

It was a beautiful day with a brilliant-blue sky and then all of a sudden the fog rolled in. At first I could see a couple of hundred yards and eventually the visibility dropped to about 75 foot. The temperature which had been steadily climbing reversed and started dropping. Jackets went back on. I trolled from sunrise to about 12:45, sometimes with Ralph trolling too, and we caught nothing. I didn't even see anything remotely resembling fish, no birds diving, no fishing boats, or anything. We were starting to wish we had gone to Patrick's tuna spot last night. We put the fishing gear away and cruised for a while.

> <u>Quote from Cross the Atlantic blog:</u> Jill said, "Bob so glad to see that you are finally blogging. Hopefully people will know that you are Notombstone. Enjoy hearing your stories. Have fun, be safe and you are in our prayers. Love, your family"

We stopped to fish at buoy number two just a couple of miles off the most southern point of Nova Scotia. In Florida, buoys are usually good places to fish. Skunked again! Later, we were just driving along and saw something grayish come up out of the water. It was kind of far away. We didn't want to scare it off, so we slowed down and got the cameras ready. Could be our first whale? All of a sudden, a swell rose up over the same spot. We looked at each other, as if to say how stupid are you? We were all set to record a swell that jacked up traveling over a shoal. The swell looked like a hump cruising on top of the water until we were ready to record and the bigger swell's top crested over. A traveling swell is not only on

Leaving Boston, Wiped Clean

the surface. If the energy "moving water" under the surface is slowed down and pushed upward, the result of going over shallow water, then the face of the swell will become steeper. If it is steep enough the top of the wave will roll down the face. When it is really shallow, then the fast moving swell will pitch forward, "break" as the underwater energy is pushed upward and slowed down.

Now that we were on the eastside of Nova Scotia, we started to see wild life. It started off with two seals. I got the handycam out, but in the sunlight I couldn't find them on the glared view finder. The seals were two-small black spots in a large area of gray water. Then we saw five or six more, but we scared them underwater. Ralph said he saw a couple of dolphins. We put out the fishing lines and again, no luck. Where were the fish? At 5:00 p.m. EST the sun popped out of the clouds and it started to finally warm up.

Ralph wanted to try trolling again. This time we trolled at a faster speed. While he was trolling, I used our little twelve-volt air pump to blow up the mattress we slept on. I guess because of the cold, it was slowly deflating. I'd been barefoot or in Flip Flops up to this time and wanted to try out my surf booties. Ralph had already changed from his Crocs to dry socks and rubber boots.

By 8:30 p.m. EST we'd lost all of our smooth seas and the sun was about to set into heavy clouds. We traveled with a strong wind, so the wind only seemed like ten mph, but the seas had grown from two to four foot and they were close together with heavy non-breaking chop. We were at least three hours away from Halifax, our destination, and about fifteen miles out to sea.

Halifax, Nova Scotia, Canada, Playing Hide and Seek

Friday July 17th

We entered the wrong channel, the south one, inside Halifax Harbour a couple of minutes before midnight EST. We met five-high school aged kids partying quietly in a really fancy speed boat. It looked brand new. It was red with black and white checkers on the sides. They gave us directions to the other harbour which was just around a peninsula inside the mouth of the bay. We were again among the tall ships, probably some of the same ones from Boston.

We stopped at Bishop's Landing, where Bruce, our logistic manager, was told to tell us to park behind the boat *Remkin*, which was nowhere to be seen. The first-security guard we met gave us permission to park at the dock and said they'd figure it all out in the morning. Ralph tied up the boat, changed into his sneakers, and went to find a bathroom. While he was gone, another security guard came and said we had to move, "No boats allowed within 150 feet of the tall ships." We were currently only about 75 foot from one. I pleaded our case and explained what we were doing. The now eight-security guards had a private meeting, about thirty foot away, where they eventually called their superior. He knew nothing of us, but agreed to give us until nine in the morning to move. They told me

Halifax, Nova Scotia, Canada, Playing Hide and Seek

with a stern voice, "If you are late we'll have the police remove you." As they walked away several turned, smiled, and said welcome to Nova Scotia. Ralph came back from the bathroom with his hands and feet burning. We suspected jelly fish particles on the dock ropes transferred from his hands to his feet when he changed his shoes.

Jim Murphy, the owner of Bishop's Landings, came out in the morning and helped us move over to Bishop's Landing Sea Side. It was his other dockage, the next opening of docks towards the sea. We spent over two hours trying to get customs on the phone. The harbour dock master came out to help us too and we were eventually cleared by calling Channel 72 on the radio.

A local fisherman named Charles came over and sat with me for sometime with a map. He grew up around Nova Scotia and explained the area to me. He said we should have gone on the other side of Nova Scotia, between Nova Scotia and mainland Canada. There would be a lot more to see and the fishing is much better. He said, "Where you are heading is where fog is created." He told us the people on the French Islands of St. Pierre Miquelon, islands further north, will love us. All the coastal Europeans loved boating stories.

We were photographed by a USO photographer and then met Tim, a crew member of the tall ship Bounty. He told us the Bounty was in three movies; *Sponge Bob Square Pants, Mutiny on the Bounty* with Marlin Brando, and *Pirates of the Caribbean*. David Goldborn, an engineer on the tall ship *Spirit of Bermuda*, gave me a tour. He remembered reading about us in the *Royal Gazette*, Bermuda newspaper, when we were in there in 2007. He knew about my *Bermuda Suicide Challenge* book from other articles and liked the name, because he really felt we were on a suicide voyage. He asked, "If you make it, what are you going to name your next book?" I told him I was leaning towards; *You've Got to be Kidding: the Whole Atlantic in a Flats Boat*, which made him laugh. He said he liked that one too.

I spent most of the day, hanging out near the boat and talking to people passing by. It felt like we were part of the tall ship assembly. Some guy tapped me on my shoulder and said Interstate Batteries were first, not second. I told him about IAmSecond.com where God is first. I think the guy was a NASCAR fan because he was wearing a NASCAR shirt. I should have asked him about the Interstate Battery race car, but I wasn't thinking.

Bob and Ralph on the boardwalk in Nova Scotia with *I Am Second* and tall ships in the background

Ralph spent most of the time at a boardwalk café on the computer. We traded off a couple of times so I could use the Internet and he'd get a break. He wanted one of us to stay near the boat to answer questions about our voyage. The town lit up the sky with fireworks, but it was my turn on the computer, so I stayed inside and looked out the window. I got a lot accomplished, but still

Halifax, Nova Scotia, Canada, Playing Hide and Seek

managed to freeze Ralph's computer and didn't have his password to turn it back on. So far on this trip, Halifax was by far the most boat friendly place, excluding the security guards early in the morning who were just doing their jobs.

A guy named Jay and his friend Craig stayed on a thirty-ish sized powerboat named *Another Woman,* four slots over from us. After talking to us for quite a while, they took us over to meet some French people on a French tall ship. Jay thought they might have high connections on the French island where we were going. They introduced us to a guy and a woman who spent sometime talking with us. The French wanted to see our boat so we all walked back where they took some pictures with us on our boat. They said they would send some of the pictures on ahead of us.

The lady from the French tall ship with Bob and Ralph

Wounded Hero Voyage I

Jay and Craig invited us on their boat, after the French went back to their tall ship. We were able to take showers and then they fed us some left-over cake and snacks. Ralph asked them if they knew of any possible business that he could contact for additional sponsorship. They were shocked to find out our voyage was so underfunded. They couldn't believe Suzuki wasn't the main sponsor of our trip. Suzuki had just lent us the motor, kicker, and gave us our blanket. We still needed money for fuel and then to get back home after we reached Germany. We stayed up for hours talking about how to fundraise and they thought if they had the right phone numbers they could get us more funding from Suzuki. Ralph didn't have the numbers of anyone high enough up in Suzuki's organization, as he had tried many times for more funding before and during the trip. We went back to our boat when they were too tired to stay awake. It rained most of the night.

> <u>Quote from Cross the Atlantic blog:</u> Patricia said, "Glad to see some comments and that you are safe. Chris is hoping you can ping your GPS more often. He follows you all the time. Stay safe and God bless. Love your sister, Patricia Marie"

Saturday July 18th

The water was so clear that I walked up and down the docks photographing the kelp, which were several foot in length, and the numerous starfish just under water. Halifax was having a "raising of the flag" ceremony on the lawn not even 75 yards away. We had to be ready to leave by the time Jim Murphy's employee brought a customer's boat over to park in our spot. Two-harbour patrol officers rode up on their jet skies to talk to us and see *the boat that was crossing the ocean*. They said we could tie up to their jet ski

Halifax, Nova Scotia, Canada, Playing Hide and Seek

floating dock if we wanted to stay longer.

We pulled away from Bishop's Landings at 8:30 a.m. in a solid-white-out fog. Several other boats were out and blasting their horns every couple of minutes. Whenever a horn is blown, an answering blast is required by any other boats on the water. Just as we cleared the docks, there was some type of battle reenactment going on. A bunch of people were dressed in 1700s militia type clothes and rowing small boats in the fog. It reminded me of the photograph of George Washington crossing the Delaware. We were inching up the harbour looking for a gas station, normally the Garmin would have identified them, but we didn't have the much needed chip yet.

A ferry went by and blasted its horn. We could hardly see it, but we definitely noticed its wake. The fog was really eerie and we both couldn't stop thinking about not having radar and more importantly a radar reflector. We asked anyone listening on their radio and got directions from an anchored sailboat several miles away. We were told Dartmouth Marina was six miles up the Narrows toward Bedford Basin. It would be open and selling gas. There was so much moisture in the air and condensation on the seat; my clothes were damp under my survivor gear... a great way to start off the day, NOT! We were navigating by one of the AAA maps I ordered from home before the trip. Stupidly, I set a map down on the water filled concaved top of one of the side gas tanks and now the map was slowly falling apart.

We passed ever so slowly through a spread out cluster of sailboats eerily moored in the fog. We were in a dead calm when each boat appeared as if by magic. With our Suzuki quietly idling we crept past the last sailboat and turned into a canal leading to a

Marina. This location was awesome. The fog was magically dissipating even as we inched past the rock jetty made of huge boulders higher than our heads. Across the hundred-foot wide canal there were small rocky areas with six-foot high boulders next to a patch of evergreen woods. Everything was so picturesque with hawks flying in and out of the edge of the fog. This image could have been taken off the cover of one of those wilderness magazines.

The canal opened up to a large Marina with boats everywhere and a 400 or so foot long two story metal building. Down by the water the marina had a large above ground gas tank mounted on a framework of steel and cement. This was going to be perfect. An easy fill up. Only there was nobody anywhere. We waited a few minutes for someone to come down to the dock. When no one came out, we tied up the boat and went ashore to find someone, but found everything locked up. We even walked around to the front of the building where we found the fence gate locked. Some people drove up in a car outside the gate and they too couldn't figure it out. It was about 11:00 a.m. on a Saturday in the summer and the boat store was locked up. This was the perfect time to hit some more musical notes from the *Twilight Zone* or maybe an Alfred Hitchcock mysterious movie.

We left and eventually found Dartmouth Yacht Club. While we waited for the gas attendant, we watched some workers mount a mast in a sailboat using a special narrow miniature crane. It was pretty cool and didn't take very long. We bought 645 liters of gas at $1.35 per liter for a total of $869. Ralph said that it translates to 168 gallons at 5.70 per gallon. Our most expensive gas yet. For comparison, the average gas in a Florida auto stations was about $2.60 per gallon. Altogether, we were carrying close to 225 gallons

Halifax, Nova Scotia, Canada, Playing Hide and Seek

of our precious fuel expecting to travel over 400 miles.

The fog thickened as we drove the six miles back toward the ocean. We drove right past Bishop's Landing, surrounded by tall ships, and didn't even see any of them in the thicker ocean fog rolling in. We ended up in the Atlantic and had to turn around because we had been told about another Marina, a couple of miles up the south harbour which might have the reflector and the chips we needed. On the way there, we came up to a really big and expensive looking yacht. It was like the kind seen in movies with all the bells and whistles. Ralph wanted to drive around hoping that someone would pop their head out and talk to him. I was really embarrassed and I told Ralph if he wanted to drive up to the yacht then he had to do it. I said, "People with money like that; don't want to be bothered by people like us." Ralph drove around idling for at least five minutes with no bites. I was thinking we were lucky that they didn't pull out a gun. Ralph's ability to put the mission ahead of being embarrassed is how he gets things done.

We made it to the yacht dockage and had to walk a mile to get to the marina store. We learned all the Garmin chips for Canada were recalled and nobody would be able to sell them. The two-story wooden marina was jam packed with gear. We were looking for the typical ball shaped reflector, but they only had the tube type. Something I'd never seen. We gladly bought it for a shocking seventy dollars. It fit right into one of the T-top rod holders where we used duct tape to secure it so it wouldn't pop out.

Quote from Cross the Atlantic blog: "God is watching over you...are you wearing your life preservers???! Blessings and Be Safe! Susan"

Wounded Hero Voyage I

To St. Pierre Miquelon, France, Flummp!

We walked back to the boat and headed out for St. Pierre Miquelon, France. It's been the kind of day that nobody likes to go boating, fog in the morning which turned into an all day rain, but we take the good with the bad.

We saw something, but it went back underwater before we could tell what it was. As soon we brought the boat to an idle, it came to the surface again. This time we both got a good look at the smooth gray roundish shaped head. "Wow, a small whale, it must be a baby," it went back under and popped up again. "Aren't whales darker?" I asked. This time we saw its dorsal fin and we were able to idle closer to it. I had the handycam recording.

"It's a shark!" I exclaimed. "But why is it acting so strangely swimming in little circles? Is that a dorsal fin or a flipper?" It was acting like it was injured and we couldn't see the lower half of its body.

"I don't think it's a shark or a whale," replied Ralph. "I think it is some type of fish, I saw its mouth and it didn't have shark's teeth."

"I don't think it has a lower body and there's no blow hole," I

To St. Pierre Miquelon, France, *Flummp*!

said. "It must be some type of parrot fish, its mouth looked more like a beak, for breaking open clams or shells."

We hung out with our weird looking fish for about twenty minutes as it just swam in little circles above and below the surface. Later, we came across what looked like the tips of rocks protruding up above the water next to an island. But something didn't seem right, as the swells reached them. We noticed that the swells weren't breaking on the rocks. We motored over closer and discovered the rocks were alive; as they quickly disappeared and swam away. We guessed that they were either very large seals or maybe walruses. Do they even have walruses in Canada? They were way bigger than the seals we'd seen the day before.

We were now down to about 220 gallons of gas and because we put some gas in both the back tanks, we had trouble planing off. In the future, we were going to put some gas into the seventy-gallon metal tank closer to the front. I smelled gas and it was making me feel a little bit sick. Something must not be clamped tight enough or maybe not vented properly. We also noticed that we were going through more fuel and figured it was because we weren't planing very well. We were pushing water instead of riding over it, plus we were mostly heading into a current.

It was still windy and raining with most of the waves in the two to three-foot range with some four and five-foot sections every once in a while. It was very choppy, but no white caps to speak of. I was cold and wearing shorts under my survivor pants, several shirts and all my jackets including my rain suit I bought in Boston. My white hands were nothing but wrinkles, even on the topside. Ralph had been using some hand cream and his weren't nearly as pruned as mine.

Wounded Hero Voyage I

Ralph relinquished the piloting and went to sleep as the waves became more consistently in the four to five-foot range. I had to goose the motor up to about 5,000 rpm to get *I Am Second* on plane and then drop back to our customary 4,500 rpm for cruising. A couple of two-liter soda bottles kept siding under my feet and instead of bending over and picking them up, I pushed them away with my feet. They eventually worked their way underneath my feet again. We came across another one of those parrot-shark-whale-fish, our name for them, and I also saw a large dead bloated bird floating all by itself.

>Quote from the Cross the Atlantic blog: Miquelon said, "Looks like really foggy weather in St. Pierre today. You can all check out the town webcams. Fog is a blessing in a sense, as when the fog hits – there is little wind."

Sunday July 19th

It was my turn to sleep so I climbed into the board bag with all my clothes and jackets on. My clothes would get all scrunched up and I couldn't move around at all. My circulation in my arms was being shut off from my armpits because my jackets were tightening up as my body slid sideways and my jackets didn't go with me. I was so cold, that I didn't use the rope tethering me to the boat, I wanted to be able to completely zip the bag shut, which by itself was rather difficult without an inside zipper. The Suzuki blanket was tucked under the bag on the forward part of the bag and draped over the bag to eliminate some of the water seeping through the bag. The bag was still roped to the boat, so I wasn't worried about sliding into the water. I had no concern about the boat capsizing, as being completely zipped would have made it difficult to get out of the bag

To St. Pierre Miquelon, France, *Flummp*!

before I drowned.

When I got up to drive for my shift, I was so cold that all I did was stand there, shiver, and shake with one hand on the wheel. At first I didn't even want to sit down because the inside of my damp stiff pants would touch my legs and I would feel even colder. I really wanted my wool beanie cap, but it was tucked away somewhere and I was too cold to go and find it. I didn't get any quality sleep in the bag, but now that I was driving, I could fall asleep in a second. I slowed the boat down to 3,000 rpm because we were in a fog and there were islands around even though we were pretty far offshore. These tiny islands were hardly ever visible on our Garmin chartplotter. It was still drizzling and totally dark out. A small flock of birds flew along side with several flying forward of the T-top light directly over our front deck.

Our big American flag was hung on a short vertical pole on top of the back of the T-top. Usually she blew straight back, but sometimes in a crosswind, or because we slowed down going up a wave, or the driver was inadvertently driving in a circle, part of the flag would hang down and surround the back facing light on the T-top. Because of the red stripes, this would cast a red flickering glow over the whole back of the boat. Sometimes this red glow would wake me up. Possibly because it reminded me of fire and as the driver I should be awake.

Yippy, at 2:30 a.m. and the moon came out. Now, we could make better time. Wait! Was that the moon or a boat? Shoot, I couldn't tell with the haze on the water! I thought I was going to have to do that *round the moon thing* again. As I got miles closer, I figured out it wasn't the moon. There were two-lower lights and one-really high light. I'd been at least ten to fifteen-miles offshore. I thought it might be an oil well where as the lower lights could be for the platform. I vectored away, a little wider, just to be safe.

An hour or so later, I thought I had passed in front of an oncoming ship about a half-mile away. I saw a red and green light coming towards me, so I turned to my left and only the green light was visible confirming my boat suspicion. Boats were supposed to have a green light on the right side of their bow and a red one on their left. Again, I kept my heading to give it a wider berth.

Around 3:30 in the morning after just doing my third 360-degree maneuver within about twenty minutes while I was trying to drive straight. I was done. Obviously I was too tired to drive. If this had been a highway, I would have already killed a bunch of people. I woke Ralph up to relieve me.

Bob sleeping on the bean bag with the soft vinyl Suzuki banner as a blanket. Bob preferred the bean bag over the board bag.

To St. Pierre Miquelon, France, *Flummp*!

The sun was up when Ralph woke me up yelling, "SHARK! SHARK! It's bigger than our boat!"

I was sleeping in the back under our Suzuki blanket. As I got up rubbing my eyes, Ralph was in this really hard U-turn, I saw something gray, blurry and fin-like, and then I heard this *fluump* sound. I turned around and saw our Suzuki blanket on top of the water getting smaller as we sped away. The wind had caught it and blown it over the side. I yelled to Ralph, "BLANKET, BLANKET! Our Blanket is sinking!" and pulled off my Interstate cap and started hitting him on his back. He really wanted to get some pictures of the shark. He immediately swung the boat back around and headed straight for the blanket. We swung by it and it was already completely underwater. From the front deck I reached in almost falling out of the boat and missed it by about six inches. Ralph swung around again. I was grabbing for poles when he handed me a spare four-foot flag pole. The Suzuki blanket was still out of reach. The fishing pole I grabbed had its line in a spaghetti tangle with the lure buried in the mess. I thrust the whole rod down into the water, including the reel, but it was just out of reach. We sat there under a blue sky with crystal clear blue-ish water and watched helplessly as our pride and joy Suzuki blanket drifted down out of sight. Ralph said he was about to jump in, but the thought of the bigger-than-the-boat shark, was enough to keep him out of the water. Atlantic's toll for this crossing was our Suzuki blanket and we soon found out that two lures were also missing off the other fishing rods. The constant pounding was too much for the lines.

Quote from Cross the Atlantic blog: "God Bless you and your adventures—we are living thru you both!! (Stay safe—wear your life preservers!!!) Fondly, S"

Quote: "You two can come home now. Now that you have seen a shark; before you see the insides of one. Those sharks are pretty savvy in the ocean. They could be checking out the situation in order to capsize the boat. And get a nice meal. Count your blessings at the next port. That is enough excitement for me. It would be just fine if that is as far as you go. Love ya, Dale"

The day was sunny with a haze near the water, visibility about a mile, and the seas were three to six foot with a little white chop. We were traveling about eighteen to twenty mph when Ralph woke me up to see this little bird that landed on the boat. It was walking around on the seat right next to him. The bird looked at Ralph and then just took off.

I had to lash down my hammock pole and the PVC pole on the roof. They were slowly sliding out. The green pole was starting to wear a hole in the canvas shade top and I was starting to question the strength of the quarter-inch white rope that weaved between the grommets of the canvas and the framework of the T-top. We'd been tying off or hooking bungees to the ropes because it was easier than wrapping around the metal framework. Many of our jackets and things were hooked by carabineers and blowing in the wind to air out.

Lunch was peanut butter and jelly sandwiches followed by luke-warm spaghetti. The wind had slowed down, so the chop was no longer white capped. My knee was still hurting, but my heels were much better and now my back was itchy. I think it was because of the salt water that dripped down my back inside my jackets. I

To St. Pierre Miquelon, France, *Flummp*!

wasn't cold, but I did feel a bit clammy. Every now and then if I moved just right, I'd get a whiff of air coming up from inside my jacket. Phew! There was something nasty brewing in that concoction of damp clothes, salt, and body odor. I was overdue for some Old Spice deodorant!

After dark, I called Jill and then Ralph called Anne and Bruce. Bruce was trying to tell Ralph the route we should take entering St. Pierre Miquelon. We had to use the expensive satellite phone ever since we've left United States waters. Most people including me hadn't known that the French had an island in the middle of Canadian waters.

Bruce suggested that we go around the two islands to get to the third. It was about 10:00 p.m. EST when we started our island loop in French waters. It was dark, calm, and foggy so we dropped down to idle speed so as not to run aground on one of the many obstructions near the water's surface. We were both leaning forward looking for any unusual disturbances as our visibility dwindled down to about 100 foot. Going around the island was so calm, it was scary. Without swells we couldn't detect near surface obstructions.

For a couple of hours, we constantly heard fog horns and continued answering them. We couldn't figure who else would be out on a night like this. We debated for a while about the likelihood that most of the fog horns were in fact lighthouses. I was so tired all I wanted to do was anchor the boat and wait until morning to get in. We were on the leeward side of the island so it was dead calm. Ralph vetoed my anchoring suggestion as he was afraid of being run over while we were sleeping. The visibility was so bad we couldn't see any lights from the island.

After driving back and forth in front of where we figured the harbour ought to be, using the rough outline of the shoreline on the Garmin, we drove right for it. The GPS showed us heading towards the center of a horse-shoe-shaped coastline. The fog was so thick that visibility was down to about ten foot. We could barely see and it looked like there were small waves breaking on the rocks up ahead. Ralph sensing danger changed his mind and we turned around and headed out again. We sat there trying to decide what to do. We finally agreed to give it another shot. This time we kept on our heading and the fog seemed to lift about a foot off the surface. All kinds of colored lights glowed from underneath making our imaginary waves. We ever so slowly pierced the hazy fog blanket and emerged surprised the fog was nonexistent on the other side. I was amazed the edge of the fog bank was so definite. We drove past an unlit small lighthouse and made our way inside the two-offset breakwaters. The town was still alive with lights, but we didn't want to hassle with trying to find a place to dock, so we drove into the corner up close to the long sand and rock breakwater and anchored. Ralph put up our yellow quarantine flag which meant we had not cleared customs yet. I put on more of my wet clothes and set up the hammock and called it a night, well after midnight.

Monday, July 20th

I woke up to the sound of someone speaking French and wondering what was going on. I removed my blacked-out eye mask, which I used to block out the city lights, and saw a guy in an inflatable red Zodiac. St. Pierre Miquelon had known we were coming and found us in their harbour. Manuel escorted us over to a sailing school next to a two-story building down near the dock. The local media was waiting there for us. I had to admit it was kind of

To St. Pierre Miquelon, France, *Flummp*!

fun to have cameramen and news reporters taking pictures and asking us questions as we were tying up the boat. The guys from the sailing school called customs and immigration for us and brought us both coffee while we waited. I love the smell of coffee especially in the morning, but the last cup I had was just a couple of sips over thirty years ago. I did not like it at all back then, but I was so cold I gladly took the coffee and managed to get about half of it down. My taste for it had not changed.

Sailing in St. Pierre is almost a prerequisite for life. Sailing is a required class in their school curriculum. There was a whole slue of kids wearing wetsuits and heading out in fourteen-foot Hobie sailboats. All the bright orange sailboats were numbered in sequence. The sailing instructor motored among them in the red Zodiac barking orders.

After finishing all the required paper work, for the government, we were both interviewed some more. Then the cameraman wanted me to move the boat out from the docks so they could get the whole boat in the background with water all around it while they interviewed Ralph. I had to keep the boat really still, because they were planning to edit the takes and they didn't want the boat to jump around too much in the finished piece. I asked them if they wanted me to anchor it, but they wanted me to run the motor and to act busy. It wasn't an easy request to keep the boat in the shot with the wind blowing the banners like sails. At one point, they stopped and had me loop around so they could continue with the boat in frame.

The Tourist Consulate bought us a room at the hotel and was going to take us out for lunch after we got organized and cleaned up. After hanging up all our damp jackets around our hotel room, so they could dry, I was the first in the shower. I wasn't too happy when I noticed I was getting a mild case of jock rot, something I had 35 years ago while wrestling in high school. I got it back then from wearing sweaty clothes too long. I didn't want to go through that again remembering how painful, itchy, and embarrassing it was. This time was most definitely from wearing wet clothes for days at time. That's was it, I'd go back to wearing my baggies as much as possible for better ventilation.

We were invited to lunch at the Restaurant Res Le Feu De Braise by Pascal Daireaux, the Tourist Consulate, and Jean-Claude Fouchard, the tour guide whom we nicknamed Van Dam because of the kickbox movie star Jean-Claude Van Dam. I had cod and scallop potatoes while Ralph had scallops with lobster sauce and we both had Cokes to drink. Lunch was great! Ralph topped his off with a coffee as he loved coffee and so far we hadn't had any out at sea, something he wanted to fix.

Jean Claude, Ralph, Bob, and Pascal Daireaux at a local restaurant

To St. Pierre Miquelon, France, *Flummp*!

Van Dam gave us, along with four paying customers, a minivan tour of the island. He started traveling along an ocean road, through a charming neighborhood and up a switchback winding hill which overlooked the whole island. We all got out near the cliff and he pointed to Canada just twelve-miles away. Newfoundland, Canada wasn't clearly visible because of the low haze over the water. Van Dam's tourist sightseeing business was named Le Caillou Blanc after the big white rock on the hill. I watched seals playing among the floating masses of kelp below near the rocks. There was a magnificent black horse grazing out on the grassy bald. I had the urge to lie down on the large dark boulders in the warm sun with the cool breeze, perfect nap weather. We finished the minivan tour down at the docks where fish were being processed.

I walked back to the boat to gather some dirty clothes and then do laundry at the sail school, while Ralph went to Pascal's office to use the Internet. Waiting for our clothes I went down to the end of the dock to talk with Miguel. We met him this morning between interviews. He was a 21-year old guy who was sailing solo around much of the Atlantic. His auto pilot system was giving him some grief so he was trying to get it fixed. Miguel traded me a small French flag for a *Bermuda Suicide Challenge* book. He was still looking for some charts of Greenland which he thought he had somewhere inside his boat.

While walking around the down town area, not far from the boat, I bought an ice cream cone and stopped to see how things were going with Ralph. After seeing the ice cream he had me go and get him one too. At our hotel, I noticed the metal stairs had snow tire treads cut to fit, spread out, and bolted to the top of each step. What a cool way to recycle old tires.

Tuesday July 21st

Pascal was a busy guy early in the morning. While he had to meet about a thousand tourists arriving by cruise ship, he made arrangements for a fuel truck to meet us at the boat. We bought 339 liters at 99 cents in Euros per liter which converted, comes to about $488 for 89 gallons at $5.48 per gallon. We said goodbye to Miguel. He had found his charts, but said they were for a different area of Greenland than where we told him we were going. Pascal made it back to our boat just before we left. He gave us some shirts and stickers from St. Pierre Miquelon and then posed for a couple of pictures with us.

As Ralph stepped over the gas tank getting in, his knee caught the plug-in wire going to our only thermos. It was our only way of warming up meals. The newly formed crack was on the outer housing around the built in female plug. After a little glue and duct tape, we hoped it would still work. Miguel was also heading to St. John's, Newfoundland and said he was sailing there in the afternoon. We pulled away from the dock and drove slowly past the cruise ship waving, hoping Pascal would see us. We were idling out into the harbour, still stuffing things into their proper location when Ralph decided to stop to make several important calls. At 9:25 a.m. we finally powered up, leaving the territory of France.

There were puffins, puffins, and more puffins. The small orange beaked cartoon birds resembling small penguins were floating in flocks, hundreds of them. As we drove close, they were the funniest things to watch. Many would sit there bobbing while

To St. Pierre Miquelon, France, *Flummp*!

the ones right next to them, the squeamish ones, would take off running on the surface of the water. They'd run as fast as they could and then lower there heads, as if to show some gumshion, and then give an additional burst of speed. When we got close, they would either take off flying or stop on a dime and dive beneath the surface.

I noticed the surfboard was bouncing again and I checked on it. The green pool noodle used for cushion had almost completely slipped out. Without it, my fragile fiberglass surfboard would get beat to a pulp against the metal frame of the T-top. It was already dinged pretty good and a chunk of foam about three-inches long and half an inch thick was missing. I found some rope and threaded it through the noodle and tied it around my board with the noodle on the bottom side of my board.

If a pilot whale is a lot bigger than a standard dolphin? Then one crossed our bow about thirty foot in front of us. Two more came up from the deep just out from the edge of boat. We had a mammal on each side of the boat and they were soon joined by eight more. I got my handycam out and began shooting. Luckily, I checked the hard-to-see record button and noticed it was out of sync taking video of my legs and the deck... again. When I thought it was recording, it wasn't. I had missed some good shots, but they were still around.

To test the thermos, we tried to heat up some of our newly purchased French hot chocolate. It worked, luke-warm as usual. It was a great moment for us, a trip like this exposed to all the elements without the possibility of having warm liquids didn't seem too appealing. Not that a trip like this would be appealing to too many people anyway. We are nearly always cold, tired, and wet, doing the majority of our driving after dark. Then to make things worse, cold water and a lot of bouncing makes for an overworked bladder. A lot of pee breaks! Often we'd tie ourselves in and then peed off the back of the boat left of the big motor. We picked the left side because the kicker was on the right and we were able to hold onto the big engine. The colder I was, the more frequent I had to pee. Unless it was rough, we hardly ever slowed down, but we'd agreed to always tell the driver in case one of us slipped.

A small group of medium sized whales showed up for just a minute or two. They were about fifty yards from us. Ralph saw a much bigger single whale breach, which is that SeaWorld thing about coming out of the water and turning a quarter turn and making a big splash. It happened about a hundred yards away. I was too busy scrambling for my handycam and missed it. We were giddy like little school girls, Ralph called his house and talked to Heath, his son, and described the whale so Heath could look it up on the Internet. They decided it was a humpback.

More whales! It was so cool being inches above the water surface with these huge mammals so close. They pretty much just ignored us. Many were surfacing and then diving. I was hoping to get a good whale's tail photo. We weren't that lucky getting one on camera although we saw several.

Around 4:00 p.m. EST we left the Atlantic and started heading into the Labrador Sea. We were no longer getting any benefit from the warm Gulf Stream... welcome to the Labrador Current! It was the really cold water which flows down from the Arctic between Greenland and Canada. It was a swift current traveling southeast. Since wind temperature is directly affected by the land or water mass which it is traveling over, our wind temperature just plummeted. "Oh, I can't wait until night time....

To St. Pierre Miquelon, France, *Flummp*!

This is going to be oh so much fun...." The water temperature in the Atlantic before our turn into the Labrador Sea was 56-degrees Fahrenheit. I knew this because only fifteen minutes earlier I accidentally came across the water temperature feature of the Garmin. Now the temperature was 48 degrees. We were hoping to see an iceberg, but I wasn't too confident.

Near the coast, right at the edge marking the start of the Labrador Sea, we stopped for Ralph to make a call to Charlie Brim of Interstate Battery. Ralph was having a tough time convincing them to have their media team leave their company names off the press releases, except in a one liner at the bottom. Ralph wanted them to include all our sponsors in that line. Ralph didn't want it to appear that our whole trip was completely funded by Interstate Battery and I Am Second. The media was reluctant to give free advertising to a profitable business when they themselves were hurting for advertising dollars. At the time of the phone call, we were at the base of a several hundred-foot rock wall with a radio tower, an out building, and a black and white lighthouse out on the end of it. If we looked really hard, we could see a guy standing out there looking down at us. We couldn't be sure, but he either had a camera or binoculars up to his face. We wondered what he thought of us and if he could read the banners.

One of us must have bumped the jack plate button because the motor was lower than Ralph thought it should be for the best fuel efficiency. He had to go down on his hands and knees, open the back storage compartment to access the hydraulic pump. Then using something metal he shorted across two of the contact screws and the electric hydraulic motor hummed to life. He raised the engine from the two-inch mark up to the four. Then from the driver's seat, he slowly lowered the motor until he felt the boat riding at its best. I double checked his final spot on the lift ruler on the jack plate; it was just over the three-inch mark.

I was sitting next to Ralph in the captain's seat trying to get comfortable underneath my yellow rain coat which I had draped over me as the replacement blanket. Ralph spotted a whale about 200 yards in front. I had just turned the handycam on as a whale breached right in front of us, but I didn't get it because the camera was still in its turning-on mode. If I hit the record button too early during the camera's turning-on stage, it took twice as long to actually start recording. I needed to stop doing that, be patient and wait until the handycam is on before I hit the record button. I didn't notice any white on the whale, so I don't think it was a killer whale. I missed another breach with the handycam because I was filming in the wrong direction when it happened. I really wanted to catch a breach in the wild.

We saw several whale tails, but they were always too far away or at a bad angle. I wanted a whale to give us that perfect "T" shot. We were motoring up on a bunch of whales we thought were feeding, because they were going up and down in the same small area. As we slowly idled in closer, a whale started to dive in what looked like slow motion. The head went down first; a slow arc appeared to roll down its spine, the bend now at its lower back, black gleaming skin reflected glistening water as if the whale had been sprayed with a high gloss clear coat. We'd seen this same scenario many times this morning, but at the last moment it doesn't happen, no "T". But this time, we were behind the whale and as both Ralph and I lean forward with anticipation, he was using his Kodak and I with my Sony, the tail cleared the water. We were no more than 25 yards away, time seemed to stand still and the tail went higher, spreading out in its perfect "T". Ralph shouted, "I've got it, I got it!" And the tail slipped quietly down as if it was the tail end of the *Titanic* with Leonardo and the girl, going under holding their breath. I'd like to think we high "fived", but there was no record of it on my audio recording of the trip, and my memory wasn't as clear as it was the first time I wrote this manuscript, so I'm not going to say we did it, because I just don't remember.

The first T-shot, the tail of a whale in the process of a deep dive

It was after dark and we were about two hours away from St. John's. We were only about half a mile off the coast of the town named Ferryland, on our Garmin. Ferryland was full of lights and beckoning us. We were both cold. Ralph was dreaming of a hot cup of coffee and I didn't need an excuse. I always want to stop and talk to the locals, especially if there was even a remote chance of getting some hot food. We hadn't made any stops in Canada since leaving

Wounded Hero Voyage I

St. Pierre Miquelon so we really weren't permitted to get off the boat. Most small towns don't have a customs office and surely none would be opened at this time of night. We'd been told in Nova Scotia that sometimes the local police can clear customs. We decided it was worth a chance, so we headed in.

We entered Ferryland's little harbour bay by going around a couple of small islands. I guessed the islands were the town's breakwater for preventing big swells from rolling into their harbour and causing havoc with their boats. Usually towns have something manmade that doesn't have multiple openings unless they make a zigzag entrance. Once on the inside of the islands, we noticed there were no boats. How could that be? Most of the shoreline around the bay had a sea wall and a few black pebble rock beaches. Nobody was out and about and we didn't want to get off the boat without someone of authority to give us permission. I suggested we just anchor and go to bed, but Ralph didn't feel comfortable, not knowing the tides and it really bothered him that there were no boats.

While motoring back and forth inside Ferryland's harbour, we noticed a canal on the south end and decided to go exploring. About a half a mile down or so down, we found a little harbour off to the right. There were several fishing boats tied up there and it looked inviting. After throwing out our anchor in the middle of the small harbour, we prepared for sleep. Of course nothing was easy, my hammock was lost again. I could've sworn that I put it away in the big right hatch on the front deck, its permanent storage spot. It was soon discovered on the floor among the jerry cans, all soaking wet. I must have put it down while I was opening the hatch and never put it in, which resulted in it falling off the deck into the hole

To St. Pierre Miquelon, France, *Flummp*!

between the jerry cans. It was made of nylon and dried quickly. Because my sleeping-wool socks were also soaking wet, I put on my clammy wetsuit booties. I never realized there was a right and left bootie. My big toe on both feet felt like they were being squeezed. I was too tired to fool with it. Tight booties are a pain to put on and worse to pull off.

Wednesday, July 22nd

We woke up with the sound of birds and a car driving along a mountain road hidden within the forest. The water was so clear we could see hundreds of starfish of many sizes and shapes. I climbed out of the boat onto the shore to get a couple pictures of our boat with some of the local fishing boats and the magnificent wilderness view in the background. An older guy came down to a dock about a quarter-mile further down the canal. He was preparing to go out in his boat, so we motored over to him to see if he knew where we could find the custom officers. He didn't know, but suggested we go to the town around the corner. I didn't ask, but I believed we were at the edge of the town of Aquafort, NF, Canada, because Aquafort was painted on the back of all the boats in the little harbour.

On our way back to Ferryland we passed a really cool waterfall cascading over the canal cliffs. Again, I can't really put into words how beautiful this whole area was especially from the vantage point of a small boat. It was breathtaking. Tall luscious green trees, clear mirror calm water, cascading waterfall, blue sky, big boulders, birds flying, fishing boats, rustic homes nestled in the woods, and of course the whales.

I Am Second in Aquafort, Newfoundland where they spent the night

Back in the Ferryland Harbour, we met four guys, Frankie, Willie, Bill, and Bailey, out on the only dock. Two of them were on four wheelers and the other two came up in pickup trucks. They educated us in some of the local fishing laws. Cod and salmon, two of the favorite fish around, were not legal to catch and keep until after the 25th of July. Salmon could be caught up rivers with a fishing license, as long as they were caught on fly fishing rods. Anyone could buy the license and it could be either seasonal or daily. There were some limitations to size and the numbers of the fish which could be kept. Frankie drove back to his shop and came back with two of his favorite lures which he recommended for catching cod. He gave them to us.

One of the guys also gave Ralph the telephone number from his cell phone to call a Mountie-police officer he knew. Ralph used the Satellite phone to call. The Mountie had never cleared anyone before, so he called his department to find the correct procedure. As

To St. Pierre Miquelon, France, *Flummp*!

it turned out, we would have to go to a bigger city with a legal port of call. Even though in most cases the customs admittance could be done over the phone, we still needed to be close enough so the officers could inspect if so desired. We made a mistake by not going to the first big city in Newfoundland, Canada after leaving St. Pierre Miquelon, France. The next big city going north was St. John's, the capital.

We were warned of a bad "Nor'easter" storm coming sometime that day or night. They told us storms in this region can be pretty bad and a small boat caught out at sea wouldn't stand much of a chance. They said it was too bad we didn't have clearance to stay since they were having a big festival on Saturday in Ferryland. We wouldn't have been able to stay anyway, because the day was only Wednesday. Saturday was too far away and again this was not a vacation, even though we were no longer on a media schedule.

A lot of cold wind got to us along the sides of the cockpit area between the gas tanks and center console. Using some of our floor mats, we made a make shift air deflector. We'd shove one side of a mat between the metal frame supports for the T-top which was bolted to the center console and the other side we'd jam between the side gas tanks and whatever we could pile up to hold them. Usually it was the fishing boxes and some of the coolers. A bungee here and there helped to contort the mat to deflect some of the air away from us.

<u>Quote from the Cross the Atlantic blog:</u> "God Bless and I'm keepin' an eye on ya since we met for the oil change in Boston. I've been emailing everyone I know! Sean C."

We came across an island which was covered with birds... covered isn't the right word, maybe blanketed is better. It was a mountainous island probably about a half-mile around with cliff face walls and tremendous caves. There were so many birds the blue sky was grey and the dark rock peaks were stained white from the bird droppings. We had to be careful and not look straight up as we were being targeted. The water was dotted with thousands of puffins. Many of the water running birds were sprinting to stay out of our way. In the movie *Batman Begins*, there is a scene when Batman summons the bats and they flood the building in such numbers he was able to escape with the poisoned girl, DA Rachel Dawes. Well that's pretty much exactly what the island looked like. The smell was pretty much like you'd expect, especially on the leeward side of the island. With all those birds around, we figured this had to be the perfect spot to catch some fish. We wanted to video some catch and release. First we did a few casts. Nothing, so we trolled at a slow pace... nothing. Where were all the fish, surely these birds ate something? We were fishing with Frankie's favorite lures.

We noticed a blue and white boat way off in the distance. We first thought it might be a sight-seeing whale watching boat and then it turned and started heading our way. We started to wonder if this island was off limits, like a nature wild life bird sanctuary, or if we needed our passports stamped before we would be allowed to fish in Canadian waters, or if fishing was even allowed near this island. We started to pull up our rods like a couple of guilty teenagers, but thought better and continued to fish. Why stop, they had probably already seen us. Our concerns vanished when the boat

To St. Pierre Miquelon, France, *Flummp*!

made a turn up the coast.

We drove into the town of Petty Harbour thinking it was St. John's, our Garmin was hard to identify locations clearly without the chip. St. John's, the capital of Newfoundland, wasn't even on the world map page of our Garmin chartplotter (probably the least expensive one they sold). We were still using the combination of Garmin chartplotter and my AAA road map to navigate. The people there told us St. John's was ten to twelve more miles up the coast. The town seemed pretty cool; it had a big fountain in the middle of its harbour.

We stopped to idle while comparing the two maps and a big whale breached about 75 yards away. My handycam was off and sitting on the dash. I kept it in a small vinyl cooler resting on a chunk of floor mat on the far left corner of the dash. It was up against the window held with a bungee going across the back of it. It was easy to grab, but always took about ten seconds to pull out and turn it on before it was ready to record. I missed many great shots by a mere couple of seconds.

The Atlantic, in cahoots with the Labrador currents and winds, stole a half a can of fruit cocktail. I set it down on top of the side gas tank, a normal resting spot for things, while I dug around under the dash for my cup. We each had our own. It might have been a mistake to set it on top of a plastic bag.... The Atlantic was always waiting for us to make careless mistakes.

St. John's, Newfoundland, Canada, Secret Benefactors

Ralph was back sleeping as I came up on St. John's in a heavy fog. I woke him up because off to the side was what I thought was a pod of whales all spouting at nearly the same time. I turned to follow them, just seeing glimpses of water spraying ten-plus-foot in the air. This was so cool, until I noticed I was gaining on them too fast, after I had already slowed down. They were still intermittently spouting, but not moving. I slowed down more and soon realized I was heading directly for a several-hundred-foot tall rock wall. The spouting was the individual chop swells crashing onto the rocks and sending water up. The fog was hiding the solid rock wall. Yeah, radar or a good chartplotter is a necessity for boating in Canada.

We pulled into St. John's Harbour at 11:25 a.m. EST after passing the lighthouse and entering through a gauntlet of cliffs. We saw a huge church with a green roof and a tower on each side. Ralph said it was named after Saint John the Baptist. Ralph called Bruce to tell him that we had arrived, only to find out that Bruce had arranged for the media to film our entrance. We had to go back out and kill an hour so the media would have time to get to the harbour entrance. I joked with Ralph about the reenactment and we agreed since we had never actually touched ground, it would still be our official entrance into St. John's. Going back out, I was reminded of my son Jonathan, the runner. I thought of him when I saw a girl

St. John's, Newfoundland, Canada, Secret Benefactors

jogging along a path high up on the cliff.

We took this time to clean up the boat and get all the banners adjusted so they'd hang straight. We idled along the cliff faces and inspected the caves down near the water's edge. There were huge cracks in the rough water sculpted rock with a florescent green moss growing everywhere. Ralph did a bad imitation of a ballerina as he stepped over the bean bag after removing the mat deflector off of our front spotlight. We hit a swell when his foot was quite elevated and I got to watch him do a spastic dance and almost go in the drink. Good save Ralph!

Off in the distance we both saw a cave that looked big enough to put a house inside. We had to check this out. It ended up being a normal car size cave which looked much bigger because of the shadows and contours on the cliff face.

We had to enter the harbour two more times to get the footage the camera people all wanted. We then tied up along side a forty-foot fishing boat for our interviews. We had to stay on *I Am Second* for customs to clear us. Two hours later with the help of Donny, one of the reporters, we were cleared. Two officers came out and also educated us on the fishing laws.... If caught fishing out of season, which was still a couple days away, we could lose the boat even if we weren't keeping the fish. The officers then warned, they wouldn't suggest eating any fish around St. John's because the water was too polluted. The town was in the process of building a sewage treatment plant, but until it is completed, they will continue dumping the city's raw sewage right into the harbour. Good to know.

We moved the boat across the harbour and tied it up extra secure. We faced the bow away from shore, threw anchors out into the water, secured ropes to shore and to the public dock at Harbour Side Park because of the wicked storm expected overnight.

Ralph went to talk to the people from Conoco Phillips, a fuel company, which had a headquarters less than 200 foot from the dock. Ralph was always trying to raise some sponsorship for fuel. They were fascinated with our mission and offered to take us to lunch the next day. They all wanted to make it happen, get us fuel, but they would have to get approval from the head office first.

We were going to be able to stay in the Murray Premises Hotel that night thanks from some anonymous donors. Well, we knew who they were, but they wanted to remain nameless. They said staying on the boat during a Nor'easter, even in the harbour would be tough. Besides the harbour was too polluted to stay on a boat with so little free-board, the nasty water would be blown all over us. I was relieved and thankful, plus to be able to get a good hot shower and sleep without bouncing all over the place.

We got a ride by a stranger from where we docked *I Am Second* to Keg's Restaurant on Pier 7. It was about a mile away. Our hotel was right next door on the other side of the torn-up street. It had something to do with waterlines for the new sewage plant which was almost finished. Kevin Butler, the General Manager, found out about our voyage through Bruce and offered us a free steak dinner. Since he wasn't there; the acting manager, Lindsey Klyne, approved it. I gobbled my steak down while Ralph let his get cold during his many cell phone calls. After dinner we signed a Bermuda book over to Lindsey and Kevin.

Ralph took a quick shower and went straight to sleep. I needed a long soak in the bath tub and did just that. My knee was doing pretty good, but my heels, although better, were still cracked

St. John's, Newfoundland, Canada, Secret Benefactors

and sore. I resisted eating Ralph's to-go steak he never finished and put it in the mini-frig for him; something that took will-power. Afterwards I gave my jackets a good washing in the bathtub and left them propped up all over the bathroom to dry. In the morning after they had finished dripping, I hung them on the heavy duty sprinkler pipes strapped across the vaulted wood ceilings to finish drying.

Thursday, July 23rd

We discussed sending the six-audio tapes from my voice recorder back to Florida by mail. I don't know whether I worried more about loosing them out at sea or in the mail. I'd read numerous stories from adventurers about how they lost all their film in the mail. I decided to keep the finished tapes with me and protect them as best I could.

Ralph received an email from Rick Myrick; he was the guy up on the rock cliff near the lighthouse when we turned into the Labrador Sea. He was able to read our website banner with binoculars and wanted to wish us luck. I thought it was pretty cool that he took the time to email us; especially since we had a conversation between us about whether he could read our banners from way up there.

The eight guys from Conoco Phillips took us to Nautical Nellie's, a fancy but still a little rustic restaurant with a boating motif. Ralph told them many stories including the one about retired General Doug Brown whom he sat across the isle from on an airplane a few months before our departure. This is one of those... "What are the odds things?" To shorten it way up; Ralph brought up the subject of our boat mission and explained how he wanted to do it in honor of the three Marines who died in the rescue mission,

Operation Eagle Claw. General Brown wanted to know why Ralph wasn't including the other five-Air Force servicemen. General Bryan Doug Brown was the guy who headed up the investigation into the crash of Operation Eagle Claw where eight-Delta Force soldiers died, including the three Marines we were honoring during our Wounded Hero Voyage; John Harvey, George Holmes, and Dewey Johnson. The Delta Force guys were on an almost impossible mission to rescue the 52-American hostages held captive in the American Embassy takeover in Tehran, Iran back when President Carter was in office. General Brown, although not a General at the time, was the person who had to testify in Congress about the events which led up to the failed mission. He was also one of the ones who started the Special Operations Wounded Warrior Foundation in honor of the eight servicemen. What are the odds these two men would be sitting next to each other in first class on an airplane especially since Ralph never sits in first class? Anne had found a special deal that time.

At another time, Ralph was telling the same General Brown story about their meeting on the airplane and when Ralph commented at the end, "What were the odds?" The other guy answered, "They were 100 percent; God was behind it." After that, whenever Ralph told that story I couldn't help thinking about how Interstate Battery and I Am Second were our sponsors. We had been trying for about a year and a half to raise enough sponsorship for this trip and then in the last possible moment (the safest time to cross the North Atlantic was in the months of June and July, other wise the storms became too unpredictable as youtube.com has showed me. We left the end of June and already it was July 23rd and we hadn't left North America yet. The safest time was about to end!)

St. John's, Newfoundland, Canada, Secret Benefactors

I couldn't get it out of my mind that God was helping us because I Am Second (God is First) was our major sponsor.

Walking around St. John's looking for a camera store, we stopped and leaned against a building to talk. The guy inside, Richard Whalen, over heard our conversation. He was having a smoke break with a window open. He was a general contractor remodeling a hundred-plus-year old building. They were turning it into a condo. He invited us inside for a tour and between explaining his remodeling stories; he educated us about St. John's, fishing, camera stores, and whales. Many whales follow and feed on the six-inch capelin and the much smaller blue fish.

We found the Celebrity Photo Studio and I was able to talk with Robert Young who wasn't too familiar with the Sony handycam, but he suggested I buy an external hard drive to load the video on. He gave me directions to some local stores which would have them. The stores were too far to walk to right then because we had to get back to the boat to meet someone.

Georgina worked at an Interstate Battery Store and came out to take us to their store for a photo shoot. While there, they also loaded us up with a few items which would help us on our trip, including a nice flashlight. On the way back to the boat, she drove us around so we could do some errands. I bought a new-twelve-volt heater thermos and an external hard drive. She also drove us up to the top of the mountain to Cabot Tower overlooking the harbour so we could get some video. Cabot tower was where the first transatlantic wireless communication was made from the Americas and Europe. It was in Morse code in Dec, 1901 from St. John's to Cornwall, England. Cabot Tower and the nearby Cape Spear are known for the most easterly spots in North America.

Wounded Hero Voyage I

We had dinner with the Conoco guys and then stayed up late downloading the videos and all the information from Ralph's laptop onto the new external hard drive. When I went to bed and hit the wall switch to turn out the light, I immediately heard the computer's fan go off and when I looked over, all the computer lights were off. The wall light switch was also connected to the power outlet, which turned off the power to the computer. We had to start the whole process over again.

The people from Conoco Phillips took Bob and Ralph out to dinner.

Friday, July 24th

When we woke, up the computer was still downloading the videos. We were afraid to stop it because we weren't sure if it would error and we'd loose all we had downloaded. Ralph went out and stopped at several businesses trying to get any kind of sponsorship. Darrell Miller didn't want us to mention his company's name, but he had his secretary, Sandra Mitten, drive back and forth from the boat to the gas station. I went with Sandra in her small hatch back. We had transferred the 100 gallons of donated gas by using our ten-jerry jugs in two trips. At the gas station, a complete stranger walked up and helped me load the jerry cans. The people in St. John's were incredibly friendly.

Panasonic donated a Toughbook laptop computer, which was supposed to be almost indestructible. They had it FedExed to us. Even though it was water resistant we still wanted to put it in a dry bag, so we headed to Outfitters, a camping store. We also bought some Long John underwear which was supposed to help keep us warm even when wet. I bought mine, the more expensive one, for 100 dollars out of my own money pretty much deleting my cash supply. I eyed the waterproof fur lined boots and gloves, but they weren't in the budget as they started at over 200 dollars.

While loading the boat, a Russian tall sailing ship went by; we seemed to be on the same tour as them. We missed them in New York (found a New York poster in Boston); saw them in Boston, then Halifax, now they were arriving in St. John's. Somehow, I don't think we've seen the last of the tall ships.

While loading the boat preparing to leave in a couple of hours, I noticed some small cracks in the T-top frame supports. Bob Ackel was down at the dock taking pictures of our boat. He volunteered to drive me to a hardware store to buy a drill bit and some self taping screws, while Ralph talked a nearby machine shop into making some metal braces for the supports. It took 32 screws, glue, and wire ties to fasten the four braces.

The water around the boat was polluted. There were big chunks of human feces and at least thirty condoms floating within ten foot of the boat. Since the big sailboat left, which was tied to the other side of the dock, we moved our boat to its spot. It was further out into the harbour away from the shoreline. The water was cleaner out where the wind and currents pushed the floating pollutants towards the shoreline. The harbour really looked beautiful from a distance, especially from the mountaintop or from our hotel. Regular sized boats with three and four-foot freeboards wouldn't have noticed what our flats boat view gave us.

The polluted water in St. John's harbour before the new sewage plant

St. John's, Newfoundland, Canada, Secret Benefactors

While waiting for the CBC (Canadian Broadcasting Company) camera team to show up, we were invited to the Crows Nest, an officers club up on the hill. Inside there was a World War II periscope which was mounted so they could see the harbour from inside the building. It was there when I noticed Darryl from CBC had pulled up in his van. His handycam was similar to mine. He told me about a program he used on his Apple computer to edit and reformat their video to make it accessible to other stations.

The guys from Conoco Phillip were sad to tell us the main headquarters turned us down. They would not be able to sponsor us with any fuel. They inferred it might be a liability issue in case something bad happened. They did give us two-small red blankets, shirts, and a couple of souvenir mugs. Almost everyone in the building came out for our five o'clock EST sendoff. CBC recorded our departure and were going to end their evening news with us driving out to sea.

Bob, Georgina, Ralph, notice the Conoco Phillips building behind

Wounded Hero Voyage I

We stopped about half a mile later near the mouth of the outer harbour so I could go onshore to video. We needed some video of the boat moving from off the boat. Ralph motored around with the pill boxes and lighthouse in the background. A cargo ship exited the harbour and headed south. We soon followed going north. A couple of miles out from of the harbour, we threw out all our anchor lines and ropes so they could drag in the water to clean them off. We then took our five-gallon bucket and sloshed about thirty buckets of water down the entire boat. It still grosses me out thinking of all that stuff in the harbour which splashed up on our boat during the night storm. It had been so rough one of our many ropes broke.

We left carrying about 180 gallons of gas with much of it in the front tanks and the boat was still having a hard time planing off. I attributed it to not having the power prop on and also not using a dolphin fin. On our Bermuda trip, we had a dolphin fin. It was an underwater wing that was attached to the motor just above the propeller nearly a square-foot in size. Its purpose was to help keep the nose of the boat down. We planned on using one, but we never had the time to take it off the other motor at Ralph's shop and mount it before leaving Tampa, Florida. Again, not a budget item to buy on the way and probably a big mistake, it could have saved us fuel. Later, Ralph suggested we check the back hull access from the top of the rear deck. One side had about an inch of water, which was normal and the other side had about three. I checked and the bilge pump was running, but nothing was going out. I took it apart and found a chunk of plastic inside blocking the impeller. I removed it and put it back together.

Harbour patrol gave us the weather report which said there would be a high over the area for the next couple of days, so we should expect perfect weather without any storms. Harbor patrol also told us to keep an eye out for any icebergs. They said we should definitely see a couple. I crossed my fingers. This Florida boy wanted one for the cover of the next book.

Ralph told me he got a call from Interstate Battery. They said we could back out of our deal to cross the Atlantic after we've reached Cartwright, Labrador. Ralph wanted to know what I thought. I said they were just concerned we might not be able to make it. They were giving us an out in case we felt it was too dangerous. It was my guess they really wanted us to finish it, especially since they made a commercial about it. I said, "We should continue the course," which is what I'm sure Ralph wanted to hear.

After dark as usual I had a hard time keeping the boat on course. This time there was an island I wanted to keep at least a mile away from. Every time I looked at the Garmin it appeared I was heading towards it as if it was magnetic. I wasn't afraid of hitting it, but the smaller ones that didn't show up on the Garmin had me concerned. I was leaning so far forward I was driving with my chest on the wheel. I preferred to drive sitting back in the chair because of the freezing wind coming up over the windshield, but right then it was more important to see. Even after passing the island, I reached down in the cooler and tore the open a bag of carrots and by the time I had the carrot in my mouth and checked the Garmin, I was back heading for the island again. I continued the 360-degree circle back to my course away from the island. We should have invested in an autopilot. The wasted gas alone would have paid for it.

Wounded Hero Voyage I

To stay awake I usually ate something, hummed, or tried to think what people at home were doing at this exact second. Ralph's watch on the dash read it was 10:08 p.m. EST, so in between munching on Cheetos, I guessed Jill was asleep with our dog Casey sleeping next to her in my spot on the bed. Jonathan was up watching TV, unless he was trying to sleep because of a race in the morning. I felt sure Bryan was out with his friends, maybe at the movies.

After staring at the lit compass for a while my eyes became blurry. After wiping them and shaking my head, I realized the "N" I was staring at was really a "W." Oops, back to the real "N", the one above the 00-degrees. Where were the stars tonight? Maybe if I brush my teeth, I might wake up. I kept my toothbrush in the hanging bag right behind the captain's seat. While rinsing my tooth brush off in the Atlantic in the spray shooting up off the side of the boat, I got three inches of the sleeve of my jacket drenched. I rinsed my mouth out with Coke because I needed the caffeine, not a great taste mixed with tooth paste.

Saturday, July 25th

Fishing season was now open in Canada. The conditions were perfect; calm, cool, and sunny. We stopped mid morning in 150 foot of water and Ralph was the first to pull one in. No not the sot-after cod, but a bright red, orange, and brown ugly fish about fourteen inches long. Ralph threw it back, as we both wondered if it was poisonous, because many bright colored things in nature are poisonous. "Warning colors" are bright-highly contrasting colors; examples would be the poison dart frog (many variations), coral snake (red, black and yellow), or the black widow (black and red).

St. John's, Newfoundland, Canada, Secret Benefactors

We saw some other guys out in a small boat and went over and asked them for the proper fishing depth for cod. They said cod are generally caught in forty to 100 foot of water. They checked out our fishing tackle and said, "Cod when biting, are caught with anything shinny with a hook on it." They told us cod were dark black or gray on top with a white belly with whiskers near their lips. They hadn't caught any cod to show us. We moved over to a big rock island, and between the both of us, we caught about fifteen of these ugly colored mud fish as I called them. They were easy to catch, didn't fight too hard, and all seemed to be meaty. Later on the Internet, I found out the colorful fish we called mud fish were called sculpins. They often had poisonous spikes on their fins which can give a potent sting, but their meat was considered to be very tasty.

Ralph with two sculpins fish caught on separate poles within seconds. Ralph caught the bigger one.

Wounded Hero Voyage I

     I tried to wake Ralph up to see a pod of eight to ten white-sided dolphins. They were darting back and forth probably feeding on small fish. I circled them trying to video tape before driving off. Ralph made no effort to get up or even glance around; he was out.

     Off in the horizon, I saw these white objects every once in a while. I couldn't decide if they were boats or icebergs. I convinced myself they weren't icebergs after first driving towards them. The closer I got, the more they began to look like big yachts, I thought I could make out some windows, so I turned away. Ralph was sound asleep, the seas were still calm. We were supposed to arrive in Saint Anthony about 5:00 p.m. and according to our GPS we'd arrive at 5:07 at our current speed of 21.9 mph.

     I noticed another white object a couple of miles away on our path. I was hoping I could get close enough to check it out without deviating from our course. I became transfixed on the object and I couldn't identify any antennas, masts, or even a wake. Most boats aren't solid white. They usually have either a stripe or they are two toned. Why didn't we have a pair of binoculars on this boat?

     Ralph woke up and looked ahead at the same thing I'd been staring down for the last half hour and screamed, "Iceberg, iceberg!" I told him when I originally saw it I thought it was about two miles away; obviously I was wrong. It must have been ten to 15 miles away. I told Ralph that if it turned out to be an iceberg, I would have to use my surfboard to get some pictures of it and the boat; this was the perfect day, calm with small rolling swells and blue skies. In the event that it was an iceberg, I was going to get wet and it would be cold. I started the slow process of heating up some soup in the new thermos.

Yep, it was an iceberg! It was big and beautiful with water streaming off of it giving it a sweaty-glistening glowing appearance in the sun. It was bigger than a football field and at least 100-foot tall. We videoed while circling it; it was completely different on each side. One side had a horseshoe shaped bay with an ice beach in the center. It had places where pieces had broken off. Some of the edges were almost transparent with the sun shining through to a darker teal color. The bottom foot above the waterline was eroded a foot back. One side looked as hard as a rock with thousands of small cracks in a white foggy shell. It was probably because it melted and refroze several times. Birds flew and landed around the peak as if it was their home.

Bob preparing to paddle around to take pictures from his board

After un-strapping my *I Am Second* surfboard, named that because of the large letters stuck on the bottom side; I posed for a couple of pictures before setting my board in the water with my surfboard leash hooked over a cleat. I pulled out my Xterra wetsuit and squeezed myself into it. It fit pretty well once I adjusted all the wrinkles out and zipped up the back. It was a thin-mil wetsuit made for triathlon swimmers, not designed for iceberg waters. I was excited but nervous as I don't like the cold. My plan was not to get wet, because the water temperature was reading 35-degrees Fahrenheit. Digging through several compartments, I couldn't find my bar of surf wax which I'd brought for traction for the top of the surfboard. The little bit of wax on my board was for Florida warm waters and was as hard as a rock after it had melted in the south and re-hardened in the north which would of made it extremely slippery.

    I attached my leash to my left ankle out of habit as there were no waves, and paddled over to within a couple foot of the iceberg. It had a sloped ice beach which I was tempted to try and climb onto, but it looked really slippery; if only I had crampons and an ice pick. Looking down through the two-foot of transparent blue-ish water and I could see I was above an underwater island of teal colored ice. The water felt unbelievably cold, just a few degrees above freezing, so I kept my feet up as much as possible. Looking up was an irregular shaped ice cliff face that was ominously beautiful, but still creaked as the whole ice-mountain slowly crept towards me. I paddled back over to Ralph to get a camera. I had to sit up, submerging parts of my body, to take several pictures and some video with the boat crossing between me and the iceberg. I felt a little vulnerable when Ralph drove about a quarter of a mile away, wondering what kinds of sharks inhabit these waters. He wanted a lot of video with his boat close to the iceberg for a size comparison and I had been steadily drifting away, traveling much faster then the massive chunk of ice. Ralph drove over and towed me back to the iceberg. I held onto the side rail of the boat, which was pretty much at my head level and made some jokes about Great Whites into the handycam.

I paddled around to try to get my blood pumping to warm up while we switched cameras and then modeled some of our sponsors' gear. I put on several shirts over my wetsuit and took some pictures of Ralph eating and drinking some of the products we had on the boat. Ralph even had me take the Toughbook computer out on my surfboard. I was getting extremely cold and it was hard to sit still on my board shivering while holding the computer with both hands. The wetsuit was slippery on my slick barely waxed fiberglass board and I had to keep my frozen-numb feet moving so I could balance myself. I was really getting nervous as I felt like I was about to slide off into the drink and didn't want to test the water resistance of the Toughbook, especially since we had just gotten it. I called for Ralph to come and get the computer, but he wanted more pictures... it didn't get wet. Ralph laughed as he kept asking, "How cold is it?"

One of my main goals on this trip was to drop into a big wave by running off the deck with my surfboard, but since we had a rope, the next logical thing was to wakeboard around the iceberg. I surprised myself and got up on the first try. I had wake boarded many times in my youth, but not for decades and getting up holding a rope handle was different that getting up on a wave especially since I couldn't feel my feet anymore. I let the rope go when it appeared Ralph was going to drive straight out into the horizon. I had to tell him he was also driving too fast as my feet had no traction slipping around. I really wanted a piece of wax. We argued a little as I wanted Ralph to drive really close to the iceberg so the iceberg's definition would be in the background, but Ralph wanted to have the whole iceberg in the videos. He was still a little nervous about a chunk of ice falling off and he didn't understand that I was going to swing wide outside on the turns and then swing inside on the straight a-ways so the iceberg would be visible on the inside shots. I wanted to spray the iceberg, but I had no control over where the boat went that was pulling me. I wake boarded for about fifteen minutes, going at least once completely around the iceberg which I christened "I Am Second Iceberg." I was getting extremely cold, tired, and had no feeling in my feet, so I let the rope slip free from my hand and dropped back down onto my board.

After almost three hours spent at the iceberg, I felt the coldest back on the boat after taking off the wetsuit and rinsing off with our water jugs. The wind had picked up and those water jugs weren't heated. Our visit at our first iceberg turned out better than I could have ever imagined. The perfect day with the perfect iceberg! It was sad to wave goodbye. I was thinking, it would be great if we could have spray painted *I Am Second* in big black letters leaving the name for others to see.

Bob paddling near the base of the iceberg heading toward ice beach

St. John's, Newfoundland, Canada, Secret Benefactors

Bob catching a ride back to the iceberg, while joking about sharks

Ralph driving back and forth with Bob in the water taking pictures

St. Anthony, Newfoundland, Best Deal Ever

I slept the three or four hours from the iceberg to just outside of St. Anthony, a town near the northern tip of Newfoundland. Ralph woke me up for another night port entry. After checking with Bruce on the layout of the harbour, Ralph made a left around an island following the red and green buoys lights. Our first stop was next to an ice plant crushing and stowing ice in the hull of a fishing boat. The harbour radio was closed for the night so the dockhands loading the ice told us to park next to a dock they pointed to across the harbour.

As we were tying up, we met Charlie and Louie who suggested we tie up to the outside rail of their boat. They were going to allow us to walk across their boat to get to the wharf. We were both parked near the Coast Guard Cutter *Harp* and several Coast Guard personal came over to check out our story. The Guards invited us aboard the *Harp* for coffee. I stayed with Charlie and Louie to finish our discussion inside their half-finished cabin, while Ralph went with the Coast Guard guys. Charlie and Louie were building a small cabin on their 25-ish-foot boat. The cabin was dried-in and they were slowly finishing the inside. I talked with them until Charlie's wife came to pick them up in her car. They said

St. Anthony, Newfoundland, Best Deal Ever

we could spend the night inside their boat and even offered us the use of their little gas heater.

I went over to the *Harp* and went aboard. Ralph had already eaten a couple of sandwiches and was still sipping his coffee. The Guards made me a couple of sandwiches and made the mistake of leaving a huge plate of chocolate chip cookies in front of us. With their help, we polished off the whole batch and I had the last one. They also invited us to stay with them for the night and gave us access to a place onshore to do laundry and to take showers. We readily accepted as they had beds. The catch was that we had to be off early in the morning since they had to go out on patrol.

After showers and starting a load of laundry, we went up and talked for a couple of hours around the dinning room table with John, the first mate and some of the crew. The Guards said they saw us two times on the news the last couple of nights from St. John's Harbour. John's hobbies were fly fishing for salmon and photographing moose and icebergs. Another guy showed us a bunch of pictures of cod fish so we'd be able to identify a real one. I finally found out how lighthouses automatically switched on their fog horns. They have an electric eye that turns on the electric horns when something blocks its visibility, much like a photo eye turns on a solar pump or a night light. The lighthouse light should be on during day and night. They corrected some of our boat lingo; beds on a boat are called berths and when referring to mileage, everything is in nautical miles when at sea; otherwise the correct term is statute miles.

Sunday July 26th

Louie came out in his black car to give us a tour of his town.

He took us over to see the stranded iceberg in Bight Harbour, a second harbour in St. Anthony. Their un-named iceberg had been there for over a month. It floated in and ran aground. We named the one I wake boarded around, *I Am Second Iceberg* after our voyage. Louie told us it is common for a chuck of ice to break off an iceberg which could cause it to lose its center of gravity and roll over in a matter of minutes. He said sometimes a chunk of ice will break off near the top and slide down the ice face picking up speed and could skim across the water for a quarter of a mile.

    Louie drove us over to the visitor center where we bought a Canadian flag. We were going to get a British flag too, but the only ones they had were bigger than our American and we couldn't do that. Louie showed us their town's newly refurbished orange decommissioned water bomber (a small float warplane). It was on permanent display in dedication to a fallen hero. We drove around the outskirts of the town looking for moose. While looking, he showed us the public garden plots which people in town could section off to grow their own vegetables. Down at the dock, we saw some fishermen repairing their nets and then some stupid kid drove across them in his truck and tried to squeeze ahead of us going through a chain link gate. Louie couldn't let that happen and put the pedal to the metal so the kid would have to go behind us like he was supposed too. The town was a shrimp and crab fishing town with tons of traps around. We saw some moose antlers laid out to dry on a dock.

    We drove by the water bottling plant where Louie's son worked. It was closed on Sundays, so Louie explained how they got fresh bottled water. They had a special boat with nets which picked up ice chunks. Sometimes they used rifles to shoot icebergs to break chunks off. There was a small battle between the tourist department who wanted to keep the icebergs to attract tourist and the bottling plant which wanted to bottle the ice.

<u>Quote from Cross the Atlantic blog:</u> "We're keeping our readers posted on your journey. Senior life Magazine"

Wood was stacked up all around the town since wood was their main source for heat. Oil was still available but more expensive. While driving through a neighborhood, Louie recognized the editor of the local newspaper out doing his yard work. We stopped for an interview while he was holding a weed whacker in his hands.

Louie dropped us off at the St. Anthony's United Church where Ralph was asked to go up front and give a presentation of our voyage. They were honoring one of their own fallen heroes that morning. Joe Walker had died driving home from a military training mission in Canada at the age of 28. What were the odds..., that on the day the Wounded Hero Voyage stopped to go to their church that they'd be honoring their Wounded Hero. More proof to us that this was a God assisted voyage.

While Ralph and I were in church, Louie found some guys and a trailer to help us pull the boat out of the water to change the oil. We met them down at the water so Ralph could decide if the trailer would work. Then Louie drove us back to the boat and Ralph and I motored down to the rock beach in the corner of a bay. I let Ralph off where he and crew hooked the old trailer to the back of a truck and backed it in the water. My first attempt to drive the boat onto the submerged trailer failed with the trailer tires rubbing the bottom of the boat. A few wood shims, a pallet, and some muscle and we got the boat out of the water.

I stood around and video taped while Ralph got help from the guys. Percy helped us change the oil, and Fred worked on the Toughbook and loaded some maps for us. Chris checked out the bilge pump which was fine. They also switched from the speed prop to the power prop since now we were traveling with more fuel. While writing this book, I couldn't make out the names of the spectators, truck driver, wrench aficionado, and mechanic overseer on my audio recorder. They wanted our old oil to be used for fuel in an oil burning furnace. Lloyd Tucker donated a Newfoundland flag to us and many of the spectators signed it.

Getting help from the local guys to pull the boat out of the water, change the oil, and program the Toughbook.

We had a little trouble getting the boat back into the water since the tide had gone out and there were only a couple of inches of water in the bay. At first, the backend of the trailer's frame was digging into the rock bottom until four guys climbed out on the

St. Anthony, Newfoundland, Best Deal Ever

trailer tongue. Their added weight changed the angle of the trailer. The trailer pivoted off the bottom and with spinning truck tires the trailer went further into the bay. Two-more guys tight roped out on the trailer's tongue as the trailer was still jerking backwards over the irregular bottom. They had to rock the boat up and down as the truck driver slowly pulled forward leaving Ralph and boat barely floating in the four inches of water. Ralph had to walk around on the boat to level it so it would not rub on the bottom and then let the gentle wind blow him into deeper water, as we had no paddle.

Locals help with refueling using a 55-gallon drum and a truck

I went with Percy to his house where he got his old-twelve-volt hot box. He used it for cooking when he was out on fishing trips. It was old and had some melted cheese petrified on the inside with a white-powder coating of fiberglass dust on the outside. We gladly bought it for twenty dollars. We also picked up his 55-gallon drum used for transferring fuel from the street gas station down to his boat, since diesel was the only fuel available down on the water. We filled the drum up in the back of his truck at a station and met Ralph at a dock, where he was working on starting the kicker motor. It hadn't been started in a while and after many attempts at starting it, one of the local mechanics suggested Ralph prime it with a straw. By pushing the straw into some gas and then capping the end with his finger, Ralph could transfer a few drops of gas right into the spark plug's hole. After reinserting the spark plug, it started right up. We made two trips to the gas station to get enough gas for tomorrow's departure going 260 miles to Cartwright, Labrador, Canada.

St. Anthony was having a festival celebration to honor one of the great Arctic explorers, Bob Bartlett (1875-1946), a Newfoundlander. He sailed many of his record number forty expeditions into the Arctic in a two-masted sailboat. Bartlett was the first person to sail north of 88-degrees north and had over fifty years of mapping the Arctic. He had rescued many people in their failed expeditions including one group stranded for four years on the ice. Bob Bartlett was a real hero!

The Bob Bartlett parade was lead by a couple of small boats followed by the reconditioned *Bowdoin*, Bartlett's boat. Following at a distance was the horn blowing Coast Guard vessel *Harp*. Much smaller boats with quieter horns including us, squeezed in front of the *Harp*. We motored up to the *Bowdoin* as the crew anchored and took down their sails. Ralph asked them some questions about their vessel before we followed the *Harp* and Jim Decker, from harbour radio in his boat, back down the harbour. Jim and his wife were going to video tape us near their town's iceberg in Bight Harbour with our handycam. Against Jim's advice, Ralph backed the *I Am*

St. Anthony, Newfoundland, Best Deal Ever

Second into the horseshoe shaped berg for some great photos. I noticed the iceberg had changed since this morning when Louie first showed it to us. A big chunk had fallen off the top and landed on a smaller section. Before heading back to the festival Jim threw us two MRE's (Meals Ready to Eat), which he kept on his boat for emergencies.

Canadian Coast Guard Cutter Harp in Bob Bartlett's boat parade

Backing *I Am Second* inside an iceberg in St. Anthony's harbour

Wounded Hero Voyage I

I was standing in line to buy a hamburger when the lady in front of me, turned around and gave us ten dollars to buy our dinner. I bought two burgers and two Cokes and walked back down to our boat, which was parked at the town's ferry dock. Ralph was easily persuaded into making a presentation using the ferry's movable steps as a podium. Several people donated some money and a few wanted to buy some books and shirts. We couldn't sell the books or shirts since we weren't sure of the legality of selling stuff in a foreign country. Everything sold would have to be done on the Internet. We posed for pictures with a bunch of people on our boat and had many of the kids sign the Newfoundland flag.

Gram and Sonya, locals at the festival, took Ralph up to the store to get some groceries. They stopped by their house to get us some home prepared rabbit and a five-gallon bucket. The Labrador Sea took ours from us after washing the boat leaving St. John's. We discovered it missing when we went to change the oil.

Monday July 27

We spent last night on the *Harp* again and asked them to wake us up at first light, around 3:00 a.m. Since it was so foggy out, they let us sleep in until four. We had a quick breakfast of eggs and toast before leaving in the still heavy fog carrying a going-away package of juice, fruit, cookies, and crackers. We went in circles trying to find our way out of the harbour. I thought they must be up in the pilot house watching us on their radar laughing because that's what I'd have been doing if I was them. Once the sun was about fifteen degrees from the horizon, the fog started to become more transparent and in less than three minutes it had completely disappeared. We had another perfect traveling day.

We passed another iceberg about a mile off to our left and debated whether we should go and visit it. John told us last night the best time to photograph icebergs was early morning or late in the evening. The best colors come out when the sun is not directly overhead. Both of us really wanted to stop, but we wanted to get to Cartwright before dark and 260 miles is a long way by small boat.

This was the coldest day so far driving in the boat. We were still in Florida mode, I had on my Flip Flops and Ralph was still in his Gator Crocs. The days of wearing these on our feet were about to end. Ralph moved his floor mat wind deflector all the way to the ground to help his feet. I was wearing my surf paddle gloves where the fingers tips are factory cut off and the fingers are webbed together. (Paddle gloves make it faster to paddle a board, but because the surfer is pushing more water, he becomes tired quicker.) Our stainless steel steering wheel was extremely cold and the gloves made it bearable.

It has been a few days since we've been on the Internet, so I used the satellite phone to call Jill. Jonathan, for the second year in a row, just won the Astronaut High School YMCA mini-triathlon. Jill also told me the case of *Running for Fun* books had arrived and Jonathan was rather upset. He wasn't ready for it to be finished and he also wanted to do the final edits. I think he was just nervous about having a book out which featured himself. I did give him plenty of time to go through the book and edit it, but he was always too busy. I wanted the book to come out before the voyage hoping to get some exposure. I've learned it is much harder to promote books than to write them. Even though I think they are both pretty tough. The profits from his book are supposed to go towards his races, coaching, and his future hike of the Appalachian Trial (AT). The AT is a hike from Georgia to Maine, some 2,172 miles. Jill also told me someone from our home church, Georgianna Methodist Church on Merritt Island, Florida, just donated a hundred dollars toward our trip.

A light fog was starting to skew our distance vision. Two more icebergs were off to our left. The Coast Guard guys told us there was a really big one out here and to keep an eye out. I think we just saw it. Too bad it was off our path. I think if it was still a clear day, and we'd position ourselves in the right spot, I think we could have seen all three at the same time. An hour later, we passed another iceberg which was close to shore. A fog bank was hovering along the coastline half hiding it.

We started to put names on some of our icebergs. The first one was *I Am Second*; the second was *Nutri-Grain*, because we made a Nutri-Grain commercial when we saw it; the third was *Too Far Away*. We decided to put a name on the grounded iceberg in St. Anthony, *In Town*, but we changed it to *Bight* after their harbour. Now that I think about it, the very first one should be called *Boat*, because I turned away from it thinking it was a boat.

While video taping an iceberg, Ralph went to wipe off the lens of the waterproof housing and it left the lens streaked. I had been eating Tostitos and attempted to spit shine the streak off but I couldn't get any spit. Then I remembered Kevin, the camera salesman, told me to clean the lens using only a soft soap and water. We had a bottle of Prell shampoo on the dash and after about five minutes of scrubbing it finally appeared to come off. We were both really relieved.

St. Anthony, Newfoundland, Best Deal Ever

At *Nutri-Grain* iceberg, we stopped so Ralph could try to copy the water bottling guys of St. Anthony who shot at icebergs with rifles. We didn't have a rifle, but we did have a bunch of flair guns. Not really expecting anything more than the flair just fizzing out on the ice, Ralph took aim and clearly missed the hundred plus-foot iceberg from fifty foot away. He commented that we weren't going to tell anyone about firing a flair for a non-emergency and he reloaded and took a second miss. I gave him a hard time, since he was in the Marines a long time ago. He said he was rated an expert with a rifle. He made some lame excuses about aiming for a crack at the top of the iceberg. While he was loading for his third shot, we had drifted so close I could have practically touched *Nutri-Grain*. I was getting nervous. Where were all those lectures he gave me about getting too close to an iceberg? We moved the boat and another unbelievable miss; I think I could have hit it blind folded. We moved away again for his forth shot. He hit it and it did just what we thought it would. It sat there and fizzled until it went out.

Ralph shooting a flare at the iceberg to see if he could get it to crack

The water temperature in the Labrador Sea has been fluctuating between 35-degrees Fahrenheit (F.) near an iceberg to as high as 55-degrees F. We were about to head into the Straight of Belle Isle (the water between Newfoundland and Labrador), and we were slowly entering heavy fog. Visibility was dropping from a couple of miles to 150 foot, then fifty foot if not less; and the water temperature was a blistering 47-degrees F.

We came up with some basic rules for naming icebergs. 1. We had to name it before leaving it, or passing it if it was far away from us. 2. If we took a picture of it, we had to name it. 3. We'd alternate responsibility for naming the bergs. If an iceberg was not named within 100 yards of leaving it, then the other person would name it on default and still get to keep their position for naming the next one.

We just left *John Koko* iceberg. It looked like three-huge icebergs, one over 200 foot tall sitting at different angles to each other on a base of ice just barely below the surface of the water. At the top of one, it looked like it was about to crack off, we even heard some loud noises. We waited as long as we could with cameras ready, but nothing happened. There is no way I can explain how magnificent these icebergs looked in real life. I have seen tons of iceberg pictures in magazines and television and never realized just how breathtaking they were when this close. There was an eerie noise they made, as if they were alive. The way the sun lit them up, waves splashed against them, birds lived on them, waterfalls formed from the melting ice, and the unique colors. So far every iceberg looked drastically different from the last. I would love to have some aerial pictures of some of these with our boat just putting on by.

St. Anthony, Newfoundland, Best Deal Ever

The Coast Guard guys recommended we stop at Battle Harbour, on Battle Island, Labrador. They said it was a refueling spot for Bob Bartlett on many of his expeditions. It was loaded with interesting things about his and other explorers' adventures. Battle Island is an outer island twenty miles northwest of Belle Isle. At one time it was recognized as the capital of Labrador where cod fish were salted to preserve and sent all over the world. Many of the buildings have been restored to how they looked in the 1800s.

The fog had long ago burned off and our blue sky with a slight breeze had returned. It was a gorgeous daytime entry into Battle Island. We traveled down the straight channel between the two islands. Battle Island was the island to the east. We passed an empty fish drying rack on our right just before reaching Battle Harbour. Most of the buildings were white with red roofs. The weathered wharf and surrounding wood buildings were old, but impeccably clean. There wasn't a scrap of trash anywhere and everything smelled clean and fresh.

Mike, the person in charge of Battle Harbour, introduced himself to us and arranged for a radio interview for Ralph over the phone. He also gave us a free lunch in the cafeteria restaurant. The restaurant served two-lunch items that day. They had some sort of fish gruel neither Ralph nor I enjoyed, but we both got seconds on the macaroni casserole. The fish gruel was the same recipe which was served back in the town's hay day and to be fair, all the other people eating there seemed to like it. Ralph tried to get on the Internet, but all they had was a really slow dialup so he gave up. All together, we were there around two hours, both of us would have loved to explore, but we were out of time, night was coming in a few hours.

Wounded Hero Voyage I

We weren't much more than 200 yards away when Ralph realized he wasn't wearing his cap. Slowly we drove back looking in the water, as we were running out of Interstate ball caps. As a last ditch attempt of finding it, Ralph ran up to the restaurant to see if by chance he left it there. Good news, it was there!

We passed a little cove along the shoreline and I counted nine-grounded icebergs. Nine-tenths of an iceberg is underwater. I know that sounds unbelievable, but for every foot visible above the waterline there were approximately nine foot below. I didn't really believe it was that much until I found an advertisement for bottled water and there was a picture shot where the camera lens was half underwater at surface level. It is an impressive photo, one I wish I had taken during the trip when I had the chance.

Ralph was asleep and this particular iceberg was calling me. It had run aground in a little cove. It was kind of tall and resembled a crown; hollow in the center with several towers all around. I wanted to get on the land side of it, out of the steadily increasing swells. We had been warned by everybody up here not to get too close. Icebergs could crack without warning. This one was loaded with cracks and there was a lot of ice floating along the shore from previous break offs. I wanted to wake Ralph up, but knowing it is better to ask for forgiveness than to get permission. Since I was second in command and in charge while the captain wasn't at his post, I went in behind the iceberg.

I admit I was a little nervous because the iceberg was tall, creaking, and the passageway was somewhat narrow if something were to fall. Once past, I immediately got out my handycam and steadied it on the most likely place I expected ice to break off next. The motor was turned off and we were sheltered from the sea on the

St. Anthony, Newfoundland, Best Deal Ever

leeward side of the iceberg. I could hear the splashing of waves and the groaning of the iceberg. I sat there waiting as long as I could until the call of nature forced me to put the camera down and hang out over the side. While in my compromising position it happened. Three sections broke off and fell knocking off more ice! It was spectacular, but my handycam was off and lying on the seat. I was surprised at the noise it had created. There was ice all over the place and Ralph was still asleep.

Before the narrow channel completely filled with big chunks of drifting ice, I slowly navigated around them with the handycam on. It would only take one big block of ice funneling down between our two hulls to possibly damage our motor; something I was always aware of. Ralph never even woke until we were out of danger. We were heading directly into the growing swells and they had become really close together making for a lot of boat ups and downs. On the sea side of the iceberg, I waited with the handycam ready in case any more ice was to break off. When I started to feel guilty for wasting too much time, I got back to traveling. I had been fooling around this iceberg for nearly one hour.

A while later, the seas were slightly angling away from us and because they were so close together; it was common for the bow to run underneath the second of two close swells and have water come over the front deck. If we weren't careful some ended up coming over the top of the windshield and drenched us. Water drained out the 2-three-inch scuppers so fast within seconds the floor was clear. Ralph was driving as I was leaning over the back gas tank filming the waves spraying up along the side of the boat. Ralph asked me to video tape over the dash with his camera, he wanted some quick usable video. Mind you, he didn't have a waterproof camera. He

Wounded Hero Voyage I

wanted to catch a wave come over the bow and hit the windshield. He adjusted his speed while we drove up and over the small swells with the top edge of the front deck coming within inches of submarining the forward swells. Why I let Ralph talk me into standing there like an idiot just waiting for the inevitable to happen, I'll never know. Maybe it seemed like fun, not remembering the water temp was in the low forties or maybe because I was already wet, but it happened. Ralph got exactly what he wanted and maybe a little more. Water was dripping from his camera in my hand as I wiped salt water out of my eyes and readjusted our ski mirror mounted on the bottom side of overhead glove box. My pocket camera also got drenched. It was being charged with an inverter inside the under dash console with the door partly opened.

We named the largest volume iceberg that we'd seen so far *Norm*, in gratitude to Norm Miller, Chairman of Interstate Battery, for being the main guy making this mission possible. Just before sunset we went through about a thousand-small islands after making our left turn out of the Labrador Sea heading for Cartwright, Labrador. The air temperature warmed up considerably now that the wind was blowing over land and not the frigid water. We passed iceberg, *The Big Guy*, after my nick name for my son Jonathan. We saw three-more icebergs off at a distance for a total of 36 icebergs spotted that day. We spotted a guy off in the distance fishing on the deck of a white sailboat with his sails down.

I came to the sad conclusion my surf booties were not any good for extended periods of time. My feet were always wet with water soaking through the seams and there was limited cushion for the soles of my feet. I voted we both get real boots sometime the next day. It is 10:30 p.m. Labrador time, an hour and a half ahead

St. Anthony, Newfoundland, Best Deal Ever

of EST. The sun had gone down a while ago, but we were still enjoying visibility by a light glow or haze off the horizon. We'd been studying the shoreline for polar bears and moose. I really wanted to get some pictures of a polar bear in the wild. But because of the possibility of polar bears Ralph would not stop to camp near any of the inviting islands.

It was now completely dark out and we've been motoring down what appeared to be a channel through a bunch of islands. We were heading for a red and green blinking light Ralph thought was our final destination, about eight miles ahead. When we were nearly there, we ran into a dead end. The marker lights which still glowed off in the distance were on the other side of a berm which might have had a road on it. While scouring the shoreline with our intermittent spotlight we found another channel. Peering through the fog down the channel we made out a blinking orange and a blinking white light. We stopped to check our almost useless Garmin without its chip and became swarmed by a literal wall of thousands of mosquitoes and flies... so much for the thought of camping and figuring it out in the morning. When we finally made it out of the narrow channels into a much larger waterway we stopped to see if the bugs were still around. Not too many, so we threw out the anchor, turned on the anchor light, and called it a night. We were too tired and frustrated to continue.

Wounded Hero Voyage I

Cartwright, Labrador, Canada, Travelers' Haven

Tuesday, July 28th (31 nights since Tampa)

I peeled my black nylon motorcycle helmet bag off my head. I was wearing it since I couldn't find my black-eye mask last night and I knew night was only dark for a short while. It was dead silent when I was woken up by really heavy breathing. I peered out into the predawn foggy haze. We were about 100 yards from shore on both sides of a straight cut through a bunch of elongated islands. There had to be a moose somewhere camouflaged in the island shrubbery. Still really tired, I stayed in the hammock and listened hard to try to pinpoint its direction. It seemed to be changing. After a while, I finally gave up and buried my head underneath my yellow raincoat I was using as a blanket. I fell asleep taking cat naps as the breathing seemed to be even closer. I tried to ignore it, but curiosity was getting the better of me. Could it be a polar bear? When it became lighter out, I climbed down and stood on the front deck peering until I finally figured it out. We had anchored in the middle of a whale feeding ground. These were smaller whales and they were barely surfacing. The sound was traveling across the water, so they really weren't close to us, maybe forty yards or more. The current was really strong heading out to sea and since it was too

Cartwright, Labrador, Canada, Travelers' Haven

dark to film the whales, I pulled out a fishing rod. I had absolutely no luck as my line swiftly swung around to drag on the surface directly behind us. I had been using a heavily weighted lure. Where were the fish?

We only had to motor a couple of miles to get to Cartwright, I could hardly believe we had camped so close. It was a cool little town with a harbour. There were a couple of king crabs boats docked at the main wharf. The view again could have been right out of a magazine. We could see long rock jetties protruding far out in the water from the individual homes tucked neatly back in the foliage. They needed these long jetties because of the tidal changes and the shallow water near shore.

We met our host, George and Pete (short for Peyton) Barrett and their son Tom with his wife Joanne. They were going to put us up while we were in Cartwright. The Barletts ran Experience Labrador, an outdoor adventure center specializing in fishing and kayak tours. After showers and some food, they helped Ralph setup his computer upstairs so he could get on the Internet above their fabulous gift shop. While Ralph was busy sending pictures, contacting the media, and looking for more sponsors; Pete gave me a tour of their gift shop while I video taped. Everything in it was from Labrador and a lot of the small detailed items were hand made by Tom. Afterwards, Tom drove me with his family to the local store to buy boots, some groceries, and to look for a new picture camera. Mine died from too much exposure to the elements.... The replacement camera and real cold weather boots were too expensive, so I bought Ralph a pair of cheap construction rubber boots similar to the pair I brought from home. Neither of us liked to wear them, but as the conditions are going to get much colder soon, I figured he'd better have something better than sneakers and Crocs.

Back at Experience Labrador, Tom took me with his nephew and niece, Dawson and Brittany, who were also visiting for the weekend, out in his little V-bottom skiff. We saw snow on some of the peaks and valleys on many of the mountains on the way to check his gill net. Tom had it buoyed out among the islands. He caught one trout, one salmon, and a mussel. Brittany grabbed the mussel attached to the top rope of the net. The native residences were allowed to keep six salmon per year while tourists were only allowed four. Yellow gill tags came with their yearly license and had to be put on immediately as the fish were pulled out of the water. Anyone caught with a salmon without a tag could loose their boat and be fined. There was an honor system for the fifty trout allowed so no trout tags were issued.

Bob in the *I Am Second* and Brittany, Dawson, and Tom in the skiff

Tom's gill net was 36 foot long with four-inch mesh. The four-inch squares were a required size so small fish could swim through and larger fish couldn't get their noses through far enough to catch their gills. The net was really for trout. If Tom caught his limit of salmon, he was supposed to relocate the net so he would hopefully not catch anymore salmon.

Tom was a handy guy to have around. He tried to find a small trailer for us to pull our boat out of the water so we could fuel it at his cousin's street gas station, which would save us a lot of money. Cartwright didn't have gasoline near the water. When he couldn't find a trailer which would fit our flats boat, he called Woodword Group, a diesel truck service. They pumped out their diesel fuel and replaced it with gasoline to fill up our tanks. They tried to pump the gas into one of the small opening on our fifty-gallon side tank, but its opening was too small for the bigger diesel nozzle. We tried to use a funnel, but the gas came out so fast it spewed all over the boat. Our boat's temporary tanks were vented poorly which has been my experience with many small powerboats; the tanks usually have to be filled slowly to keep them from belching gas out around the fill nozzle. Tom suggested removing the whole cap assembly on the tanks making for a much bigger opening. It worked and didn't take very long. The bad part was the gasoline which sprayed the deck ate some of the black rubber off the bottom of Tom's shoes and we had black foot prints all over the boat's white deck.

Tom and I loaded the small-nozzled empty jerry jugs in Tom's truck and filled them at his cousin's gas station, for a total of 310 gallons of gas on the boat. We didn't feel the need to carry our full capacity of 347 gallons since we were only going about 625 miles to Nuuk, Greenland. We used the jerry cans because they could be loaded in the front area of the boat to help with planning instead of topping off the back tanks. The weather report said we'd have three to four-foot seas with slight winds later turning out of the west. On the Bermuda trip, we traveled 774 miles on about 300 gallons. While I was carrying two jerry jugs down to the boat and walking along the rock jetties, the jugs were swing one way and I was stepping the other. Splat, I fell in front of everyone, no worries, the caps were on tight. Nobody laughed out loud, but once they realized I wasn't hurt, they had a hard time holding back their snickers.

The tides changed so drastically around Cartwright the Barretts kept a tide chart on their kitchen wall. Depending on the tide and the amount of time between using their boats, determined how close to shore they parked their boats. After loading the jerry jugs close to shore, we moved the boat out near the end of the jetty. This was so we wouldn't later be land locked when the tide went out. Before we re-docked at the jetty, Tom threw out the back anchor while we were heading in. He left enough slack so we could inch into the jetty before tying the line to a cleat. When everyone was out, he took the separate bow line and walked along the jetty about a hundred foot pulling the boat so it angled and slowly pulled away from the rocks. The longer he walked with the rope, the further the boat pulled away from the jetty. The boat was in a straight line between the anchor off the back of the boat and where we tied the rope to the rocks.

We met another traveler, Tommy Cook aboard the *CAP'N LEM*, a tri-hull sailboat. George picked Tommy up from the wharf and drove him over to the Experience Labrador complex. As it turned out, he was the same guy we passed coming in yesterday, who was fishing. I never thought to ask him if he caught anything, but I wish I had. Tommy was attempting to solo sail the North-West Passage above Canada connecting the Atlantic to the Pacific. He had about the most beautiful midsized sailboat I'd ever seen. I am a big fan of the movie *Waterworld* with Kevin Costner. The *CAP'N LEM* was a cleaned up version of the sailboat in *Waterworld*. It was basically an all white boat with black rope netting spanning all three hulls, and a graphite looking jib rolled up. His website is: *Arcticsolosail.com*. We all ate lunch together and hung out for a few hours.

Some people showed up in a rugged white four-wheel drive elongated jeep with off road tires and stuff strapped to the roof rack. They were from the "Drive the Globe; over land adventures." They donated some money to our voyage, and didn't stay long. They were doing their adventure of their own, exploring Labrador.

The Barretts, Bob, the people from Drive the Globe, then Tommy, George, and Pete

Ralph had been on the computer all day, except for meals, so I went upstairs to help for a couple of hours until George offered to take Tommy and I to the abandoned US military radar station on top of a nearby mountain. All that was left were a few concrete slabs and some columns, but it was a good break from the computers and a neat ride up some old roads.

Did I say there were a lot of flying bugs in Labrador? If not, well there was and nobody seemed to put on any bug spray. I asked Tom about that and he said the bite wasn't as bad as the poison in repellant that's absorbed through the skin. And to be honest, I don't think the bugs in Labrador were nearly as ferocious as the ones in Florida, although much bigger. I did notice Cartwright sold a lot of shirts that said things like; I survived Cartwright with a picture of a huge mosquito.

Ralph told me while I was gone; someone from E-Pec Motors came by to see our boat. He offered to switch out the Suzuki with one of their motors. But just like Suzuki, they offered no additional money. Ralph was happy with the performance of our Suzuki and without additional money; there was no benefit in changing.

It was suggested to Ralph by several people during our trip, the best way to get Suzuki to donate some real trip expense money was to threaten to have their motor breakdown while out at sea. Ralph immediately said there was no way he could or would be apart of something like that. I have the same belief that Ralph had... NO WAY!

Ralph had a bunch of pictures and video on his multi-purpose camera which had stopped working shortly after the wave-over-the-dash video incident. After removing the SD card and capturing all its pictures, there was still a bunch on his camera's full internal memory. Ralph had the camera drying out in front of a fan all day and it started working again. For some reason, the computer wouldn't recognize Ralph's camera. So Tom and Ralph decided to try to move the pictures to a new SD card and after disregarding Tom's warnings. Ralph checked all the small boxes corresponding to

Cartwright, Labrador, Canada, Travelers' Haven

the picture files and hit "ok". Tom cringed knowing these were a lot of the surfboard-iceberg pictures and could not be reproduced. Ralph insisted he had not erased them, saying a check mark is for saving and an "X" mark is for deleting. After he couldn't find the pictures, he still believed when he turned the camera off and then back on they would be re-filed on the SD. Wrong... they were gone. We had just joined the ranks of adventurers with lost pictures. One of them might have been used for my book cover.

There is a "Brown" theme running through our adventure. We found out George Barrett was adopted; his birth name was George Brown, which was the same as our Dad, George Brown. And what about General (Bryan) Doug Brown who was in charge of the investigation of Operation Eagle Claw, he met Ralph on the airplane. He has the same first name as my son Bryan Brown. Oh, and the Don Brown who trailered the boat from Ralph's shop in Florida to the sendoff at the beginning of the trip. He was also one of the guys in the camera boat following us the first couple of miles out into the Bay. One of our Dad's brothers is named Don Brown. (There are more Brown name things in the end of the second book.)

We stayed up late on the computers and then walked over to the Barrett's small travel camper they had set up for us to sleep in. Thanks Barretts, another soft dry bed. The next day we'd be leaving, heading out into our coldest weather yet, still without all the proper cold weather gear. We'd be leaving during the last two days of what was considered the safest two months of the year. In reality, we should have been ending our trip in Europe around this time instead of just starting out....

To Greenland, Calling for a Fuel Drop

Wednesday, July 29th

While Brittany and Pete cooked pancakes, Tom and Joanne's four year old son Jackson Barrett collected his saving of $8.10 from recycled bottles and cans. Jackson wanted to donate his money to the Wounded Hero Voyage. With his parents' permission Ralph accepted Jackson's savings and made sure to get his picture, so he could upload it to his website.

Brittany said she could make thinner pancakes than her grandmother, Pete. They were getting so thin Ralph called them French crepes. As Ralph tried to explain what crepes were, Brittany interrupted him and said they were road kill. The rest of the morning Ralph was calling Brittany, "Road Kill." I think she thought it was cool. We finished loading the boat with Brittany and Dawson filming with my handycam. Oops, I forgot to tell them to move the camera slowly.... Tom had to keep a close watch of Stephan, their two year old, who was trying to keep up with his older brother throwing rocks into the bay. Joanne came out with a big bag of chocolate chip cookies and a note which she said to read after we'd left. George and Pete gave us a Labrador wind sock. We had all the kids sign it and hung it up on one of the fishing poles.

To Greenland, Calling for a Fuel Drop

Most of us went over to see Tommy and get an up close and personal look at his boat. Since we were leaving right after, we all drove over in *I Am Second* and George took his truck. I had to check out Tommy's boat, so I again let the kids do most of the filming. This had to be one of the coolest sailboats I'd ever seen. Tommy said she was a fast boat as long as she didn't have to head too much into the wind. The reason the tri-hull was so fast was because most sailboats keel over when they have a full sail, which causes the sail to dump wind. Wind is the force needed to push the boat. But with the three hulls, keeling is much more difficult so she goes much faster and is more stable. We wished each other good luck and off we went.

Tommy Cook's boat, he is attempting to sail the East-West Passage alone

We left Cartwright almost three hours later than we'd planned. It was really hard leaving new friends, people who we'd probably never see again. Hopefully we'll be able to keep in contact, thanks to the Internet.

It didn't take us long to dip into the Barretts' cookies.

Joanne's note:
"Bob and Ralph as you enjoy these cookies; remember it is not only your loved ones back home that will be thinking of you, praying for you. We pray that the North Star, the good Lord, and whatever guides you, keeps you both safe, leads you home and blesses you and yours. Sometimes it takes a complete stranger to make us realize how much we have, how lucky we are. We should all count our blessing more often. You might not consider yourself heroes, but you are definitely both brave brave men. May the wind always be at your back. May you safely find your way home. Thank you for all your inspirations. Safe travels, calm waters, deepest respect. Joanne, Tom, Jackson, Stephan Barrett from Cartwright, Labrador."

I got just a tad-bit chocked up reading Joanne's note, but I'm going to blame it on the cold wind in my eyes and I needed something to drink.... Thanks guys. We timed our departure wrong. Now that we were leaving late, we were battling the strong incoming tide. Seeing everything in the daytime, we realized before on our way to Cartwright we had plotted our Garmin the wrong way. It appeared we had tried to drive through the small islands instead of going around the outside of all the small islands. That would have put us in the main channel, where the big boats operated in. I think the real problem was we had the Garmin zoomed in too close so we never saw the whole picture. We never knew there was a main channel. We were zoomed in looking for obstructions which would have showed up normally if we had the right chip or a larger plotter.

To Greenland, Calling for a Fuel Drop

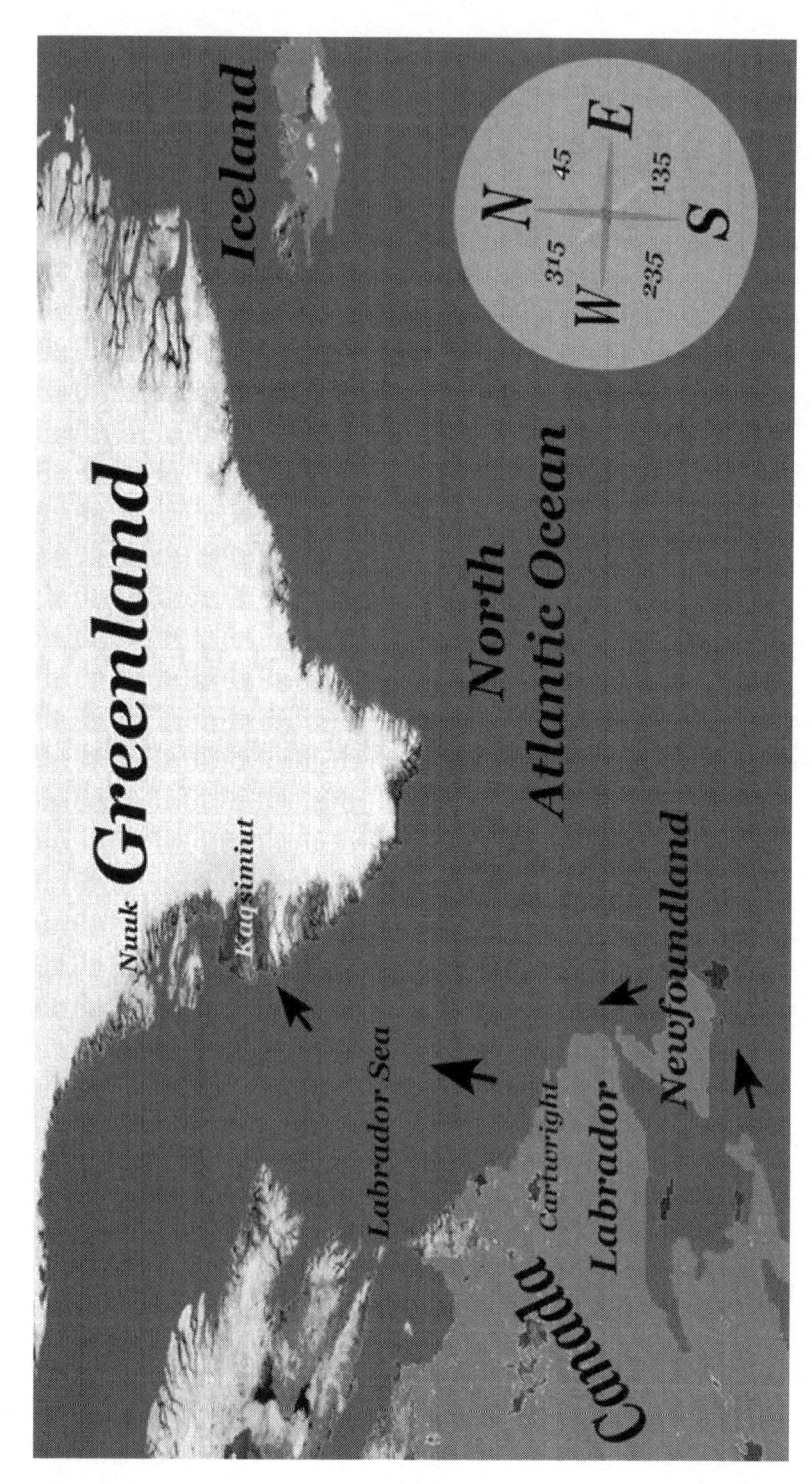

Wounded Hero Voyage I

I polished off the last of Joanne's cookies just as we cleared the coastline heading out to sea. This was the heaviest the boat has been on the whole trip to date. Ralph did a weather check and the seas were supposed to be three to four with the wind changing from out of the northeast, to out of the northwest. So far, the swells were only one to two, and the wind was out of the northeast. We almost lost one of our floor mats, but I caught it just before it went over. I prayed the Atlantic toll for this leg wasn't going to be too demanding.

There were a couple of icebergs just off our path, but since we'd gotten such a late start we weren't going to be able to do much more than slow down to take some pictures. We had to get to Greenland soon. They were predicting a bad storm to come down through the Labrador Sea in a couple of days; something we didn't want to see first hand out on the open sea. We were hoping to arrive in Nuke, Greenland sometime during the night on Thursday or early morning on Friday. Hopefully it would be around a two-day trip. Ralph was sitting backwards facing the motor just starring at the water churning up behind the boat. We were driving slower than usual with Suzuki turning 4,000 rpm instead of the usual 4,500 rpm. I didn't really expect such a strong head current and there was no sense in wasting more fuel than we had to. Our maps showed the Labrador current as generally heading to the southeast, but it was going almost directly southwest exactly opposite of our northeast heading.

Ralph went to store his sneakers in the center front deck hatch behind the anchor hatch and discovered it was full of water. This hatch was normally used as a bait well with a three-quarter-inch hole going through the floor. When used as a bait well, there is a overflow pipe that goes in the hole and any water above the pipe drains out through the floor. We were not using the overflow pipe. There was an upside down stainless steel half clamshell covering the hole on the bottom side of the boat. Its opening faced towards the back of the boat. With the monocat hull design, the hole was usually several-inches above the water flowing between the two hulls. The idea is as the boat is going forward; water is siphoned out caused by wind rushing past the opening. But because the boat was so weighted down, it was sitting lower in the water. I stuffed a home made wooden plug in the hole from the top, but because of the thickness of the bottom there isn't enough fiberglass floor for the plug to grip firmly. Most of the water probably came in while the boat was docked in Cartwright, weighted down with the extra fuel. The compartment wasn't able to drain because of some plastic bags blocking the hole. Now that we were moving, the hatch drained fast and Ralph replaced the plug.

We unsnapped and pivoted up the ten-inch wide eight-foot long cushion on top of the access hatch on the front part of the back deck. It covered the compartment which was designed for skis and fishing poles. The compartment was full of miscellaneous stuff: oil, some tools, ropes, extra water, etc. Anyway, the two-inch thick cushion added height to the forward part of the back deck. Before, as we were trying to sleep part of the air mattress was on top of the cushion causing added slope which gave the person trying to sleep the feeling that he was sliding towards the engine.

Because it was getting so cold, we worked on making a wind block on the driver's side of the boat. We took the deck banner, which we used in port for displaying our sponsors. Its original purpose and shape required grommets to be mounted on the top, but its new purpose and because of its shape, the grommets needed to be on the bottom to hang right. Our solution was to hang the wind block upside down so the sponsors would be displayed upside down. There wasn't much we could do about that, so we just went with it. We also added floor mats near the back sides to attempt to deflect some water off of both the sleeper's head and feet. The improvements seemed to be helping. The back wasn't getting showered as much in these small seas.

We lost audio tape number 7 out of the 15 in my house fire, November 15, 2009 (Two months after I returned home). This section of the book would have been more detailed, but with the help from the recovered videos, pictures, blogs, Ralph, and because I wrote this section once before (all copies were lost in the fire); I am hoping it all comes back to me.... As soon as I was back listening to the tapes again, I put the player in my backpack and accidentally hit the record button, losing one side of the next tape. (It seemed a mysterious force was trying to prevent our story from being written.)

Quote from Cross the Atlantic blog: Bob Brown said... "This is Bob Brown I am also sorry for all the people waiting for the book and HD video documentary. All computers, flash drives, CD's, camera, and external hard drives were burnt in the fire. I believe I have lost everything except the audio recordings. I only lost the one tape of the Canada to Greenland crossing and possibly some of the Greenland tape. That was one out of fifteen. I plan to attempt to have someone who knows what they are doing attempt to retrieve the information off the hard drives, but it doesn't look good. Most everything is partly melted.

If it is recovered, which I highly doubt, I will probably publish a part-I soon and a part-II when I have time to get back to it.

To Greenland, Calling for a Fuel Drop

If I can't get the book recovered (70,000 words), I don't know if I will write the book at all. I have over 300 hours in writing the book so far (every chance I had since I've been back and don't know if I will ever have that much time (at least for quite a while... sorry...books are not a profitable business, more of a hobby) Bob Brown"

Our house fire on November 15, 2009, started while we were at church. My computer and handycam with all the videos and the only copy of the manuscript were inside. The computer was on the desk against the sliding glass door on the left. The handycam and external hard drive were about five foot away on a shelf on the entertainment unit. The picture was taken by Steve Cupach, the Publix Pharmacist, who thought a plane had crashed into the neighborhood because of the mushroom cloud of black smoke.

We passed a couple of icebergs and now that Ralph was asleep, I was getting the subliminal call from an iceberg to vector over a mile or so out of the way to get some video. I debated with myself and decided since the current was heading in a southwest direction; all the icebergs might be over on the westside of the

Labrador Sea. We were heading for the eastside. This could be our last iceberg. I would only stay a couple of minutes, and we'd only waste about a gallon or two of gas. The seas were small and the wind was supposed to change sometime soon. When would I ever get a chance to do something like this again? Live the moment. I vectored. I named this berg *Igloo*.

The wind was still in the same general direction, maybe a little more from the east, but it was now much stronger. Our one to two-foot swells had changed to three to five and building. Before we were quartering them and now we were taking them head on. It was getting cold and eerie out. We never had a really good sky, but now the gray to darker gray clouds had completely surrounded our horizon. Water was misting us all the time and we had taken quite a few over the windshield, but not more than a gallon at a time. We had burned up 100 gallons of gas and had just barely gone 100 miles from Cartwright. We had 210 gallons of gas left and about 525 miles before we hit land. We burned one-third of our gas while going only one-sixth the distance. I kept telling myself, "The lighter we get, the higher out of the water we'll be, the better we'll be able to plane, the faster we will go, the dryer we'll be, and the better fuel mileage we'll get. The wind would be changing soon, knocking down some of the swell, and with that expected tail wind we'll greatly improve our mileage."

To Greenland, Calling for a Fuel Drop

First day since leaving Labrador and we were already freezing and going through a lot of fuel.

Bob passing icebergs

Wounded Hero Voyage I

With the naming of iceberg *Dude*, we decided to stop naming and counting icebergs. The list was getting way too long. To date we have named 17 iceberg; *Boat, I Am Second, Bight, Too Far Away, Fishing, Nutri-Grain, John Koko, Lost, Norm, The Big Kahuna, The Big Guy, Trucker, Three Studs, Greeny, Igloo,* and *Dude*. Our list of un-named icebergs had grown to 44, for a total of 61 icebergs. I had originally thought I would be lucky to see just one.

Dash: list of Marines, icebergs, compass taped and glued to windshield

Thursday, July 30th

Driving through the night was miserably cold. We were always on the lookout for an iceberg to pop into our forward light. During my shift, all I could think about was how warm and dry the Barrett's camper was, and thank God for Percy's hot box. Our soup cooked relatively quick and was good and hot. We had to work fast whenever we had the lid opened to prevent spillage and seawater from splashing onto our food. If we were both up, we took turns eating right out of the hot box. Whenever we changed drivers we'd

To Greenland, Calling for a Fuel Drop

heat up some soup or stew for the shivering sleeper.

Hot box with hot dogs and noodles

Both of us were very observant of the amount of fuel we were burning. We slowed the boat down a little more, still hoping for the weather report predictions to come true. Where was that northwesterly wind? We were nowhere near where we were supposed to be. Ralph asked me several times if I was okay with going ahead. I said yes, but I still kept doing the math in my head and looking at the gas. I'm sure he was doing the same thing. We should have bought a dolphin fin for the motor and left fully fueled.

Titanic was always in the back of my mind when driving at night. I wasn't worried about the boat hitting an iceberg and it sinking us. Our boat NOT like the Titanic really was unsinkable. If we cut our boat in half, it would float; the hulls and floor were injected full with foam. We had maneuverability, but that wouldn't

Wounded Hero Voyage I

have helped if I fell asleep and hit one. When we did see them at night, they didn't glow white. Instead they looked more like a big gray boat until we lit them up with our spotlight.

The winds were now in the 25 mph range with seas from five to eight foot. We had blown through our second-hundred gallons of gas and still we had about 400 miles to go on the remaining 110 gallons. We had just burned two-thirds of our gas and we had only traveled one-third the way across to Greenland. We slowed down even more. Ralph hit on the topic of possible turning back to Canada. Traveling with the strong wind and current we would get great mileage and could easily get back traveling 225 miles to Canada. We discussed our finances and there was nowhere near enough money to complete the trip especially if we had to replace our Canada to Greenland gas for a duplicate time. As it was, we were still doubtful we'd have enough money to get to Iceland let alone get us and the boat back to the states. We kept telling ourselves God would help us, we were on the I Am Second Wounded Hero Voyage, and quitting is not an option. To Greenland we go!

Our white cockpit light was no longer working as was our back mounted light over the back deck. On many boats, there is a red light over the dash used mainly for reading maps. It is used because it doesn't reflect back off of the plastic gloss waterproof coating on most nautical maps, and it is also easier on the eyes of the boat navigator and pilot. At night, we usually drove without an overhead cockpit light unless we were eating or looking for something. In my case, I used it when video taping myself or Ralph since I couldn't get my handycam into night mode without opening its protective waterproof case. Tonight's video productions were cooking spaghetti, boat surfing, and the proper way to wash out the

To Greenland, Calling for a Fuel Drop

hot box using just bread.

Bob eating spaghetti using the red light while making a video

Friday, July 31st

The swells started to shrink and shift around a little more out of the north, instead of our wishful northwest. At least this was good for boat surfing since it wasn't always done by going with the swells. Our heading was still on a northeasterly heading, but as long as I wasn't hitting the swells head on, I could drive at a sharp angle to the wave and ride the swell's face. If the swell was just right, I could get about a three or four-second ride before running out of wave. Ideally it would be much better for boat surfing if the swells were coming from behind at about 45 degrees, kind of what we had on our Bermuda voyage going to Bermuda from North Carolina. I had to resist the urge to turn east, which would give me a great ride, but not in the right direction. Sometimes, like any guy who has grown up surfing, I had to follow my free spirit and tweak my heading to get the most out of a wave. I'm sure, no, I know for a fact

Ralph had done the same thing many times, just like I did.

It seemed to warm up just a bit as the wind slowed down to about fifteen mph; the water temperature was 46-degrees F. We were now lighter and making much better time. Our spirits were more positive with just 300 miles to go. We had passed the halfway point.

While Ralph slept, I decided to make a video on how to make Maple and Brown Sugar Oatmeal by way of the hot box. While it was heating up, I videotaped some boat surfing and made a commercial for Chap Stick. The oatmeal was great, the perfect warm-up your belly breakfast food.

The wintery gray sky didn't let up. The winds and swells had clocked around now coming out of the east-northeast and building to six to eight-foot with 25 mph winds. The wind was blowing the droplets of water from the sea sideways as if were misting, plus continually throwing sprays of water from the boat crashing into the waves over us. We were no longer making good time and the boat surfing thing just wasn't going to happen. If we were heading north, we'd be flying. Where was this supposedly west wind?

Whenever we stood up to drive, we'd usually keep one hand on the T-top support poles. We both started to notice there was quite a bit of movement in the T-top. The support poles were bolted to the floor and the center brace connecting the midpoints of all four corners wrapped around the sides and front of the center console. The braces were attached to the center console with bolts accessed from the inside of the console compartment. I held the bolts on the outside of the braces with a wrench. And Ralph had to squeeze down between the captain's bench seat and the console to tighten the nuts among all the wires and steering mechanisms, not to mention all the junk we'd crammed in there. This was accomplished wearing all his jackets and a big bulky rain coat. It sounds easy, but we were like a cork floating in a bathtub with three rowdy kids playing with their power ranger action figures. Ralph's fingers had lost most of their dexterity because of cold weather numbness.

Our air mattress was made up of eight connecting tubes running long ways with a built in pillow at the top. Water would collect in the valleys and eventually soak up through the board bag, but most of the water penetration came through the zipper. This usually happened when the sleeper would try to curl up in the fetal position or roll over inside the bag putting the zipper in one of the mattress valleys. Also since a lot of water was being blown across the back of the boat, it made sense if we could raise the sleeping area up a couple of inches, then it would be a little dryer. Ralph tried using the bean bag between the board bag and the air mattress. This was now the new back sleeping position. We started using our green spare deflated vinyl air mattress as a blanket and rain shield for the sleeper. Not to repeat our earlier mistake, it was tied to the back of the captain's chair with a string around the one-inch fill nozzle with the cap screwed down tightly against the string for insurance.

I was having a hard time keeping warm. My whole body was shivering and my feet were freezing. I was alternating between my white rubber construction boots with blended wool socks and my bare feet in Flip Flops. In the boots, my feet stayed wet, turned white, became wrinkly, and were still freezing. In the Flip Flops, they seemed to be able to dry out a little. Ralph was swearing by his Crocs, but still goes for the boots occasionally. My fingers were too cold wearing my fingerless surf paddle gloves and since I found my simulated thin leather craftsman work gloves, I switched. My work gloves were really thin with a nylon reinforced breathable back. I had to switch back when they became soaked. I clipped the wet work gloves to the storage box on the dash in a doubtful attempt to dry them. The winds are close to 35 mph and the seas were up to nine foot. We are being peppered by a continuous spray of frigid water. The storm we were warned about had caught us.

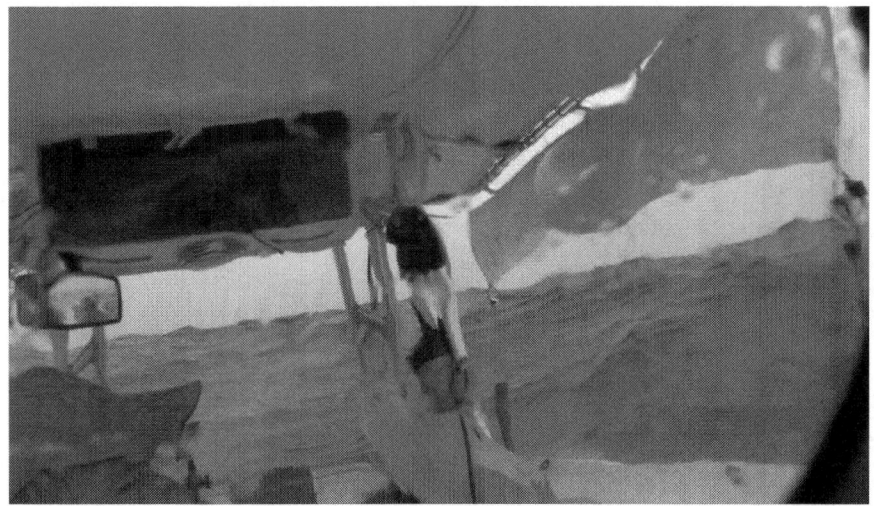

Bob driving as Ralph films through the cockpit, he is in the mirror

Frostbite and hypothermia were in the back of my mind as I was sure they were in Ralph's. After our Bermuda trip, I did a little research: A body needs to be able to produce as much heat as it loses. Heat lost is transferred 25 times faster immersed in water than in air. Wet clothes transfer heat five times faster than dry clothes. When the body's core temperature drops down below 95-degrees F, it is considered at risk; normal is 95 to 100 and ideal is 98.6 F. Mild hypothermia is 90 to 95-degrees F and the body starts to shiver to warm itself back up causing mild mental confusion. Moderate is 82 to 90-degrees F with violent shivering, poor muscle coordination, movements are slowed and difficult. The body starts

To Greenland, Calling for a Fuel Drop

to constrict its outer blood vessels to divert the blood to its vital organs. Small extremities, lips, ears, fingers and toes, start to turn blue. Severe is 68 to 82-degrees F, the person is slowly dying. Often the person has difficultly speaking, is slow to respond, has loss of memory, and lack of dexterity. The exposed skin becomes blue and bloated, pulse and respiration slows considerably then the major organs start to fail.

After the trip, I found out that world famous modern day adventurer Bear Grylls (Man vs Wild) did a similar voyage in 2003 with four companions in an open-mid-thirty-foot-aluminum-bottomed inflatable boat. According to his book, *BEAR GRYLLS Facing the Frozen Ocean*, he traveled from Canada to Greenland, Iceland, Faroe Island, finishing in north-western Scotland. Bear is the youngest British person to climb Mount Everest and he said he was colder on his crossing from Canada to Greenland than he was on top of Mount Everest. He and his team were all wearing several layers of the warmest clothes available underneath a full cold weather dry-suit including insulated boots, gloves, and helmets.

Bob driving, cold, red faced, and wet

To pour gas from our jerry cans into the bigger tanks wasn't an easy task. The seas were still rough and trying to tilt the jug far enough to get its screw-on-pour tube into the tank filler tube always resulted in some spillage. We didn't have any gas to waste. Our next solution was to pour off some fuel into our little one-gallon plastic bucket and then attempt to bend its rim to make a pour spout and then empting it into the front fifty-gallon side tank, again some spillage. Next we went to cutting up a plastic one-gallon tropical fruit drink container with its cap still on and setting it inside our one-gallon bucket so it wouldn't fall over. I'd pour about a quart of gas into it, set the jerry jug down, pick up the quart of gas and then pour it into the top half of a large cut in half Gatorade jug used to funnel the gas into the front fifty-gallon tank. Once I'd poured off about a gallon of gas out of the five-gallon jerry jug, it wasn't too hard to pour the rest as long as I was fast at inserting its pour spout tube into the fifty before tilting it too far. I had to time the pour with the coming swells.

Bruce was keeping track of us via Ralph and his satellite phone. Ralph wanted Bruce to see if he could get a military fuel drop since it was something they could easily do. Well maybe not easily, but they are trained in that sort of thing and we were underneath their normal flight path going to Europe. I guessed they'd just strap a 55-gallon drum to a parachute and shove it out of a plane. The drum would float as gas is lighter than water. I wondered how much something like that would cost us. It would also make for a good video.

We were also in contact with the Canadian Coast Guard and they said they could come and get us. But we both felt sure if they did, that would be the end of the trip. They would probably prevent us from leaving their coast heading to Greenland again.

Ralph discussed the possibility of drifting back to Canada and saving some gas so we could still drive into a harbour. I didn't like the thought of spending at least a week drifting, I was already a Popsicle. I rejected that plan. His next idea was to use the sea anchor attached to the front of the boat and wait-out some of the worst weather. A sea anchor is an underwater parachute designed to drag in the water. As the boat is pushed by the wind and waves, the chute opens up and catches the water, which acts like an underwater break. The sea anchor causes the boat to turn and face into the wind and waves. The boat will still drift with the current but will cut through most of the wind and waves pushing it.

With the sea anchor out and the boat facing into the wind, we moved the back sleeping area to underneath the steering wheel by cramming the bean bag down on the floor. I went to sleep there while Ralph slept on the captain's seat inside the surf bag. We were both using our Conoco red blankets. We thanked God for them as they were not water absorbent. They were presented to us at our St. John's sendoff. I also used the green air mattress blanket. I bundled up with a synthetic wool gray ski cap, wet socks, and still froze. We were miserable, wet, frozen, and becoming grouchy. My feet were so cold that they burned. I spent hours just rubbing them and wrapping them snug inside my Conoco blanket. Sometimes I caught myself thinking; what was I doing out here? And does anybody really care? I could be home, warm and toasty. It would be so easy to just quit, get rescued and just go home. Then a minute later I'd see the adventure side of it. The grass is always greener on the other side... at home I would want to be out here and out here I would want to be home.

When the seas calmed down and we were pulling the sea anchor in, we made the mistake of not keeping the rope tight. We were using the motor to help relieve the tension on the rope when some of it got caught around the prop. Ralph lifted the motor out of the water, I hooked my leg around the rope going from the T-top down to the kicker and I leaned down over our Suzuki 115. It only took a couple of seconds to unwind the rope. Ralph didn't want to bother filming it, but I made him. I told him we had to document the good, the bad, and the stupid. Another stupid thing I did, was to get my almost dry work gloves wet again.

Bob untangling the sea anchor rope from the prop

Saturday, August 1st

We drove when it wasn't so rough and sea anchored when conditions worsened. One of our four fifty-gallon gas tanks was accidentally installed backwards with the fuel pickup in the front of the tank. As the boat goes forward, the fuel travels to the back of the tank. In an effort to get all the gas out, I had to unscrew the straps holding it down to the deck and turn it around. When I was finished

To Greenland, Calling for a Fuel Drop

re-screwing the last strap and stood up my left flip flop was gone. My feet were so numb I didn't feel my Flip Flop fall off my foot. It was a bright yellow with a green toe strap. It was rubber and should have floated, but it was nowhere to be seen... a toll.

Ralph had maintained communications with Bernie and was able to update the blog using the satellite phone. They had a service which recorded Ralph's comments and converted them into a word document which Bernie could edit and then post on the CrossTheAtlantic.com website. Sometimes the service couldn't identify Ralph's speech over the whistling winds and banging seas so some of the blogs were incomplete.

I didn't call Jill as much as I should have because I knew we were going to quickly run through our prepaid expensive satellite minutes. Jill did tell me Anne called her almost everyday worried about us out at sea. A lot of our friends called Jill to get the lowdown on us. Jill's attitude about the trip wavered depending on the attitude with whoever she was talking to. The ones who thought it was neat brought up Jill's attitude as well as the ones who thought it was stupid and ridiculously dangerous brought her down. My oldest, Bryan, thought it was crazy and said he had no desire to go on a trip out in the open sea in a small boat, while Jonathan said he'd be right there with us if he could.

At around 180 miles to Greenland, Ralph decided that in an effort to conserve our dwindling fuel supply, we'd stop using our big engine and drive with our emergency 9.9 horse power kicker. I wasn't too excited about extending our frigid crossing traveling at a snail's pace, but agreed it was better going slow then to run fast until empty. We were already a day late arriving in Greenland, we had emptied all four of the fifties, emptied all ten of the jerry jugs, drained off about eight gallons out of the 27-gallon tank under the console, before switching to the remaining seventy-gallon tank with an unknown amount. We stopped using our under the console tank since it was a semi-transparent tank , we'd save it for after our metal seventy was emptied that way we could better judge our remaining amount of fuel.

Bob using the kicker, Suzuki 9.9 horse power engine

Quote from Cross the Atlantic blog: "Worried after last Blog (Only 250-miles...). Was very concerned with your gas consumption in HEAD-ON SEAS and WIND. I have been praying for a following sea and mild wind/waves for your journey. Please take all precautions to stay warm as Hypothermia will sneak up on you and it may be too late once you recognize the symptoms (if you do) Stay as DRY as Possible Please. Make sure Your EPIRB is in top form. God Bless...God watches over those who seek to help others... Your Friend in Cocoa, Mark B."

To Greenland, Calling for a Fuel Drop

Tired Ralph bundled up inside his raincoat.

This was not one of those luxury cruises where we were pampered and got to relax out in the basting sun. Heck, we had hardly even seen the sun. It was out for only a short time after leaving Cartwright. The haze started close to a mile away from us and continued upward almost covering the whole dome of the sky. Every once in a while a couple of the clouds would part and we'd get one of those glorious radiating beams which could have been copied from a church baptism invitation. The weird thing was several times during the day, the only beams that opened up in the clouds were exactly on our heading. Since most of the sky was an even gray haze without individual clouds to use as a navigational position to head for, I was able to use the beams. I'd check my heading on the compass or Garmin and then compare it to the beam and adjust my heading. I felt God was helping us drive on a straight path, because the more we zigzagged, the more fuel we'd burn up.

Bruce had done some fancy Internet work and found a guy in Greenland, Niels Chemnitz, who would come out and refuel us. It wouldn't be cheap, I believe the price was $2,500, but at least we

Wounded Hero Voyage I

had a good backup option.

> <u>Quote from Cross the Atlantic blog:</u> "Hello Brown Brothers!! Good to know you are both well—hang in there! I am wearing; my shirt with pride! Stay Safe, Peace and Prayers, S and T"

Sunday, August 2nd (37th day since leaving Tampa)

It was our fifth day at sea since leaving Cartwright, Labrador. My face and lips were raw from the cold and the wind, my wrist were covered with hundreds of painful little puss blisters, my feet especially my toes felt like thousands of needles were constantly sticking me, my heels were still cracked, my hands were numb, and I needed a shave. I must have looked like a real mess, because I felt like I had been through a meat grinder and then put away in the freezer. I don't think Ralph looked any better.

I had rigged up the handle on the kicker with a short wooden flag pole and a piece of PVC pipe duct tapped to the throttle so it reached the top of the captain's chair. With the help of a bungee I put a downward force on it against the seat cushion so it would stay in position. I would only have to tweak it every once in a while. While I was driving I kept my feet curled up inside my Conoco blanket and pulled my ski cap down over my ears. I was never comfortable but I still managed to fall asleep driving. I even knew I was going to fall asleep, so I rigged up the handycam to record it, as sleep would only last till I hit the next swell.

Ralph made the decision to cancel Nuuk as our point of entry into Greenland. We were now more concerned where the closest gas station was. With the help of Bruce our heading was adjusted more eastwardly. The wind had begun to slow a little and crept a little more around from the north. The current also appeared to be

To Greenland, Calling for a Fuel Drop

heading more towards the southeast which made me happy.

Ralph had been blogging our mileage count down. He tried to get me to agree with him when we were within a hundred miles from Greenland, that we were in European waters; so we had

successfully crossed the Atlantic Ocean. I argued to really cross the Atlantic; we had to be on the European continent, not a territory.

> <u>Quote from Cross the Atlantic blog:</u> "I am anxious for you two to get your hot bath, shower, and some warm food. I have been following you a lot. You must be headed somewhere besides Nuuk. I am so glad to see you are making progress. Dale"

Monday, August 3rd

We started to see more icebergs again, changing my theory that the icebergs would only be on the westside of the Labrador Sea. What did I know, I'm from Florida. The water temperature was now in the lower forties. Our slurred conversations were starting to include a hotel with a hot shower and then we were out of gas in the big seventy tank. Night driving in soaked clothes was incredibly cold with chattering teeth, shivering bodies, and numbing pin cushioning feet. I was wishing we had purchased a couple pairs of electric heat socks, real boots and water proof gloves; many of the things we had talked about bringing months before our departure. I wondered how a couple of days and nights aboard the *I Am Second* compares to the hit TV show *Most Dangerous Catch*, where they still get to go inside, eat hot food, get dry and warm every couple of hours. Do they have hot showers and beds on their boats?

Wounded Hero Voyage I

Tuesday, August 4th

Ralph pulled out the Toughbook and by plugging in our coordinates off the Garmin and using some downloaded maps, he zoomed into our location. We were really close to Greenland, but the gas station was still a-ways away. We hadn't used the big Suzuki for days. We were dead tired and agreed to fire up the big guy to quickly knockoff some distance. It felt so exhilarating to really be moving again. The water was relatively calm with one to two-foot swells with a little ripple on top. With a couple of visual checks at the remaining fuel tank looking under the console with the door opened, we couldn't chance it any longer and reverted back to the kicker. Both of us wondered if we had just made a huge mistake.

Ralph using the Toughbook computer to check the heading

Soon we had entered where our Garmin showed us we were within Greenland. We were amongst hundreds of icebergs and a few rock islands all nestled in a gray clouded mist without hardly a ripple in the water. This was like something out of a science fiction

To Greenland, Calling for a Fuel Drop

movie. These unique shapes were something only to be appreciated by a few and we were alone. We putted along ogling like little kids. This was so different than anything I imagined. I expected to see some ice, maybe frozen lakes with some ice here and there, but these were huge icebergs and they were everywhere.

We drove for a couple of hours until according to our Garmin, we were just about there. Funny, there was nothing that resembled any type of civilization. We were literally running on fumes and there were no signs, no trash, nothing but water, ice and rock. We had less than half an inch of gas across the bottom of the tank. The Garmin had the town labeled and we were there at the end, and all there was was a rock shoreline. That was it! I was pooped mentally and physically. Ralph set out motoring along the shoreline as I told him I didn't care any more, I was going to sleep.

Ralph woke me up when he saw a couple of radio towers. Soon a line of really small houses appeared clustered around an opening in the brown-green-gray rock. We pulled into Kagsimiut, population 47, with barely any gas visible in the bottom of the tank. I was one happy fist mate and after thanking God, I estimated we might have had about a half of a cup of gas total on the boat. God had brought us in. If we had run the big motor just a few more minutes, if I had vectored one more time, if we had zigzagged another couple of times, spilled much more gas, we would have been paddling with our hands. Well not really, my hands weren't going to spend much time in the now 35-degree water. I don't know what we would have done, I suppose we would have had Bruce get in contact with that guy and he would have brought us some gas. Anyway, we made it. Just for grins, I double checked the Garmin and added up

Wounded Hero Voyage I

all our backward drifts with the sea anchor. It totaled out to be 16 miles.

Quotes from Cross the Atlantic blog: "Great job!!! You made it across!! We never doubted you guys would make it. Get plenty of rest and hot food, maybe you could find some Gortex boots or waterproof boots or Gortex jackets, they really help. So continue on the great job of your journey and may God continue to bless and watch over you. Cathy L"

Our Mother's thoughts during the Canada to Greenland Crossing: "When I learned from a family member, that Ralph and Bob were far from land, very low on gas, and very cold, I pictured the worst.... They were not going to make it safely back and I did panic. It was worst than panic. In the morning I thought I would hear it was all over for the two of them. I left everything in the hands of the Lord and by the Grace of God, they did make it and I thanked our Maker for it. Amen.

Bob, the middle of five boys, was a good child and stayed out of trouble. He worried me not in that respect. Ralph, the forth boy, was accident prone and expected to be adventurous. I had a hard time believing Bob had joined Ralph on the Bermuda trip. I knew of the plan for the Wounded Hero trip but only wanted to talk to family members and Bob's Godmother, Mary Beth, about it. My Prayer Request was made in the name of all who were traveling be it by land or sea. Ralph and Bob's Mom."

Quote from the Cross the Atlantic blog: "Hi Bob and Ralph, Congratulations!! Hope you have a safe and warmer trip to Iceland. We check the website several times a day and Jill gives us reports in the morning and after lunch. All the girls think you are nuts but the guys wish they were there with you. What a blast. Keep safe, Jim and Susan"

Quote from the Cross the Atlantic blog: "You guys are my new heroes! Georgs"

Ralph and Bob's voyage is long from over; the story is continued in the **Wounded Hero Voyage II**; *Smallest Powerboat Crossing the Atlantic* soon to be available at www.RobertBrownBooks.com

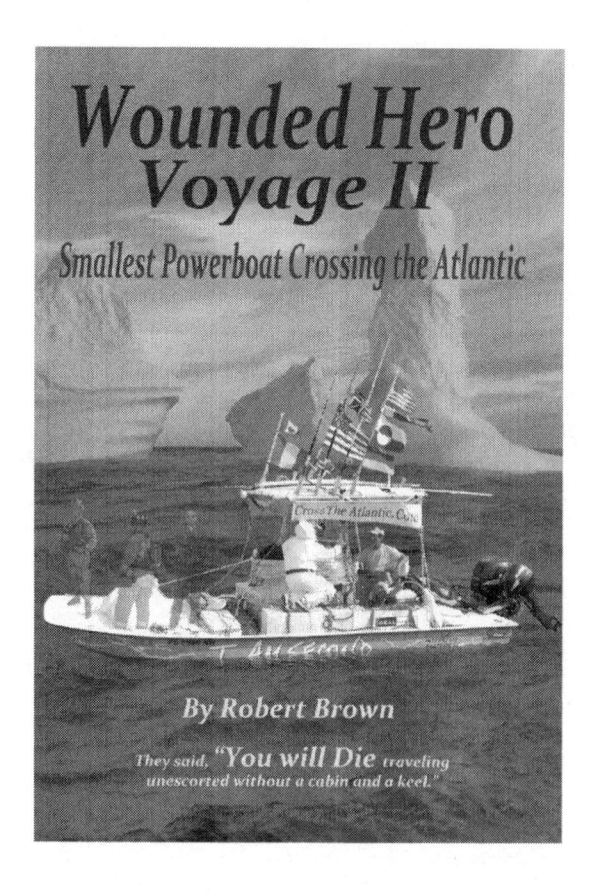

Our Toll Crossing the Atlantic Ocean

Login sale sign, Ralph's Don't-Go-Anywhere-Without-Notebook, American flag, Fifteen-foot flag pole, Four small military flags, Hammock strap, Blue jeans and red shirt, Paul's special lure, Flip Flop, Two Interstate Battery hats, Suzuki blanket, wallet receipts, and a five-gallon bucket.

Our Boat Stops and the Big Mileages

United States of America

Tampa, Florida

Ft. Meyers, Florida

Islamorada, Florida Keys........... (Tampa to the Keys------400 miles)

Miami, Florida

Sebastian Inlet, Florida

Cape Canaveral, Florida

Atlantic Tolls and Mileages

Jacksonville, Florida ... (Cape Canaveral to Jacksonville --130-miles)

Charleston, South Carolina.. (Jacksonville to Charleston--200 miles)

Beaufort, North Carolina

Norfolk, Virginia

Virginia Beach, Virginia

New York, New York .... (Tampa to New York -- 1,675 miles)

Boston, Massachusetts .... (New York to Boston –270 miles)

Canada

Halifax, Nova Scotia .... (Boston to Halifax – 450 miles)

France

St. Pierre Miquelon..... (Halifax to St. Pierre Miquelon – 400 miles)

Canada

Aquafort, Newfoundland

St. John's, Newfoundland

St. Anthony, Newfoundland

Cartwright, Labrador

Greenland

Kagsimiut .... (Cartwright to Greenland ---------- 625 miles)

Total miles from
Tampa, Florida to Kagsimiut, Greenland approximately
4,100 miles in 37 days

Thank you!!!!

To start off, I have to say there were so many people involved in making our voyage from Tampa to Greenland a success. It would be impossible for me to even begin to try to name them all. It is a fact that I don't know and have never met the majority of them. But they all know who they are and I personally wish to say thanks.

God was always there for us.

My family, Jill, Bryan and Jonathan, for allowing me go. They know that Ralph and I are just two regular guys, dreamers. They never really expected us to go. They gave me permission to go knowing full well that we'd never get funded. It was as much a shock to me as it was to them, when Ralph called to tell me nine-days before we left telling me that the trip was funded, at least enough to start.

Ralph for inviting me on another trip of a lifetime. After our first trip was a success, he could have easily found a more experienced seamen than me.

Anne Brown and their kids, Phillip, Heath, and Brittany for the sacrifices they made so Ralph could do the trip and their road support in the States.

Norm Miller, because we were dead in the water until Ralph conveniently ran into him. Scott Miller, his behind the scene help and Charlie Brim, Ralph's communication window to Norm.

The I Am Second organization our major sponsor and because it is such a cool organization... God is first therefore you put yourself second. But I felt honored to spread God's message in such

Thank you!!!!

a unique way, since I am not an outspoken person, I let the voyage and the signs do most of the talking.

Peter Rostel, the actual owner of the Intruder (*I Am Second* boat).

Bruce Schulman, our logistic man behind the scenes, he was always there for us.

Bernie Heckmann, Trey Hacker, and Renee taking care of the website.

Marino for helping prepare the Intruder (*I Am Second*).

John and Jeff Carroll, our support guys onshore during the early stages of the trip.

Jason McKean and Julio Salazar, our Wounded Heroes who took part in our voyage.

John McDaniel for help with the Wounded Heroes.

Rebecca and the SPM team, phone calls and media support.

Jody and Larry Ross Communications help with media.

All of our sponsors and the many people who helped us:
I Am Second, Interstate Battery, Boat US, Benco Insurance Planners, Ideal Image, Cape Surf, NGR Manager, Mustang Survivor, Spot, Suzuki, Icelandic Seafood, 66 degrees North, Panasonic, Xterra Wet Suits, Georgianna Methodist Church, Experience Labrador, BugBaffler, Louie, Percy, Canadian Coast Guard, Drive the Globe, RNLI, Jim Murphy, Anders N Mathiesen (Hot Springs),WYC, Eldings Whale Tours, CA Cruising Association, Magnus Scheving (Lazy Town, Iceland), Hallmar, Linjohn Christiansen, Hahns, Barretts, Elin Brimheim Heinesen, Maurice, Heidi, Kevin and Heike Brown, Guys from Conoco, Patrick Lyons and Jim Pike from Shipyard Quarters, Peter, Scalloway Hotel; all the guys in Wells; Wendy Hodkinson, and Konrad E. Braun.

Wounded Hero Voyage I

Richard Cullison for recovering the video from the external hard drive after the fire.

Jeff Michalsky for his help keeping my computer working.

Tamara McHatton, Cindie Robinson, Dean Schaaf, and Donna Chesher for their help with this book.

Cody Dotsun for help with the pictures and the cover.

Jim Suber (Jacksonville Dock Master), Garrison Rudisill (Dock Master Charleston Harbor Resort), Pat Vargo and James Scruggs (Norfolk Cityfest management), Rudee's Inlet Marina (Virginia Beach), Nate Grove (NYC Parks Department), Conrad Kreuter and Judy (Moriches Inlet, NY), Brian Johnston (Ponquoque Power Sports, Hamptons, Long Island), Patrick, Charlestown Navy Yard, Dan Mullett (Prossers Boat Basin, St. John's Newfoundland), Poul Erik Pederson, Elerttson (Brokey Yacht Club, Reykjavik) Oskar Petur Frioriksson (Vestmannaeyjar, Iceland), Torshavn, Faroe Islands Coast Guard, David Boyd, and all the other people who donated either directly to us or through www.crosstheatlantic.com.

Thank you!

Now that the trip is over, I want to thank the readers who help promote my books so that one day soon, I can get the videos turned into a documentary. Thank you!

Thank you!!!!

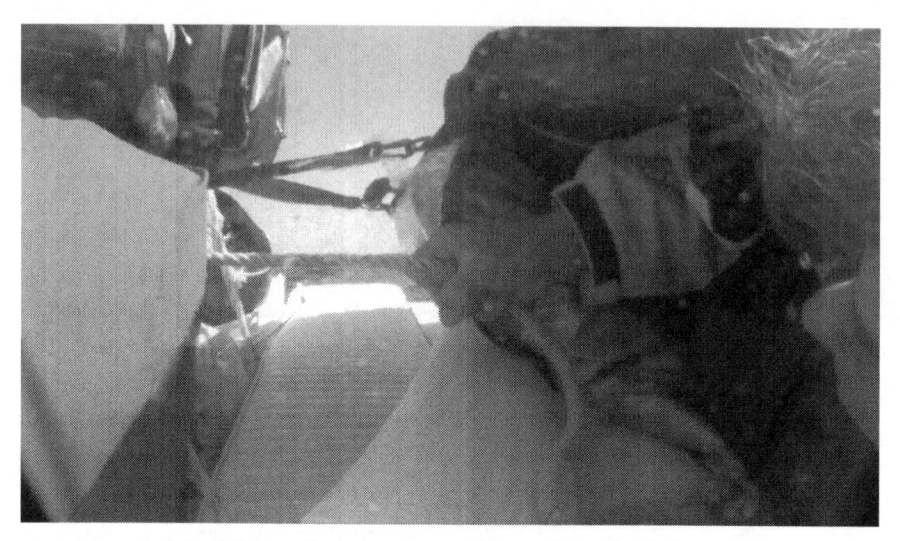

Bob holding safety rope to pull board bag bed forward

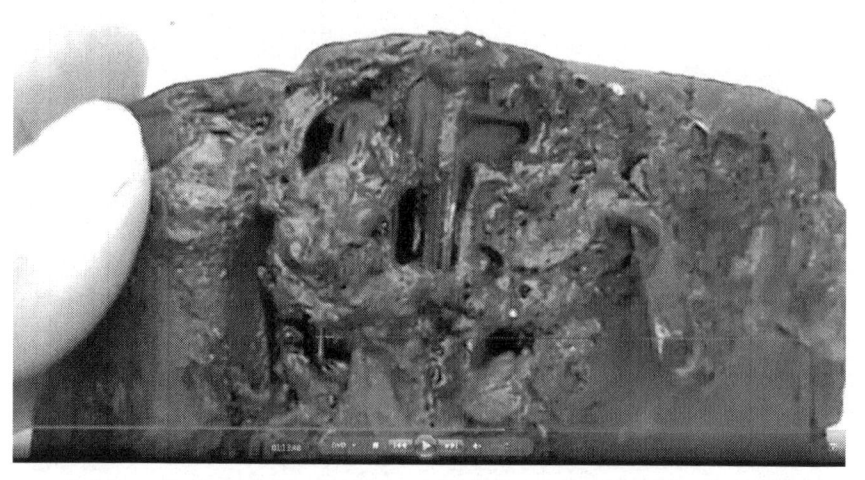

Bob's melted Sony handycam with all the video from the boat trip

About the Author Robert Brown

Robert usually goes by Bob, was born in Waltham, Massachusetts, at a military hospital in 1957. He is fourth in line of eight children. Ralph was also born in Waltham and he is number five. Like many military families, they moved a few times: Massachusetts to California; Satellite Beach, Florida; to the island of Grand Turk (southeast of Cuba); Satellite Beach, Florida; to Cocoa Beach, Florida; and finally Merritt Island, Florida, after high school.

Bob grew up in a Catholic family, accepted Jesus into his life in the fourth grade, and baptized a second time as a Baptist in his twenties. Bob married Jill in 1986 and became Presbyterian and finally Methodist. The important thing is that they are a Bible believing family.

After a move, while Bob attended a partial year, in a private Catholic school, it was discovered that he had dyslexia (read words from the right to left instead of left to right) and repeated fourth grade in a public school. That explains how both Bob and Ralph graduated from Cocoa Beach High School in 1976. Bob earned his AA at Brevard Community College.

Bob's parents were divorced and Bob along with most of his brothers and sisters lived in Country Acres, a juvenile foster care center in Titusville. The Cullison family temporarily adopted Bob and he moved back to Cocoa Beach and then eventually back with

About the Author, Robert Brown

his mom. She did an incredible job as a single mother.

Bob has worked since the age of 13 starting his own lawn mowing business, became a dog groomer, bus boy, salad worker, dish washer at Bernard Surf, started working at McDonald's Hamburgers and became a store manager, a little UPS work around the Christmas rush, became self employed as a painter/builder. He built and rebuilt several homes including a spec house (a two story which he lost his shirt on when the real estate market crashed in the 90's).

Bob grew up around the water, and has surfed for over 35 years, likes to sail Hobie Cats, scuba dive, and swim. His other interests are hanging out with his family, movies, riding motorcycles, camping, hiking, climbing, snow skiing, wrestling, making videos, reading, eating... once he won a weight gaining contest and ate 11 and a three-quarter pounds of food in two hours (something he trained for) just after wrestling season in high school.

Bob and Jill have two boys who have been sports oriented since they were big enough to throw a ball. Bob has been fortunate enough to be able to attend almost every sporting events in kids were in, usually video taping. He believes in is important to be there and support his family whenever possible.

Recently his house (uninsured) was destroyed by fire while he was at church and with the help of his Dad and brother, Dana, friends, nearby churches and schools, they have rebuilt the house. Special thanks to Rick Chrisman who helped a lot (died Jan, 2012)

Bob started writing after a couple of years of listening to audio books while working. His first manuscript was a surf novel which he has finished but yet to have published.

We are still in the process of making a documentary

film or a mini series with the footage taken during the Wounded Hero Voyage.

Front Cover Heroes
(Ghost riders representing all Wounded Heroes)

Army National Guard: James Tyson served in Iraq on two deployments. He grew up with my kids, Bryan and Jonathan. He's in his eight year in the National Guards and is currently attending college. In the service he was trained as a mechanic.

Fireman: Kevin Falk of station 43 was one of the many firemen including ones from stations 41, 42, and 44 that came to my rescue and put our house fire out. Without them, there would not be the audio tapes or the videos from the trip so instrumental in writing these books. Kevin is a Marine (once a Marine, always a Marine) is a third generation service man. In the Marines, he worked with crash fire rescue, so combined he has fourteen years experience as a firefighter.

Deputy Sheriff: Barbara Ann Pill, 52 years old was taken from her husband of over thirty years, her two boys who grew up to become police officers, and her grandchild. She died in the line of duty, after thirty plus years of service, arresting two robbery suspects she pulled over in a car identified as being in the robbery. She was shot multiple times over a few pieces of hotel furniture. She was a highly decorated hard working officer that could both be tough yet incredibly nice. An old saying comes to mind by the people that knew her. It says a lot about Barbara, "Don't mistake my kindness for weakness." Picture and information credited to: Nessie for True Blue Warriors (A Hero Remembered... Never Dies) End of watch March 6, 2012

(Photoshop work on the front cover: Bob took the actual picture from his surfboard and then he was inserted into the picture on his surfboard, the three Wounded Heroes were ghosted onto the boat, extra sky and water were added along with extra height on the *iceberg)*

Books available at: www.RobertBrownBooks.com

Bermuda Suicide Challenge;
in a Flats Boat

Running for Fun;
High School Runner, Jonathan Brown

Wounded Hero Voyage I;
Smallest Powerboat Crossing the Atlantic

Wounded Hero Voyage II;
Smallest Powerboat Crossing the Atlantic

There are some videos and pictures on
Facebook page: "Robert Brown Books" and on his website:
www.RobertBrownBooks.com

Wounded Hero Voyage I

Robert Brown

Wounded Hero Voyage I

Made in the USA
Charleston, SC
30 November 2015